Design of
User-Friendly Programs
for Small Computers

Design of User-Friendly Programs for Small Computers

Henry Simpson

McGRAW-HILL BOOK COMPANY

New York   St. Louis   San Francisco   Auckland
Bogotá   Hamburg   Johannesburg   London   Madrid
Mexico   Montreal   New Delhi   Panama   Paris
São Paulo   Singapore   Sydney   Tokyo   Toronto

Library of Congress Cataloging in Publication Data
Simpson, Henry.
    Design of user-friendly programs for small computers.

    Bibliography: p.
    Includes index.
    1. Microcomputers — Programming.   2. Minicomputers —
Programming.   I. Title.
QA76.6.S5728   1984   001.64'2   84-10070
ISBN 0-07-057300-X

1234567890   DOC/DOC   8987654

ISBN 0-07-057300-X

The editors for this book were Stephen Guty and Georgia
Kornbluth, the designer was Mary Ann Felice, and the production supervisor was Sally Fleiss. It was set in Century Schoolbook
by Achorn Graphics.

Printed and bound by R. R. Donnelley & Sons Company.

Contents

Preface

What makes a program user-friendly?

The answer to this question depends very much on whom you talk to. To some, the essence of user friendliness is menus, help screens, and crash proofing. To others, it is speed and flexibility. What serves the computer novice will very often frustrate the computer expert — and what serves the expert will usually befuddle the novice. In short, user friendliness is not a fixed thing that you can put your finger on.

The term is mushy enough that you can use it any way you like. This is no help to the system designer or programmer, who wants to design a program that people can use effectively. Ad hype aside, the meaning of the term is not very clear, and still less clear is how to write a program that will be user-friendly.

Another problem for the designer is the fragmented way that user friendliness is often thought of. The programmer, told that operators cannot use the new system, will blame them at first; after regaining composure, however, the programmer will sit down and try to figure out how to patch things up so that operators will like it more. "Let's see now," thinks the programmer, "I'll redesign the menus, put in some additional error tests, and use color. That should do it." It may, but patching afterward is not as good as planning beforehand. You need to take the users into account before you design, not afterward.

What the foregoing points illustrate is that we need a better definition of user friendliness and of the process required to design and develop programs that have it. These are the two main goals of this book.

My definition of user friendliness appears in Chapter 1, but I won't be giving away too much by telling you that the test of a program's user friendliness is how well it meets user needs. Doing this takes more than tacking on so-called user-friendliness features such as menus. It requires an awareness of and a responsiveness to operator needs. That is why the first three chapters of this book focus mainly on the operator.

Of course, there is more to writing user-friendly programs than understanding operators. You also need a systematic strategy for taking these needs into account during design and development. Chapter 4 presents such a strategy. Chapters 5 through 11 then fill in details on how to follow it.

This book is directed primarily at people who will be involved in designing, developing, or evaluating software for microcomputers. It is written as if to a programmer, with many dos and don'ts, but the audience is assumed to include not only programmers but also systems analysts, designers, testers, evaluators, and perhaps a researcher or two. The book assumes a knowledge of computer hardware and software concepts, and does not stop to define such terms as CPU, record field, or cursor. This is not a book for the beginning programmer; it assumes that the reader is familiar with at least one programming language and is fluent enough in its use to be able to write programs that are technically sound.

This book reflects three major influences. The first influence is research. In recent years, an enormous amount of research has been done concerning the interactions between operators and computers. This research has been conducted mainly by psychologists, computer scientists, engineers, and human factors specialists. Several different literatures exist, and the list of relevant publications grows longer every day. Researchers have made valuable contributions to our understanding in many different areas. Notable recent contributions are the work of cognitive psychologists in developing the human information-processing model and the work of human factors specialists in compiling design guidelines for hardware selection, data input, data output, and program control.

Unfortunately, most research studies are narrowly focused on a single question. Not all the important questions have yet been asked, and no one has yet linked together the available answers into a strategy for program design and development. Providing such a strategy is really the province of software engineering, which is more of a technology or art than a science. As always, the program designer and developer will be the point man or woman when a problem needs solving. If the answer is not in a research journal — and it probably is not — the designer must use common sense and expert judgment to come up with a solution anyway. The researchers are always going to be a few steps behind. Therefore, the second influence reflected in this book is software engineering techniques and the so-called systems approach to design. This influence is most evident in Chapters 1 and 4.

The third major influence on the book is my experience as a programmer, system designer, and developer. I would like to say that my own opinions have had little to do with the way this book turned out, but that would be untrue. There were too many places where I had to interpret a research finding more broadly than an academician would like, answer a question that no one had asked before, or devise a technique for doing something out of my own best judgment. It is probably inevitable that opinion will creep in any time one writes anything, for people lack the objectivity of their computers. The chapters in this book that reflect my opinions most strongly are Chapters 8, 10, and 11.

Application of human factors in any design enterprise is a creative activity. The designer must analyze the problem and solve it systematically. Since no two problems are ever exactly the same, design guidelines that emerge from one situation — whether research or actual practice — never apply precisely in another. Thus, it is impossible to write a cookbook that gives the recipe for solving every design problem. However, there are general principles that apply universally and many specific design guidelines that apply in solving common design problems. If you know these principles and guidelines, you can design user-friendly programs and avoid human factors blunders.

This book is divided into eleven chapters. The first three provide an introduction to human factors and to the characteristics of the human operator. These are designed to help readers understand the nature of the human part of the human-computer system. Readers who are not familiar with the human parameters around which they must design — memory, vision, information-processing capabilities, and so forth — may be in for surprises. Human beings have many characteristics that are not obvious to intuition or common sense.

Chapters 4 through 9 cover program design and development. The program development process is described in Chapter 4. (Use of the definite article is not meant to imply that this is the only program development process — rather, that it is representative of the family of "top-down," systems-oriented program development approaches.) Chapter 5 deals with hardware. The next three chapters deal with various aspects of design: Chapter 6 with data output, Chapter 7 with data input, Chapter 8 with utilities, and Chapter 9 with program control.

Chapters 10 and 11 cover program documentation and testing. These are important and usually boring topics. They are also written about almost endlessly, which suggests that they concern a lot of people and that no one has yet put them to rest. I don't claim the final say, but I do attempt to define and distill the key factors you must consider as a programmer.

I would like to acknowledge the help of members of the Anacapa

Sciences staff for their careful review of early drafts of portions of this book. Doug Harris was particularly helpful. Also thanks to Barbara Gates, who did the word processing with grace and good spirits.

HENRY SIMPSON

Design of
User-Friendly Programs
for Small Computers

One

Introduction

What is a "user-friendly" program?
What does it take to write one?
This chapter will attempt to answer these two questions and introduce you to some of the human factors concepts that underlie the design of user-friendly programs. These concepts are not very exciting, but they are important. Once you understand them, they can influence the way that you approach and solve a problem, such as designing a computer program. The concepts discussed are the human-machine system, human-computer interface, and systems approach to design. Along the way, there will be a view of the microcomputer revolution that is now rolling with full force, and why it is making user friendliness so important.

USER FRIENDLINESS — WHAT IT IS

The term "user friendly" is new but has already become a cliché. It is used indiscriminately by program publishers, industry journalists, and program users to refer to things they like about how a program works. What does it really mean?

An Operational Definition

Basically, a "user-friendly" program is one with features that acknowledge *human factors*. Human factors are the various characteristics of people which influence their performance — memory, ability to see and hear, intelligence, motivation, motor skills, and so on. User-friendly programs are designed by people with an awareness of human factors. This awareness may be conscious or intuitive. It may be based on instinct, experience, or the careful application of design guidelines obtained from handbooks.

In general, a user-friendly program is easy to use, tolerant of operator errors, easy to learn, and acknowledges that human beings are imperfect creatures. Few experienced programmers show a total indifference to human factors. At the same time, few pay as much attention to them as they should.

What is required to write user-friendly programs? The answer to this question is not obvious. Clearly, a basic prerequisite is that one must be a competent programmer. One must have a thorough understanding of the programming language and how to use its capabilities and overcome its weaknesses. But this is only for starters. Besides being a competent programmer in a technical sense, the programmer who wishes to write a user-friendly program must meet some addi-

2

tional requirements. These requirements fall into three different realms — those of *attitude, knowledge,* and *skill.*

The Importance of Attitude

Of the three requirements, perhaps the most difficult to meet is attitude. The attitude requirement is more than simply the desire to write user-friendly programs; this desire, it is assumed, exists already. Rather, the concern is with something more fundamental — a philosophy of programming which starts with human operators (the "users"), places them in the foreground of the programmer's concerns, and relegates the technicalities of software design and hardware selection to the background.

This is much easier to talk about than actually to do. It is particularly difficult for people with a scientific or technical orientation. For example, the computer scientist, engineer, or mathematician typically approaches the programming process from the point of view of software or hardware design. Very often the operator is taken for granted. Sophisticated designers such as these typically have a rational view of the world and work with others of like mind. They thoroughly understand the inner workings of their programming language and machines and work in a community of others who share a common vocabulary and technical knowledge. It is no surprise that they should have some difficulty attempting to see the world through the eyes of program users who may know little or nothing about programming languages, to whom a computer is a mysterious and perhaps threatening machine, and who may not really care. It is not easy for a programmer to take the user's viewpoint, but this is the first step in writing a user-friendly program.

Incidentally, this example is not intended to single out a particular group (computer scientists, mathematicians, engineers) and stereotype them as being myopic. This would be a nasty slander, and besides, the author happens to belong to this group. In fact, no profession is immune to the criticism of being insensitive to the needs of program users. This includes people who are professionally trained and who make their living as human factors specialists.

Another important aspect of our attitude is how we think of and approach the design process. Many designers tend to think of it as having two separate and independent parts. The first of these is the technical design, or "engineering." The second is the user-friendliness part, or human factoring. When we split design in two this way we inevitably put user friendliness in second place. This is not the way it should be.

It is neither cost-effective nor sound design practice to add on afterward what should have been present from the start. The only reasonable way to come up with a design that is truly user-friendly is to intend to do so from the start and to have the "engineer" in us work hand in hand with the "human factors specialist" in us. We must, at all costs, avoid compartmentalizing the design process. How do we do this? Simple: Every time we ask a technical question, concerning design, we need also to address and answer the related human factors questions. Every time we design a part of our program that will have an effect on what the operator does (most things do), we must make sure that the operator's needs are considered.

The foregoing is what we mean by *attitude*. In exploring this issue, we have wandered a bit, possibly slandered some good professions, and come to a simple but important conclusion: *Every design starts with the designer's attitude*. Obviously, attitude is of profound importance.

Human Factors Knowledge

What must you know to create a user-friendly program? The required knowledge falls into three general categories:

1. Capabilities and limitations of the human operator
2. General design principles
3. Context-specific design guidelines

These three types of knowledge are hierarchical. That is, the capabilities and limitations of the operator permit researchers and designers to develop general design principles. When these principles are applied in specific situations, context-specific design guidelines are the result.

If you understand human capabilities and limitations, certain design principles emerge, and these can in many cases be translated into design guidelines that apply in specific contexts. To give a concrete example, research has shown that, without extensive training, typical human operators can accurately recognize about five different brightness levels on a cathode ray tube (CRT) display. It follows from this that if you attempt to code information using more than five brightness levels, human operators will compress the levels within their visual apparatus and make errors. From this basic limitation, a design principle can be derived: Do not code information using more than five brightness levels on a CRT display. Now, suppose we wished to apply this principle in a specific context, namely, a CRT display that will be used for presenting the population density on the map of a particular city. The map is divided into sections of equal area and, the higher the population density in an area, the brighter the display. Given the above design principle, it is clear that we can have no more than five different population densities since that is the maximum number we can portray using a monochrome screen. Given this limitation, we might have second thoughts about using monochrome and consider using color. (The human perceptual apparatus can distinguish among many more colors than brightness levels.)

This should give you a general idea of the type of knowledge you must possess to begin to design user-friendly programs. It starts with knowledge of the human operator, which leads to general design principles, and ends with context-specific design guidelines. This book contains some information in all these areas. A friendly warning. Some readers may not be interested in learning about the human operator or in reading general design principles. They may want to skip this stuff and get to the "real data" — design guidelines. This would be a mistake. This is not a handbook. You cannot look up an answer to your problem in it. There are human factors handbooks, but none of them covers the complexities of human-computer interface design in the depth you need to solve your design problem. You will find some of the answers in this book, but more often you will be breaking new ground and have to solve the problem yourself. That is when it is important to understand the human operator and have the general design principles at your fingertips. That way you can write your own design guidelines to solve the specific problem you face. In other words, do not skip the early chapters.

Human Factors Skills

Finally, we come to skill. For the purposes of this book, skill may be defined as the ability to perform the design task effectively, while taking human factors into account. As in most worthwhile enterprises — cutting hair, making an omelet, performing open-heart surgery — skill is acquired through practice and a lot of feedback from the people who have direct contact with the products of our work. The feedback part is important. You can never be great in your eyes alone, despite what some folks with Napoleonic delusions may think. In other words, you cannot be your own judge and referee. You must write your program, have people try it out, and then have them tell you what they think. It is amazing how fast this helps you learn, recognize errors, improve, and gain skill — provided, of course, that you do not start clenching your teeth when someone suggests that your program has one or two shortcomings and could use this or that improvement . . .

Those three things, then, are what it takes to write user-friendly programs. It starts with your attitude. This text may have preached a bit in an attempt to shape *your* attitude about certain design ideas, but there will be no more preaching. Most of this book concerns the second factor — knowledge. It will provide the factual information you need to write user-friendly programs. Study it carefully, apply it, practice it, get feedback on your efforts, and you will become a skilled designer of user-friendly programs.

SOME KEY HUMAN FACTORS CONCEPTS

This section will introduce you to some of the basic and most important concepts of human factors. The concepts covered are the human-machine system, the human-computer interface, and the systems approach to design.

The Human-Machine System

The concept of a human-machine system appears to have had its origin during World War II in the context of research concerning human performance using complex electronic equipment such as sonars and radars. It became evident that old ways of thinking about hardware, and human interaction with it, were very limiting. It made much more sense to think about the human operator and the equipment as separate components in a larger system.

Here is how this works. Consider, as an example, a sonar system. The issue, so far as the captain of a destroyer is concerned, is to detect enemy submarines in order to attack them. The sonar designer, for obvious reasons, works to design a system that will detect submarines at as great a range and depth as possible. In analyzing the problem, the designer sits down and starts thinking about what factors influence when detection can take place. The usual line of thought goes something like this. First, there are the characteristics of submarines themselves. For an active ("pinging") sonar, the bigger the submarine, the more sound energy it will reflect back to the destroyer. The designer has no control over this. Next, there is the transmission medium, the ocean. From acoustics, the designer knows that the amount of sound that is reflected back from the target depends primarily on target range and the clarity of the water.

Once the sound has reached the destroyer, it must be detected by the transducer (a sort of underwater microphone array), amplified, processed, and presented on a display of some sort. The designer has a good deal of control over what happens between transducer and display

— for example, the designer can vary the size, shape, and number of elements in the detecting array; can filter and amplify at will; can perform all sorts of esoteric processing of the signals; and can present the output on video, graphic, or audio displays, using as many display formats as desired.

Now we come to the sonar operator, the sailor who looks at the display to decide whether or not an enemy target has been detected. The sonar designer has absolutely no control over sonar operators and does not like to think about them because they are so unpredictable. Yet it is obvious that the characteristics of operators are just as important for the designer to know about as the characteristics of enemy submarines; the transmission properties of the sea; or the design of transducers, amplifiers, signal processors, or displays. Operators have certain properties, too — visual and auditory senses with definite limitations. These will affect how readily they will detect an enemy target that is displayed by the sonar. They have a limited attention span and will become fatigued; this will influence whether or not they are alert enough to detect the target, when it is there. There is also a social factor involved. The sailor is a fairly junior member of a ship's crew — and a sailor who reports an enemy submarine when none is there may get in trouble. This tends to make the sonar operator cautious.

This example illustrates the general concept of a human-machine system. Where one draws the line between the system and the outside world is somewhat arbitrary, but it can be argued that the system includes everything from the submarine to the commander of the destroyer. The designer certainly needs to take these end points and everything in between into account. That is, designers need to know about submarines; about the transmission medium; about transducers, amplifiers, and processors; about human operators; and even about ship commanders. Each of these factors will affect whether or not the system accomplishes its *mission*. The system's mission is to detect and destroy enemy submarines. Since anything between the submarine and the ship's commander may influence whether or not detection takes place, all those things in between are important and should be considered by the designer. From this perspective, cloudy water, barnacles on a transducer, a burned-out preamplifier, a hung-over sonar operator, and a Queeg-like commander all have degrading effects on mission success; one is pretty much like another with respect to catching the submarine. Obviously, hardware problems are only part of the picture. People problems are only part of the picture, too. It takes both — human and machine — to fill out the picture completely.

Most human factors specialists would probably consider the system to consist of the sonar operator and the sonar equipment. Some might extend the limits to the ship's captain, but probably not to the ocean or the enemy submarine. But, as you can see, where one draws the line between the system and the outside world depends upon the point of view. At any rate, even if we do not include certain factors within the system, we must still take them into account during design if they will affect the mission. In short, we cannot afford to limit our view of the world during design to hardware or software alone.

The Human-Computer Interface

The human-computer interface is a type of human-machine interface. However, it represents a different sort of design problem from the usual hardware interface. This becomes clear when you consider what exactly it is that the designer must design first with a conventional machine (e.g., an electric oven or an automobile), and then with a computer program. In the first case the designer worries about hardware, in the second about software.

Traditionally, an interface has been thought of as a piece of *hardware*. In designing a machine, the designer is mainly concerned with the physical displays that present information to the user, and the controls that the user manipulates to manage the internal workings of the system. For example, in designing an oven, the designer is concerned with such display questions as whether or not the oven should have a window in it and how temperature and timer status should be displayed. The designer's concerns include such control issues as the design and arrangement of temperature and timing controls. In other words, the interface is hardware and the designer's task is to select or design hardware and arrange it appropriately.

In computer systems, the interface is not so easy to define. It still has a hardware aspect, to be sure, but *software* also is a part of it. What is displayed to the operator is a function of both hardware and software. The hardware chosen — CRT display, printer, sound generator, etc. — basically becomes a channel or medium for information that is created and controlled by software.

The control aspect of the interface is, analogously, part hardware and part software. Software can be used to govern how control takes place. For example, software can be used to assign control functions to keys. Hardware only limits what can be done. Figure 1-1 illustrates the basic human-computer interface.

Clearly, the concept of a human-computer interface is more subtle than that of the traditional human-machine interface. As we have illustrated, this is because software permits the programmer to manipulate the way information is displayed and the system is controlled. In

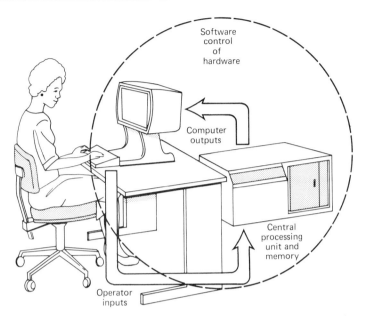

Figure 1-1 The human-computer interface has both a hardware and a software aspect: Hardware is a channel or medium for presenting information to the operator and for operator control of the computer, whereas software governs the hardware through which this interaction occurs.

the traditional human-machine system, displays and controls are fixed and are, quite literally, the hardware itself.

Now, for the sake of stretching our minds a little, let us look beyond the operator and the computer and think about the human-computer interface a bit more globally. This, you will recall, is what we did when considering the problems of the sonar operator, not only with the sonar equipment, but also with the size of the enemy submarine and the ship commander's temperament. The interface, it was indicated, could be extended beyond the operator and machine alone to other things that influence mission success. Let us perform the same sort of analysis for the human operator and the computer.

The human-computer interface is usually thought of as involving only an interchange, or dialog, between an operator and a computer. It is true that this is the primary interface we are concerned with in this book. However, if we take a "systems" view, we can easily identify other interfaces as well. Before we start writing software, we should define just how far our "system" extends, locate the various interfaces, and take them all into account.

To illustrate how this is done, let us consider an example. Suppose that we are about to design a management information system (MIS) that will be used to keep track of the amount of time required to perform different types of maintenance tasks on automobiles. We will design data-collection cards that will be completed by the mechanics performing the work. The cards will be entered through a computer keyboard into a data base by a data-entry clerk. Later, a system operator will review the data for completeness and accuracy, and will generate hard-copy reports. These reports will be distributed to the mechanics, their supervisor, and the owner of the repair shop. Here are the questions:

- What is the "system"?
- Where does the human-computer interface lie?

Let us start with the first question. The general rule for deciding what the system consists of is to start by defining the mission that underlies all this data collection, data entry, report generation, and so forth. After you have defined the mission, then put your magnifying glass on all these activities and identify those that influence mission success. The mission of this system, apparently, is to keep track of maintenance worker hours. The boss is getting the reports to see how efficiently the mechanics are working. The supervisors and mechanics are getting reports so that they can evaluate their own performance. The motivation behind all this is to maintain work standards in terms of efficiency and productivity.

What will influence mission success? The main factor is report accuracy. This, in turn, depends on several other factors, which extend back in a chainlike succession to the mechanics: the quality of the data base, as determined by the system operator; data-entry accuracy by the clerk; checks on data made by the supervisor; completeness and accuracy of the cards completed by the mechanics. On this basis, then, your "system" extends from the mechanics to the report recipients and includes everything in between.

How do you like that? From a systems viewpoint, you cannot be content with worrying just about the interactions between the system operator and his computer. You need also to take into account all these other factors as well.

Now let us attack the second question — and define the human-computer interface. Answering this question is rather like one of those hidden figure tests one occasionally finds in the Sunday morning comics — you know, "How many hidden animals can you find in this picture?" Let us start by enumerating the interfaces.

First, and obviously, there is an interface between the data-entry clerk and the computer. Second, there is an interface between the system operator and the computer. Is that it? Not quite. There are also interfaces between the computer and the report recipients. They do not interact directly with the computer — they do not control anything — but they do see and use a computer-generated report. There are three such interfaces, since three different user groups — mechanics, supervisor, and shop owner — receive reports.

But (in the words of a certain hard-sell television commercial), "Wait, there's more." There is another, less obvious and more distant interface on the data-input side. Mechanics complete data-entry cards for entry into the computer data base. They do not interact with the computer directly, but the accuracy and completeness of their efforts profoundly influence the system.

Now we come to the lesson in all this. By taking the systems view of things, we uncovered several design-related issues that we must take into account:

- *The mechanic-computer interface.* The data-collection cards must be designed to suit the needs of both the mechanics who complete them and the clerk who enters them into the computer. For the mechanics, completing these cards is an extra chore, something besides their "real" work. For this reason, the cards must be designed so that they can be completed quickly and accurately. At the same time, the cards must be designed for ease of data entry into the computer by the clerk. Meeting both these requirements is sometimes difficult. A trade-off usually must be made. The smart designer will make the trade-off in favor of the people who complete the cards, rather than in favor of the data-entry clerk.

- *The clerk-computer interface.* The designer must assure that the clerk can enter data into the computer data base quickly and accurately. Some techniques that might assure this are a correspondence between the data-entry screens and the data-entry cards (they should look the same), and comprehensive tests of all entered data for accuracy in terms of type, range limits, and duplication with previously entered data.

- *The system operator-computer interface.* This must be designed so that the operator can quickly and accurately check the data base and generate required reports.

- *The report recipient–computer interface.* The reports must be designed with the needs and abilities of each group — mechanics, supervisors, owners — in mind. The information requirements of the three audiences differ and reports should be designed accordingly. Mechanics are primarily concerned with learning how well they are doing, individually; reports for this group should focus on individual performance. Supervisors will want to compare the performance of the mechanics and should receive summaries that permit this comparison to be made. Owners are interested in overall performance, not individuals, and should receive a summary that integrates data in an overall index, such as average worker hours per maintenance task.

The total system and its interfaces are illustrated in Figure 1-2. This example should not be taken too literally. It was presented primarily to illustrate how a systems view might influence the way we think about the human-computer interface. One often oversimplifies the matter. The most common oversight is to assume that one need only be concerned with what happens when someone sits down before a computer. Often, the system extends beyond a single operator and computer and involves users who, though they never see or touch the computer, have an interface with it through the information they provide or the reports they receive. Designers overlook such interfaces only at their own peril.

What is the system, and how many interfaces are there? As you can see, the answer to this question may require a little analysis.

The Systems Approach to Design

The field of human factors did not originate the systems approach, but this approach has certainly become a cornerstone of what human factors specialists do. Actually, the "system" in the name has a double meaning. First, it refers to the system being designed. Second, it refers to a particular strategy for deciding what that system should consist of.

The systems approach to design is perhaps best characterized in terms of two features: (1) early definition of system end goals, or objectives, and a movement "backward" to define the hardware and software required to meet the goals; and (2) careful definition of system modules, and their interactions, before design is begun.

The first point — starting with design objectives and working backward to define required hardware and software — is certainly not intuitively obvious. In many ways, in fact, it runs counter to our instinctive approach to problem solving. For example, inexperienced programmers are inclined to sit down at a computer keyboard and start writing code before developing a design plan. This might be termed the in medias res design strategy. Such programmers confuse motion with progress. Programming instructors pull their hair out when they see this happen, and they rail at their students to do more planning before

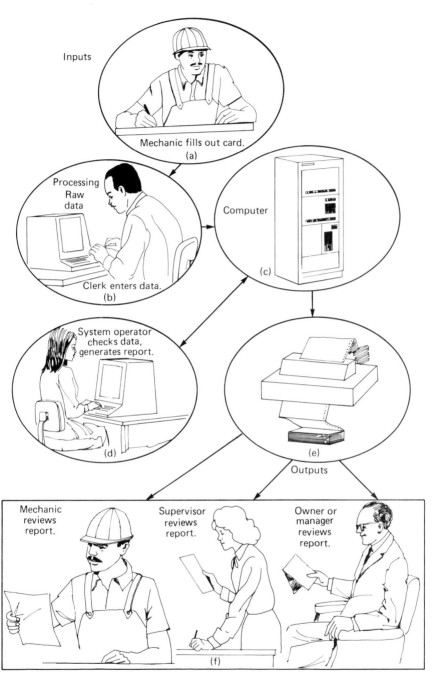

Figure 1-2 The human-computer interface is often multifaceted. In a management information system it may involve several different people, not all of whom interact directly with the computer: the originator of raw data (mechanic), data entry clerk, and system operator and report recipients — mechanic, supervisor, and owner or manager.

they start coding. The systems approach requires you to define your end goals, or objectives, before you do *anything* else. While it is much more fun to get on with the action, hard experience has shown that it will save work in the end.

In fact, the systems approach is effective not only for programmers, but also for real estate salespeople, navigators, artillery men, and anyone else who has a clear and definable job to do. In each of these occupations, the most sensible way to start is by defining where you want to go — how many houses to sell this month, what latitude and longitude to set the course for, what map coordinates to hit. Once the goal has been defined, you can work your way systematically backward to find out what that goal means in terms of what you must do. If you are a real estate salesperson, this means figuring out how many telephone calls and personal contacts you must make each month. If you are a navigator, it means plotting a course from your present position to where you want to go. If you are an artillery man, it means drawing a big X on the map and making sure the battery commanders know which way to point their weapons. And, if you are a software designer who wants to build a user-friendly program, it means starting with a clear and explicit statement of the things you want your program to be able to do.

The second point — definition of system modules and their interactions — is like the military strategy of dividing and conquering. That is, break down the design into modules, design each module separately, and then integrate the modules together. This approach is particularly helpful in the design of complex systems. In designing an aircraft, for example, the overall aircraft system may be broken down into subsystems, such as flight control, navigation, communication, and avionics. Separate teams are assigned to work on each subsystem. Each team then designs its assigned module. The teams meet periodically to do "system integration," that is, put the modules together. You can see that this approach is a practical necessity when a system becomes complex and it is impractical or impossible for one individual to design everything. On the other hand, as soon as design is being done by more than one person, it escapes the grasp of a single mind and certain new types of problems develop — the modules do not always fit together as they should. However, the more carefully we plan our design, the less of a problem this is.

The divide and conquer technique also makes sense for designing smaller systems — such as microcomputer programs — when the entire design team consists of a single person. By analyzing the design problem and dividing it up into modules, you make it possible to perform the design one logical step at a time. And since system integration is being done by one person, fewer problems are likely to occur.

Note that the key to success with this approach is to do adequate advance analysis and planning, and to avoid simply jumping in and starting to code.

This section introduced a few of the basic concepts of program planning and design. These concepts will be developed further in Chapter 4, which contains a recommended procedure for program development — from initial planning through to program testing and delivery.

THE MICROCOMPUTER REVOLUTION

Why is there so much interest these days in making programs user-friendly? There was not much talk about it 5 years ago, and 10 years ago the term had not even been invented. The major reason, probably, is that the advent of microcomputers has made computing power available to a far wider audience. The operator of a microcomputer is typically less sophisticated than the operator of a minicomputer or mainframe. As the microcomputer revolution progresses, people from all walks of life are coming into contact with computers. Often, they have had no prior experience with computers at all. This truly is a revolutionary change from the way things once were. In the old days, the only people who talked to computers were the experts in data-processing centers and computer science departments. They spoke a strange language, cast mysterious spells, and intimidated the world with their knowledge. However, things have changed. The secret has got out that computers are not that complicated after all; a lot of people who used to be frightened by computers now own them and put them on tables in their living rooms.

The trouble is, much of the software available for these machines still reflects the mentality of the data-processing center and the computer science department. That is, programs written by computer experts for computer experts still very much influence the way people write programs today. Gradually, however, the industry is waking up. The software publishers look at their balance sheets and discover that programs that are easy to use sell better than those that confuse their users. The lesson from all this is fairly clear: The key to the success of the microcomputer is software, and no less than this, the key to the success of that software is its user friendliness.

The Case for Making Programs User-Friendly

We suggested above that user-friendly programs will sell better and that program users will like them more. The first is a marketing consideration, the second a matter of user acceptance. While these are important, it is doubtful that either one would rank very high on a human factors–oriented designer's list of reasons for applying human factors in a design. This designer's concern is primarily with the *performance* of the human-computer system. Human factors are applied in the design because its creator knows that they will improve system performance. In many designs, with many types of equipment, with many types of operators, and in a wide variety of environments, conscious application of human factors improves performance. It does this because designs which are properly human-factored increase efficiency of use, increase effectiveness of use, reduce errors, and ease the learning process. People generally tend to prefer designs with good human factors as well, which suggests that they will have a better attitude toward those designs than others and that this may, in turn, influence their performance indirectly.

In an engineering sense, efficiency is the amount of output achieved for a given input. Translated into programming terms, efficiency is reflected in how much effort the program user must expend to achieve a particular program objective. Suppose that the objective is to enter a certain piece of data. In a user-friendly program, the computer would display a prompt to the operator requesting the required data, and it would test that entry for validity according to certain rules. If the entry were invalid, an error message would be displayed, telling the operator what error had been made and how to recover from it. In a non-user-friendly program, no prompt would be presented and there would be no error testing. The operator would have to know, from memory, what entry was required, what values of it were acceptable for entry, and how to restart the program when it crashed because of an invalid entry. Lack of user friendliness results in delays and lost time as the operator looks up things in manuals or attempts to recover from errors. This simple example illustrates how user friendliness can increase *efficiency.*

Effectiveness is a matter of accomplishing objectives. People are effective in using programs when they successfully do what they set out to do. Here, again, the probability of accomplishing the mission is much higher in a user-friendly program. This is not entirely due to the fact that the designers are more attentive to certain data input, output, and control features; it is also a consequence of the way such programs are planned. Designers must anticipate possible operator errors and protect against them. They must make the program as simple as possible, achieve a high degree of internal consistency, and avoid redundancy within the program. Strict adherence to these and other design principles results in a design which is fully integrated. As in a work of art, each part relates to every other part and to the whole. Without adherence to such design principles, the program may be more like a collection of independent subprograms, with bridges built between them. The net result of an integrated design is that the program becomes more effective for operators to use. They are then in a better position to accomplish their goals.

One of the most important reasons for human-factoring programs is *reduction of errors*. This consideration, in fact, is overriding in a number of computer applications — control of nuclear power systems, navigation, mixing of chemicals. The human factors design philosophy requires the designer to anticipate possible operator errors and to protect the operator and system against them.

While the consequences of operator error in the use of microcomputer programs are seldom as serious as they might be for applications with larger systems, they can be serious. Time or data may be lost, or if the program is being used in a control operation, the functions being controlled may run amok. Operator errors waste time, cost money, endanger someone, or do some combination of all three things. These are good reasons for error-proofing programs.

Finally, user-friendly programs are generally *easier to learn to use*. This ease of learning is not the result of built-in training features, but rather is an outgrowth of everything else. If you write a program that has a well-organized control structure, clear and simple displays, and ample prompting, the user's learning burden is eased considerably.

Still, there is another side to this story. Though much is to be gained by human-factoring a program, there are some things to be said against it. Readers with a human factors orientation will probably choke as they read what follows, but both sides of this story need telling.

The Case against Making Programs User-Friendly

Human-factoring a program takes time, effort, and ingenuity. For some programmers, these factors equate to program development costs, that is, dollars. What are the costs? These are very difficult to define in quantitative terms.

How much effort, how much extra ingenuity, how much extra time make the difference between a program that is user-friendly and one that is not? The answer depends not only on one's notion of what a user-friendly program is, but also upon the program designer. The experienced designer of user-friendly programs will build in certain features that the less experienced programmer will not. A best guess (and it is really little more than that) is that the experienced programmer must spend between 25 and 50 percent more time on a program when consciously attending to making it user-friendly. On complex programs, this may amount to a large cost in time and, if the programmer is being paid (most insist on it), *money*.

So what does all this mean? It means that, in certain cases, building these features in simply does not pay. Here are some cases in which extensive human factoring does not make sense:

• Simple programs designed for the use of one or two people

• Programs without serious error consequences

• Programs designed to answer a single question, i.e., the type of program written by engineers to solve a specific, one-of-a-kind design problem

The opposites of these three factors define when human factoring *is* important in design — namely, when many people will use the program, when error consequences are serious, or when the program will be used repeatedly.

This issue is really one of cost effectiveness. The question reduces to the following: How much will human-factoring the design improve system performance, and does the cost of the performance improvement counterbalance the additional development costs?

THE CREATIVE NATURE OF DESIGN

Though most human factors principles have been recognized through scientific research, their application in a particular design problem is anything but scientific. Each problem a designer faces is a little different from those previously faced. Therefore, several decisions must be made in solving the new problem. Each decision, in a sense, represents a potential study question itself. Designers of large systems — for example, aircraft manufacturers who sell jet fighter aircraft to the government — often run elaborate and expensive experimental studies to evaluate alternative designs objectively.

It is doubtful that most readers of this book have such resources. For them, design decisions therefore become judgment calls. They must make the best decision they can.

The process is creative in the sense that one comes to the design problem armed with a few general principles and a grab bag full of context-specific design guidelines which have been found to be preferable in this situation or that. The *design principles,* which are discussed in Chapter 3, amount to a kind of design philosophy. Each design principle can be applied in innumerable ways. For example, one of the key principles is *feedback.* Feedback is the information that you give to the operators to show them that something they have done has had an effect on the computer. In general, research findings indicate that feedback is necessary and helpful to operators. Feedback shows them that they are having an effect. However, in actual design terms, how do you apply the feedback principle? The following are some examples of ways in which feedback can be given:

• Every time the operator presses a key, the computer displays the entry on the screen.

• Every time the operator enters something into the program data base, the computer provides some explicit indication (for example, a sound) that shows that the information has been accepted.

• If the operator requests that a report be generated, the computer displays a message to show that data are being processed and that there will be a delay before the reports are generated.

The above are some specific and arbitrary examples of the application of a general design principle. These features do not come off a list of rules. Rather, they emerge from the designer's understanding of the feedback principle and its creative application to a specific design problem.

It should be no surprise that this is the case. Many people have commented on the creative nature of program design. Few occupations require more originality or greater ability to turn abstract ideas into tangible achievements.

The "cookbook" approach to human factoring, or for that matter to program design itself, is unworkable. In human factoring, the designer must internalize general design principles and then apply them to specific design problems. An understanding of the human operator must underlie design. The designer need not be a psychologist, biologist, or ergonomist, but must know some basic facts about human strengths and limitations in terms of human characteristics such as memory, vision, and information processing. Moreover, the designer must know what problems routinely plague the operator. (These topics are covered in Chapter 2.) Since any program that must be operated by a human being requires a human-computer interaction, it is only reasonable for a programmer to know as much about the human side of this equation as about the computer side.

Two

The Human Operator

What a piece of work is man!

Shakespeare

This chapter introduces you to the human operator, the man or woman who will use your program. Its objective is to make you aware of some of the basic characteristics of this operator that should influence your program design.

Operators are a diverse lot, and so the chapter starts with a discussion of some of the common types (or stereotypes) you are likely to encounter. This discussion is a bit oversimplified, but it has enough generality and truth to get you thinking about the differing needs and abilities of differing operator groups. In this chapter, as well as later in the book, the particular concern is with what some people label the "naive" operator.

We will look inside naive operators and see what makes them tick according to some of the theories of cognitive psychology. In recent years, cognitive psychologists have developed what is termed the "information processing" approach to the analysis of human cognition. These psychologists have drawn an analogy between the way the human mind and a computer process information. There are some surprising parallels. More important, however, this model has implications for the design of interactive computer programs.

We will take a close look at the two key human senses that are involved in human-computer interactions: audition (hearing) and vision.

People have internal mental models of how things work. In using computer programs, they have certain ideas about the cause-and-effect relationships between their actions and what is going on inside the computer. The accuracy of these models varies with the operator's sophistication. In addition, the strategies people employ to accomplish a task using a computer program vary with the mental model they possess.

This chapter will discuss all these topics. When you finish it, you may have a different way of thinking about the folks who use your programs.

TYPES OF OPERATORS

Any attempt to classify operators is a gross oversimplification, but necessary nonetheless. The programmer is forced to make assumptions about the audience before writing the program. Four stereotypes are presented here: sophisticated users, technical professionals, naive users, and skilled clerks. The universe of operators can be sliced in many other ways, but these four classes of operators are fairly typical.

By and large, microcomputers are owned and operated by individuals who use them at home or in their professional pursuits. The owner-operator of a microcomputer will often perform several different functions with this computer — functions that would be assigned to different people if a minicomputer or mainframe were being used. Thus, the operator of a microcomputer may at different times act as systems analyst, programmer, data-entry clerk, and report analyst. The operator of a larger computer is likely to play only one of these roles. It is true that as the power of microcomputers increases, the roles of operators are becoming more specialized and more similar to the roles involved in the use of larger computers. Still, three of the four classes of operators to be discussed are owner-operators of the all-around type. Only skilled clerks are specialized for one job function.

Naturally, you should recognize that these types represent points on a continuum and that actual operators will show certain characteristics, which will be described, in varying degrees.

The Importance of Defining Your Audience

One of the earliest lessons fledgling writers learn is to define their audience. The writer must know as much as possible about the audience — their intelligence, education, interests, and so forth — in order to tailor the book, article, etc., accordingly. A common error is for the writer to assume that readers know more than they actually do — more particularly, that readers will bring to the written page what the writer brings to it. It often comes as a shock, then, when readers scratch their heads, look puzzled, ask questions that reveal their confusion, or scribble question marks, exclamation points, or snide remarks on the manuscript. Such feedback is educational, builds humility, and sensitizes the writer to errors.

An analogous process occurs in computer programming. That is, the programmer must define the audience (the program users), understand what they bring to the program (their degree of sophistication about computers and their knowledge of computer programs, as well as their intelligence and motivation), and then write the program accordingly. Unfortunately, the feedback that programmers get is seldom as revealing as the feedback that writers get. However, feedback does come, and if the programmer has made wrong assumptions about the audience, the feedback may be traumatic.

An additional problem is that, as in writing, it is often difficult to define the audience precisely. Either we lack the knowledge, or the program user audience is so diverse as to make its definition meaning-less. In such cases, we cannot write the program for a single audience; we must take into account the needs of a range of users. The tech-niques for doing this are covered later in this book. The place to start, however, is with the best definition of the audience that we can make. Let us take a look at four user stereotypes.

Computer Professionals

You are, presumably, one of these. But for the moment, try not to take what is said personally. Remember, this discussion concerns the com-puter professional as a user of a program that you have written. This particular program user is, in other words, on the opposite side of the fence from you.

Computer professionals may or may not make their living as pro-grammers. If they do not, they probably could if they wanted to. These users have done considerable programming, probably in several lan-guages. They understand software design concepts. They also under-stand computer hardware — the interplay among CPU, memory, and input-output (I/O) devices. They are intelligent, well educated, and highly motivated. They are as smart as, or smarter than, you are. Some may have very high opinions of themselves. (On the other hand, some computer professionals are very humble.) Given your program, they will quickly grasp how it works in a technical sense.

Computer professionals are not intimidated by software, and if a particular program does not work quite as they would wish, they will want to customize it to suit their own needs. These are the kinds of people who call up the programmer and want to know the file structure so that they can modify it for their own purposes.

They have little patience. They like programs to be fast. Many of them care less about user-friendliness features than about finding ways to speed up their use of the program.

These users, since they are programmers themselves, are very sen-sitive to the shortcomings of a program. It is good to have one or two as friends who can test your program before it goes to market.

On the other hand, these users are not typical of the population that is using programs on today's microcomputers. Unless you are writing a specialized program aimed specifically at this audience, you would be best advised to target one of the other groups described below.

Professionals without Computer Experience

Most microcomputer users fall into this category. They are intelligent and well educated, and they know that a computer can help them do their job better. Typically, they do not have technical training in engineering or the sciences. They may use their computer to manage a stock portfolio, calculate a budget, plan their diet, or perform other data-base planning and management functions.

Unlike computer professionals, these users lack computer expertise — they do not have a particularly good understanding of what is happening inside their computer. They also lack broad experience in using different types of programs.

However, since they are intelligent and well educated, they share certain traits with computer professionals. They lack patience, set high standards for program performance, and are intolerant of program errors. Since they lack technical expertise, they are in no position to modify programs that do not work properly. Instead, they will return them to the dealer, condemn them to their friends, fire off angry letters to journals that potential users might read, and make the programmer miserable. These are the users who make careless programmers release early revisions to their programs or, worse, change the program's name to escape ignominy.

Here are some other defining characteristics of these users:

- They know little about computers.
- They are not interested in knowing about computers — in fact, they may not even like them.
- They know how to turn the computer on.
- They (probably) know how to load the program and bring up the first menu.
- They have probably not read any program documentation.
- They cannot be expected to remember anything that is not presented within the context of the program.
- They will consistently ignore screen prompts, and will enter data that have inappropriate type, format, length, and other characteristics.
- They are motivated to accomplish the function the program was designed to serve.
- They resent it when things go wrong and will blame it on you.
- They will write data to the program disk, if possible.
- They will attempt to load data from an empty disk drive.

The picture drawn here is of program users who are intelligent yet arbitrary, who are demanding but lazy, and who set impossible standards. These are users to whom user friendliness in a computer program is critical. In most cases, this is the best audience to keep in mind when you write your program.

Naive Users

Naive users know next to nothing about computers or about how computer programs are supposed to work. They seldom use programs. You should assume that their first exposure to a program is in your program — that they have never used a program before. Naive users are children and adults who have little or no exposure to computers in their daily lives. When they sit down before a microcomputer, it is usually to play a game or to use some simple home or entertainment program.

The most that one can assume about this audience is that they know how to turn their computers on and off. The programmer must therefore manage the human-computer interaction very carefully. Every step of the interaction must be guided with menus or detailed on-screen explanations. Every possible error must be trapped. This audience is even more likely to make the careless errors described above than are professionals without computer experience. Along these lines, Murphy's Law comes to mind: If something can be done incorrectly, the naive operator will do it. This is not meant as an insult to the thousands of people who use microcomputer programs. It is being realistic — recognizing that mistakes are inevitable in this imperfect world. If you are writing programs for the naive user, you must carefully anticipate them and protect the user against them.

Most programs being written for microcomputers today are directed at professionals without computer experience and at naive users. The requirements of these two groups are basically identical. The naive user requires more careful handling, in terms of on-screen prompts and status information, but both groups are inclined to make the same types of errors of commission or omission.

Skilled Clerks

Skilled clerks are not programmers, but they use a microcomputer for several hours per week and develop very strong user skills. Operators falling into this class are word-processing operators, data-entry clerks, and others who use a program frequently enough to master it. These operators do not have a high degree of computer sophistication, but they do become highly skilled. They are like computer professionals in their interest in speed. They quickly grow impatient with features designed for less experienced operators, which tend to slow them down.

Skilled clerks are expert operators, but not programmers. In a sense, they are what naive users or professionals without computer experience can develop into after several years of experience.

Operator Stereotypes and Program Design

Now that we have considered some generalizations about program users, what do we do? The best advice is to use these generalizations as reference points in planning and designing your program. Consider, before you start writing the program, whether it will be used by one or more of these groups — or some other group not mentioned here.

Plan, design, and write the program with the particular group in mind. If the program will be used by computer professionals or skilled clerks, then *speed of operation* is of the essence. If it will be used by operators without computer experience or naive users, then *careful hand-holding* is the prime consideration. If the program will cross the boundary between the more and less skilled users — for example, used by both professionals without computer experience and skilled clerks — then the needs of both groups must be taken into account. This can be done in one of two ways. The first is to design the program to serve the needs of the least sophisticated operator (lowest common denominator). The second, and preferred, method is to make the program flexible so that it can function at two different levels. One way of doing this is to provide an operator-selectable level of prompting. This permits users to specify at the outset how much prompting they want. Prompting takes time and will slow down skilled operators. By providing this and similar features, you can permit operators to tailor the program to suit their individual needs.

HUMAN INFORMATION-PROCESSING MODEL

Suppose a friend calls you on the telephone and tells you that she has discovered a sensational new type of portable computer. This computer, she says, requires no electrical power; has a seemingly unlimited information storage capacity; will accept input in the form of light or sound and three other forms; and functions quite effectively in hostile environments.

You might be intrigued enough to inquire whether this computer has any obvious shortcomings. At this point, your friend remarks that it has a few. It is true that it has an almost unlimited storage capacity, but its input buffer is limited to about five bytes and all input data must move through this buffer before being processed. It can accept input in five different forms, but it is essentially a single-channel processor and can handle only one of these at a time. But its most serious problem, she remarks after a pause, is that it is somewhat unreliable. When you turn it on, it usually works quite well, but after it has been running for a while, it has a tendency to lose or distort data or, in some cases, fabricate data from thin air. It also seems to be sensitive to the time of day, to the amount of sunlight it receives, to the quality of its interactions with other computers of its type, and to a number of mysterious factors.

Are you interested? If this were an actual machine, which it obviously is not, you would probably not be interested. Despite the machine's impressive memory and portability, its unreliability would make it impractical for most applications. Unfortunately, since the machine just described is your human operator, you will have to live with it anyway.

The Human as an Information Processor

The comparison of a human operator with a computer is very relevant. The two have much in common — enough that many psychologists today are using the parallel as a jumping-off point in their investigations. If you put the two — human being and computer — side by side, as in the anecdote above — you quickly see that the human information processor has some impressive capabilities as well as some striking weaknesses. To illustrate this more clearly, let us take a closer look at human information processing. Assume in what follows that the human information processor is acting in the capacity of a computer operator, seated before and monitoring a CRT display of computer-generated information. A sequence of actions occurs as the operator monitors the computer display. This sequence is illustrated in Figure 2-1 and described below.

Sensation. When information appears on the display, light waves travel through the air and affect the operator's sensory apparatus — the eyes and the part of the brain that sense light. If the operator is looking away from the display, or otherwise occupied, nothing will register on the senses. Sensation is not conscious, but it is a precondition of the conscious awareness that information is being received. Human operators are single-channel processors. They cannot monitor two displays simultaneously, or even two senses. They are, however, capable of quickly switching their processing resources back and forth among different displays, and so in some cases they may achieve the seeming equivalent of parallel processing.

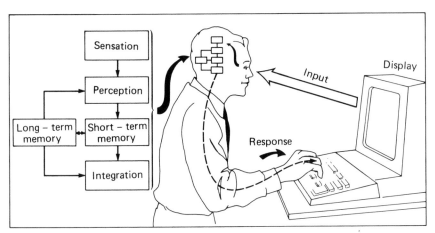

Figure 2-1 Human information processing involves several stages: Incoming information must first be sensed, which is done preconsciously. Next, sensation is integrated into a conscious awareness of the stimulus; perception occurs. Active, deliberate processing begins with short-term memory, in which an interplay occurs between incoming information and the content of long-term memory, and meaning is assigned. Eventually, the information becomes fully integrated and the operator responds to it, "closing the loop" with the computer.

Perception. Following sensation, there comes the act of perception. Perception amounts to the integration of sensation into some meaningful awareness — that light has been seen, sound has been heard, something has been felt — though meaning has not yet been assigned. Perception is influenced by learning and by what has happened to the individual in the past. It is also influenced by the state of arousal and fatigue. When one is fresh and wide awake, perception works well. When one is disinterested or fatigued, perception is less effective. You may have heard of a phenomenon called the "vigilance decrement." This term is used in reference to a decline in detection performance of sonar or radar operators as time passes and they sit before a detection display. They will be quite good at detecting targets early in their watch, but later on, as they become fatigued, they detect fewer and fewer targets. In signal-processing terms, they become less sensitive detectors. A typical vigilance decrement curve is shown in Figure 2-2.

Short-Term Memory. Active, deliberate human information processing commences with short-term, or "working," memory. The term "short-term memory" is something of a misnomer. This "memory" is really much more like a processing buffer. It is a location in which there is an interplay between information coming in from the senses and long-term memory, the information is processed, and the human being makes sense of it. If this sounds a bit vague, it should, because short-term memory is not fully understood.

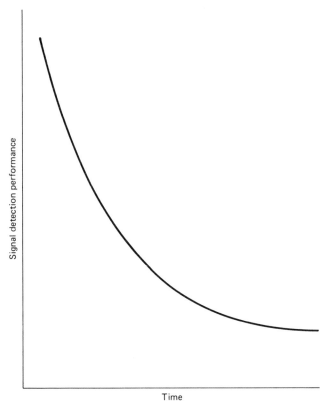

Figure 2-2   Vigilance decrement curve. Operator vigilance is tested in long (½ hour or more), monotonous tasks. In such tasks, detection performance is usually high at the beginning of the watch, but it rapidly declines and levels out as time goes on. (Not shown, but also characteristic, is that detection performance will improve as the watch nears its end, if the operator knows that the watch is almost over.)

What is known, however, is of profound significance. The contents of short-term memory are what you are currently attending to. If you look up a telephone number and walk to the telephone, your short-term memory holds that number. As soon as you dial the number, the contents of short-term memory are rapidly lost. Many people think of short-term memory as memory for recent events — for example, what they had for lunch yesterday. This is a misapprehension. The contents of short-term memory are constantly updated. It is like a buffer. Old information is shifted out as new information enters.

The capacity of short-term memory is well-defined and surprisingly limited. In a research review that has now become a classic, G. A. Miller showed that its capacity is around seven items. (He coined the term "magic number 7 ± 2," since the studies he reviewed indicated that short-term memory typically ranges between five and nine items; see the Bibliography.) More recent studies have shown that the number may be somewhat less, perhaps as low as three items.

When we speak of the human being as a limited-capacity, single-channel information processor, you can see that short-term memory is one of the key limitations. A buffer this small does not have much excess capacity. There are some wrinkles on this limitation that may be of interest. First, the contents of short-term memory can be preserved for a while by "rehearsal," that is, by consciously attending to what is in memory. Rehearsal is what you do when you repeat over and over again the license number of the car that sideswiped you so that you do not forget the number before you get a chance to stop and write it down. Second, people seem to be able to handle more than seven things in their memory through a process called "chunking." Chunking occurs when you let one concept stand for several things (for example, when you form a word from the first letters of several related things you want to remember). In chunking, you increase your effective short-term storage capacity by coding information.

While rehearsal may be used to extend the time the information is kept in short-term memory, and chunking may be used to increase storage capacity, these phenomena have little practical significance to the programmer. It would be foolish to recommend the writing of programs that require their users to rehearse or to chunk to overcome these built-in limitations. What these laboratory phenomena do pinpoint is the basic limitation of the processor itself. And here is where the human factors considerations come in. In designing programs, you need to make sure that you do not overstress the human processor. Do not, for example, expect people to remember fifteen things for 5 minutes. They can hang on to *about five things for about 15 seconds*. The items may be letters, numbers, names, or any other single cognitive entity. If you present three such items on a display screen and then erase the display, the operator has a reasonable chance of remembering them long enough to do something with them in the next few seconds. If you present five such items, most people will be operating at the limit of their capacity. If you present ten such items, the person will not be able to perform.

Laboratory studies have shown that, without rehearsal, information will be retained in short-term memory for about 15 seconds. After that, it will decay and be lost. Decay is one way that information can be lost from short-term memory.

A second way that information can be lost is through displacement. With such a small capacity, short-term memory is filled very quickly and, as new information comes in, old must be shifted out. In this sense, short-term memory is like a shift register.

Extensive research has been done concerning short-term memory in both vision and hearing. Basically, the same limitation applies in both cases.

Long-Term Memory. The information coming in through the sensory channel must be decoded and integrated. For example, sound vibrations must be converted to phonemes, to words, to sentences, to meanings — in other words, through a series of integrative transformations that involve an interplay between short-term memory and the content and decision rules contained in long-term memory.

Long-term memory is quite different from short-term memory. The capacity of long-term memory probably has limits, but they are not yet known. If short-term memory is analogous to a buffer, long-term memory is more like permanent disk memory. Long-term memory contains all the information a person has encoded throughout a lifetime. Like the disk, the information in long-term memory appears to be organized. The disk has a directory that can be used to access any piece of information. Human beings have a similar directory — actually several directories — that permit them to access what they need to know. Much research of late has focused on what is termed "semantic" memory. This research views the memory as a complex network structure in which each item is located at a node of the network and is accessed through links that correspond to various semantic categories. If somebody asks you to name all the people you know whose first names start with A, for example, you can access those names by using a semantic feature, the letter A. You can access such information by using a number of other semantic categories, as well. The organization of memory is not well understood, although all researchers seem to agree that long-term memory does have a structure and is organized. Research findings also show that you can code (i.e., put things into memory) and recall (i.e., extract things from memory) better by capitalizing on this structure.

The information may be encoded to different degrees in human memory. In general, the more "deeply" the information is processed, the stronger the memory trace. The less it is processed, the weaker the memory trace. This is one way in which human memory differs from disk memory. On a disk, information is either encoded or not encoded. In human memory, it may be encoded at different levels.

In extracting information from memory, you may be put in the position of either *recalling* it or *recognizing* it. In a recall task, you are presented with a question (explicit or implicit) and must answer it — for example, "Name all your friends whose names begin with A."

In a recognition task, you are presented with information and must determine whether or not you are familiar with it. Recognition tasks are easier than recall tasks because you do not have to organize a search of your own memory. This is one of the reasons that menu-driven programs are easier for inexperienced operators to use than are programs that require operators to make use of commands that they have memorized. The menu poses a simple recognition task, but program commands must be recalled from memory.

Operator Response.   There is a mind, will, or intelligence involved in all this processing. After the information has been processed, operators deal with it at a conscious level. They may ignore it, maintain it in their short-term memories, or make some response — write something down or manipulate controls to modify their displays. If they do the latter, then the loop is finally closed. That is, information originating on the display and processed in the human operator leads to a decision to adjust the control, which modifies the display. In this case we have what can be thought of as a closed-loop system.

The following is a summary of the basic limitations of the human information processing system:

- It is a single-channel processor.
- It must be focused on display to sense information.
- It depends upon perception, a function of attention, which in turn depends upon state of arousal and fatigue.
- Its short-term memory has a capacity of roughly seven items.

    Information is lost through decay in about 15 seconds.

    Old information is displaced by new information.

- Its long-term memory has unlimited capacity.

    Information is organized in semantic structures.

    Recognition tasks are easier than recall tasks.

In this section, the human information-processing model has been presented in highly simplified form. To readers who want a more detailed description, see Card, Moran, and Newell's book *The Psychology of Human-Computer Interaction* (see the Bibliography).

HEARING

While stereo manufacturers make a point of advertising frequency ranges from below 10 to more than 20,000 hertz (Hz), human hearing (or audition) is most sensitive in a range between about 1000 and 4000 Hz. This is a fairly safe range to use in presenting auditory informa-

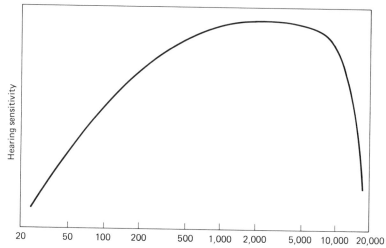

Figure 2-3 Human hearing sensitivity curve. Human hearing sensitivity extends from a few hertz to more than 10 kilohertz (kHz), but the range of greatest sensitivity is between about 1 kHz and 4 kHz.

tion. As people age, their ability to hear the higher frequencies (above 10,000 Hz) declines. Also, in any given population, there is considerable variability in hearing. Thus, one is well advised to present auditory information in the safe range given. Figure 2-3 shows a human hearing sensitivity curve.

The perception of sound does depend upon the orientation of the listener (i.e., which way the head is pointed) but for most computer applications can be considered not to matter. That is, hearing is influenced little by which way the head of the computer operator is facing. This is an obvious but important difference between the senses of hearing and vision. For you to see something, it must fall within your visual field — your eye must be pointed at or close to it. This is not required for hearing, which is one reason that sound is often used in warning signals. Though sound is probably used most commonly as a warning signal in programs written for small computers, it can be and is used in a number of other ways as well. Here are some of the possibilities:

- *Uncoded sound alone.* An example is computer-generated speech.
- *Coded sound alone.* Examples are intermittent beeps as a warning signal, a sequence of tones to indicate a particular program status, a Bronx cheer to indicate a bad move in a game.
- *Sound (coded or uncoded) that is redundant with the visual display.* An example is a computer game with sound effects that rein-

force what is happening on the screen, such as explosions, laser firing, rocket movements.

• *Sound to supplement the visual display.* Some information is presented by using sound and some by using the visual display.

Each of these four uses of sound is a little different. The differences are based on whether or not the sound is coded, whether it is used alone or with a visual display, and, if used with visual display, whether it presents redundant information.

Sound is coded when the listener must interpret it to determine a meaning. It can be argued that all sound is coded in some form, but some types of sound are certainly much more directly and automatically interpretable than others. Speech, for example, is interpreted so quickly that for all practical purposes it can be considered uncoded. Information coded by other means, such as frequency, number of beeps, frequency pattern (melody), and so forth, is not as directly interpretable by the user but can become so with practice.

When audio and visual displays are used together, they are mutually reinforcing. The observer may use both senses to interpret information that is presented — this has greater impact than using either sense alone. In many cases it is desirable to present some information through sound and other information through visual images, without the two necessarily being coordinated. This makes sense when one of the channels (for example, the visual), is already heavily loaded — in this case, the audio channel can be used to present additional information.

Hearing is a complex subject, and this section has highlighted only some basic ideas that will help you put it in perspective. The use of sound in programs is discussed further in Chapter 5.

VISION

Vision is our most important sense. It is also the sense most directly involved in the majority of human-computer interactions, which typically take place by way of a CRT display. This display may be either monochrome (single color) or capable of presenting color, and it may be used under varying degrees of ambient (background) illumination. In addition to CRT displays, computer output may be presented on other visual media such as printers. Since the properties of human vision govern how a person perceives what appears on these displays, it is obviously important for the designer to have a basic understanding of vision.

The Visual Field

The visual field of the eye is the area that can be seen when the head and the eyes are motionless. A single, stationary eye is capable of registering visual information across an angle of nearly 180° — essentially, everything in front of the viewer. With two-eyed vision, this field is extended even farther. Sensitivity is greatest at the center of this field and decreases toward the periphery.

Despite the width of the visual field, in viewing a display the human operator typically attends to a much smaller field. While reading text, for example, the brain will typically register about 5 characters at a time. However, the eye moves rapidly, starting and stopping, and thereby giving the impression of a much wider field of apprehension.

The characteristics of the eye are important in designing displays. A warning signal, for example, must either be presented where the eyeball is looking or be made conspicuous in some other way so that it will attract attention. One method is to use a flashing message in the peripheral visual field. Another is to forego the visual warning altogether and use sound, which is not dependent on visual search and detection; sound produces a sort of automatic "interrupt" of the human information-processing system.

Brightness and Color Perception

The eye is sensitive to brightness and to hue (color) and color saturation (purity).

Brightness Perception. Light brightness is equivalent to intensity. The brighter something is, the more readily we see it. The human visual apparatus has a very wide dynamic range (i.e., the range, from dimmest to brightest, over which light can be perceived). This range is far wider than that of the visual displays associated with computers.

While absolute brightness is important in visual perception, the perception of information on CRT and other visual displays is typically more influenced by *contrast* — the difference in brightness level between the message and the background field. The greater the contrast, the more readily perceptible the message. The influence of poor contrast on message legibility is as evident in an out-of-adjustment video monitor or worn-out television tube as it is on a page that was typed with a worn-out ribbon. In all these cases, poor contrast between message and background reduces message legibility.

Brightness can be used to code information on a display. For example, brightness level might be used to represent temperature on a graphic cross section of a jet engine. The brighter the display, the higher the corresponding temperature. People do not have a very good *absolute* sense of brightness, that is, the ability to remember what a particular brightness level represents in terms of the variable being coded. Without extensive training, they can remember about five different brightness levels. The perception of *relative* brightness levels is better than this, and performance can be improved by presenting a brightness key on the display. In planning brightness-coded displays, the designer must assure that the contrast between different coded levels is sufficient to enable the eye to tell the difference.

A blinking message appearing on a screen is attention-getting in part because it represents a systematic variation in brightness across time. The more extreme the range of brightnesses from displayed message to background field, the more attention-getting the message. Attention is also influenced by other variables, such as blink rate, message location, and use of color.

Color Perception. The second aspect of visual sensitivity is the eye's ability to perceive different hues, or spectral frequencies. Visual sensitivity is not constant across the spectrum, but varies systematically as a function of hue. In addition, the sensitivity of the light-adapted eye is different from that of the dark-adapted eye. Figure 2-4 is a curve which indicates human visual sensitivity as a function of spectral frequency for both the dark- and the light-adapted eye.

The eye is least sensitive to the extremes of the visual spectrum — to black, violet, and blue at the shorter wavelengths, and red at the longer. This holds true for both the dark- and the light-adapted eye. The dark-adapted eye is most sensitive to green. The light-adapted eye is most sensitive to yellow and orange. Since sensitivity varies with dark adaptation, the program designer should take this into account in selecting colors for display. If a color CRT is used in a darkened room, then the eye will be dark-adapted and most sensitive to green. If the CRT is used in a bright room, then color sensitivity will shift toward the yellow and orange.

That the eye is less sensitive to the spectral extremes (blue and red) does not mean that these colors should be altogether avoided. Rather they can serve as suitable background fields for colors that the eye is more sensitive to. In setting up contrasts, however, it is important to avoid certain color combinations which can cause confusion by producing a sensation of shadows and afterimages. Color combinations to avoid are red and green, blue and yellow, green and blue, and red and blue.

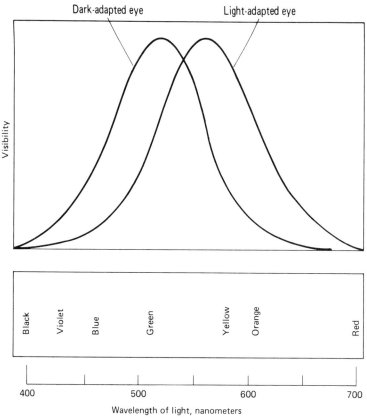

Figure 2-4 Human visual sensitivity versus spectral frequency for the dark-adapted and light-adapted eye. *(Adapted from Cakir, Hart, and Stewart:* Visual Display Terminals, *copyright 1980, by permission of John Wiley & Sons, Ltd.)*

Because of the physical construction of the eye, it is less sensitive to red or green when these colors appear at the periphery of the visual field. The perception of other colors, such as yellow or white, is less degraded in equivalent parts of the peripheral field. Since this is the case, the designer should avoid using red or green for information that will appear in the periphery, and instead use yellow or white.

As much as 10 percent of the male population is color-blind, but color-blindness among females is so small as to be numerically insignificant. The percentage of males who are color-blind is large enough that it cannot be ignored. You take a significant risk if you design a program that requires color vision for effective use.

A reasonable strategy for handling color-blindness is to use redundant coding. For example, color is quite desirable in map displays, on which various features may be indicated by different symbols. These symbols are easier to identify and discriminate when they are both shape- and color-coded — that is, *dual-coded*. Information coding is discussed in greater detail in Chapter 6.

Whereas the eye can discriminate differences among many different colors, most people do not have a very good absolute color sense. When viewing their own color photographs, for example, people are often surprised at the striking difference between the colors in the photos and those they remember from the time the picture was taken (assuming the picture portrays the colors of the scene fairly accurately). People do not have a built-in sense of color, or an "absolute color pitch" that permits them to recognize a color in some absolute sense. Most people are capable of recognizing between four and nine distinct colors when these colors are presented independently and used to code information. This recall number is in the same range as short-term memory, but the color memory limitation is caused by another mechanism. As in brightness coding, color discrimination can be increased through training or by the use of an on-screen color key.

There are a number of different philosophies about the use of color in displays. The most shallow is to use color for its own sake, without any real attempt to capitalize on its advantages and compensate for its disadvantages in human perception. A first advantage is that color provides a far greater range of contrast and coding options than does monochrome display. Even with the relatively inexpensive and primitive color capabilities of microcomputers, an enormous number of colors can be generated and used effectively to code different types of information. A second advantage of color is that it significantly aids visual search. Color may be used for reasons other than these, but it is then essentially window dressing.

Some disadvantages of color are that some people are color-blind and cannot use it effectively, that designing color displays is more demanding than designing monochrome displays, and that color equipment is more expensive.

COGNITIVE MODELS

A cognitive model is a person's internal representation of something in the external world. Since the phenomena of the external world are many and varied, people's models of them can take many different forms.

A Mental Map

One type of cognitive model is a sort of internal mental map that permits you to find your way around the physical world of your daily life without getting lost. On this map are the physical locations of your home, the place you work, the grocery store, and so forth. You built up this map through practice and probably do not think about it. However, you become very conscious of the need for such an internal representation — or an actual, paper map — when you visit an unfamiliar area and cannot find your way around.

This happens when you move to a new area or when you go, for example, on a business trip to a place that you have not been to before. Then you suddenly realize that getting from point A to point B — from Yonkers to Whippany — requires you to make scores of checks of street signs, cross-checks to maps, and decisions. And unless you are lightning-fast and brilliant, it also involves your making a lot of mistakes. However, the second time you make the trip it becomes easier, the third time still easier, and so on. After you have made that trip a few times, you build up your internal map to the point that you no longer need the paper one and can make the trip without even thinking about it.

In addition, there are individual differences in people's skills at building maps. If you travel for a living, you have probably learned some techniques or *strategies* for finding your way around an unfamiliar place. You may, for example, sit down with a map and plot your route before you put your car in gear. You may mark certain landmarks and keep your eyes open for them. On the other hand, if you have little experience as a traveler, you may find that a high level of anxiety greets you in a strange place, that the maps appear incorrect, that all the other drivers seem crazy, that there are not enough road signs, and that you cannot seem to keep street names in your mind long enough to look for them (anxiety reduces short-term memory capacity).

Using a new computer program involves many of the same processes as finding your way around an unfamiliar geographic area. Programs vary in complexity, of course, but the typical business program will consist of several subprograms which are linked together in some fashion through a control structure. The subprograms may allow various types of data entry, display, operating modes, and so forth. Before operators can use such programs effectively, they must know their destination (the subprograms they want to use) and what streets to turn on (sequence control actions) to get there. They will have to check signs (display indications of current subprogram, status, operating mode, etc.), make decisions, make incorrect turns (incorrect keyboard entries), and so forth, until they get to their destination.

As in using a road map, skill in using a computer program increases with practice. There are also individual user differences. As a computer professional who is familiar with many types of programs, you will quickly find your way around a new program, largely through the transfer of skills that were developed using other programs. On the other hand, unfamiliar users will have more difficulty finding their way around, make more errors, experience greater anxiety, and have far more frequent short-term memory lapses.

As a designer, there are certain things you can do to help users remain oriented and find their way around your program and its various subprograms without getting lost or making a large number of errors. The key is to provide an adequate user map of the program in the documentation and to give ample prompting within the program.

Mental Models of Computers

In addition to mental maps, people seem to possess and use internal models of how things work. The accuracy and completeness of these models varies with the individual and the device. One person may have a very good idea of how the various systems in an automobile — fuel, ignition, cooling, power transmission, hydraulics — function to make the car move and stop, while another's knowledge may be limited to knowing that putting gas into the thing makes it go and stepping on the brakes stops it. In reality, one need not have an entirely accurate or complete model of a system to use it effectively, but the model must be good enough for accurate prediction. (Many of the models of science have acknowledged limitations but are still quite useful.)

The idea of a cognitive model has direct relevance in the design of computer programs. In order for people to use a program that you have written, they must have some understanding of computer hardware and software. How much understanding do they need? This, of course, depends upon how you write your program. If you write the program so that it has extensive prompting and holds the user's hand throughout, then all that is required is for the user to understand that computers require electricity, programs are stored on magnetic media, and that the user must turn the computer on and perhaps make a few keyboard entries in order to get things moving. With such a limited understanding of computers, you could expect little of the operator and could not write a very complex program. Such an operator could probably play a computer game or use a program that performed one simple function, such as balancing a checkbook, but not much more.

Since your ambitions probably extend beyond such simple applications, your program will generally be designed based on the assumption that the operator will have a somewhat more sophisticated mental model of the functioning of a computer and the program that drives it. Suppose, for example, that you are designing a word processor. This program will be used to compose text at the keyboard; manipulate that text in various ways; save text blocks to files that are written to disk; merge, read, and purge files; link files so that they can be printed out in hard-copy form; and perform various text editing functions, such as insertion, deletion, and search and replacement. The program just described would require the operator to understand the following basic concepts:

- What computer files are, and how they are stored, retrieved, and edited
- That computers have a "working" memory (RAM) — a working area that can be used to store text as it is composed, edited, and used during hard-copy printout; that this working memory has limitations that should not be exceeded; and that power failures can sometimes be traumatic.
- That some keyboard entries control the computer and others become text

These ideas are not complex, but without them, an operator would have little idea of how to use your word processor. Research has shown that people can use computers and other devices without having a full understanding of them. When they do so, they are at a distinct disadvantage, however. For example, some studies have shown that such users cannot take full advantage of the capabilities of the system. They will learn some of its features and master them, but they will be reluctant to try procedures that exercise capabilities that they do not fully understand. Sometimes they will show what is called "superstitious" behavior, repeatedly performing a rote procedure which fails to produce the desired result but which they learned elsewhere and trust. If you want to have some fun and see this for yourself, get a reverse polish notation (RPN) calculator and ask someone who has never used one before to perform some basic arithmetic operations.

If you suspect that the users of your program will have incomplete mental models of how computers or programs function, you have a number of options. In some cases, you can educate your audience. You can conduct a class or provide the required information and documentation. Another option is to design the program so that detailed knowledge of computers or programs is not required. You can provide extensive prompting and other forms of help to the operator. As noted earlier, however, this may limit program utility.

Yet another option, which may or may not be practical, is to design software that will conform with a mental model that the program user already possesses. This may sound rather farfetched, but it is precisely the idea that underlies the Xerox Star interface, Apple's Lisa, and the state-of-the-art software being produced by some of the more visionary software developers. In such programs, extensive graphics are used to convey familiar visual analogs of the computer world: File records look like index cards, a text editor screen looks like a piece of paper, a purging routine is represented by a wastebasket, and so forth. The operator uses a mouse or light pen to point to visual icons (graphic representations) to make the program perform functions such as filing or purging information. Developing this kind of software is expensive. There are also obvious limits to what you can do with this kind of interface. However, the development of such interfaces underlines the need that progressive software firms have recognized for users to be able to relate to computers in a more natural way than they have in the past. What is implicit in such developments is that program users possess or will develop mental models of how their hardware and software systems work and, if the software can provide analogs that are familiar in everyday experience, human-computer interactions will be simplified.

Cognitive models and maps are useful concepts for discussing how people seem to represent the world. However, these are basically research constructs or metaphors and must not be taken too literally. The way that people actually represent the world is far from well understood and is undoubtedly more complex than these simple metaphors suggest. However, these are useful tools to help us structure our thought and discussion and they can help us in deciding how we should and should not design a human-computer interface.

STRATEGIES

A strategy may be thought of as a set of decision rules one uses to solve a problem or accomplish a goal. Generally, strategies enable solving the problem or accomplishing the goal more efficiently, or at least their users think that they do. For example, one may have a strategy for getting a salary increase that involves coming to work conspicuously early and staying conspicuously late on days when the boss will see; being particularly responsive to memos from those who matter (boss, boss's secretary, senior vice presidents); implicitly or explicitly taking

credit for good ideas and blaming mistakes on inarticulate subordi-
nates; socializing only with a certain strata of the staff; and perhaps, if
time is left over, attempting to do a good job. Strategies such as these
— as described in Machiavelli's *The Prince* — though not generally
acknowledged, and perhaps not followed consciously, nonetheless exert
a powerful influence on behavior.

Similarly, a program designer will often have in mind strategies for
using a program that involve, for example, using a series of subprograms in a particular order to accomplish some goal. The designer of
an investment program might intend that the first thing the operator
should do when starting the program is to update the files by entering
all purchases and sales, the second thing is to compute a new portfolio
profile, and the third thing is to print out a profit and loss statement.
This, in fact, may be the only intelligent way to use the program. Still,
there is nothing requiring the program user to use it this way, and if
the program designer has not taken the time to articulate a strategy in
some explicit form (such as provided directions in the program user's
guide), it is likely that many operators will misuse the program. In
other words, the existence of a powerful tool (a program) does not
guarantee its effective use. *Before someone can use your strategy in
your program, you must tell them what it is.*

Three

Design Principles

Certain key principles support the design of user-friendly programs. These principles are not arbitrary, but follow logically from the nature and characteristics of the human operator. This chapter will translate the characteristics of the human operator discussed during Chapter 2 into twelve practical design principles that you can follow as you design your software. Many of these principles will be familiar. That is because you have encountered at least some of them before, either in a technical or other context. For example, principles such as simplicity and consistency apply equally to software design, to writing, and to a variety of technical or aesthetic activities. Still, the principles are not universally recognized and are by no means universally followed.

How should you use these principles? Study this chapter carefully and assemble a mental checklist that you install in the back of your mind. Think of these twelve principles as human factors commandments whose violation is a sort of sin. Well, perhaps you need not attach that much significance to them, but they are important.

In what follows, each of the design principles is discussed separately. The design principle is first defined, and then examples are given of its application in one or more aspects of program design.

1. DEFINE THE USERS

Designing a program is much like writing a letter. In either case, one of the first steps is to identify the audience and design or write accordingly. Differing audiences have differing needs and expectations. If you ignore them, you will disappoint expectations or, worse, fail to meet needs.

Chapter 2 described four operator types: (1) computer professionals, (2) professionals without computer experience, (3) naive users, and (4) skilled clerks. These operator types are really points on a continuum rather than narrow categories, but they are useful classifications for thinking about the potential audience for your program. As noted in Chapter 2, computer professionals are probably the smallest audience, the most demanding in terms of program flexibility, the least patient, and the least in need of prompting and other operator help. The requirements of skilled clerks are similar. Naive operators are at the other extreme, often in need of constant hand-holding and likely to make every blunder in the book as well as a lot of others that no one thought to put in the book. Somewhere in a gray area between these extremes lies the realm of the professional without computer experience. Such operators represent a range of needs depending upon where they fall in the continuum.

46

Sometimes you will be writing a program for just one of these audiences. That makes your task fairly simple. Define the audience, and plan your program accordingly. Often you will be writing your program for more than one audience — typically, for some combination of professionals without computer experience and naive users. In these cases, you must anticipate the needs of both audiences. How do you write a program for two different audiences? There are two basic approaches: (1) write for the lowest common denominator, and (2) provide different features for different audiences. The first approach is the simplest but will be unsatisfactory for more sophisticated program users. However, if there are not many such users, it is a reasonable solution. The second approach is more difficult for the programmer but preferable for program users. Essentially, this amounts to *providing for operator growth* in the use of the program. Operators may, for example, need prompting today that they will not need next week, after they have used the program a few times. Obviously, as operators gain skill with your program, they need less hand-holding.

2. ANTICIPATE THE ENVIRONMENT IN WHICH YOUR PROGRAM WILL BE USED

How well a program works is influenced by the environment where it is used. The main factors to consider are light, noise, and distractions. If you live alone in a cabin on a mountaintop in Colorado and code only at night with the lights out, the program you produce could very well reflect this serene and somewhat unrepresentative environment. Program users who attempt to use the program in a noisy office with the lights on and with constant interruptions from coworkers may find it impossible.

Here are some reasons.

When you turn the lights on, you reduce the contrast range that can be displayed on a CRT display. This means that something you can see in a darkened room when writing the program may not show when the lights are turned on.

Another environmental factor is noise; it will affect the program user in two ways. First, surrounding noise may mask meaningful sounds (alerting signals or coded information) produced by your program. Second, this noise will sap some of the operator's processing resources. Some people are quite effective at reading and watching television at the same time, or performing other kinds of time-sharing activities, but the fact is that when you share your resources in this way, your performance is not as good as it would be if you focused on one activity alone. The distractions of noise work in much the same way. The louder and more frequent the noise, the more the operator's performance will be degraded.

Finally, distractions (telephone calls, interruptions from people, spilled coffee, etc.) interrupt the continuity of what program users are doing. If the program cannot be stopped temporarily and then started up again later, users may very well be forced to go back to the beginning and start over. Video game players know how handy it is to be able to freeze the attacking aliens in midair while they run to the refrigerator for another soda. This feature is an example of the principle we are discussing.

You may find it difficult or impossible to anticipate where and how your program might be used. In this case, you have your choice of designing the program for the worst possible environment (bright, noisy, distracting) or forgetting about this principle and moving on to something that you can get a handle on. On the other hand, on your mountaintop you may be receiving visions that permit you to have complete prescience. Make the best of the situation that you can.

3. GIVE THE OPERATORS CONTROL

Ideally, operators should be able to control the rate, amount, and importance of the information that is presented to them. There is a limit to the rate at which operators can process information. Your program can be used successfully only if you do not exceed their processing limits.

Operators vary in the rate at which they can process information. Also, these rates change as they learn and develop skill. People have built-in mechanisms that permit them to assess how successfully they are processing information that comes in, and to adapt their behavior accordingly. For example, experienced readers are able to evaluate how successfully they have obtained the relevant meaning from what they have just read. This self-assessment capability is quite different from reading skill itself — it is what is termed a "metacognitive" skill. In simple terms, a metacognitive skill permits people to assess the effectiveness of their own cognitive performance. In computer operation, these skills provide a feedback mechanism that permits operators to assess their performance and adapt it accordingly. If they are sitting before computers and being overwhelmed by the amount of information flowing across the screen, then they can recognize the need to slow it down and, if the program permits them to do so, slow it to match their processing capacity.

While this explanation may help you understand why you should give operators control, you can also see the need based on common sense. In commonsense terms, this principle reduces to a number of different admonitions, such as the following:

- *Do not present information too quickly.* Let operators control the rate, or start and stop the information as necessary.

- *Do not present too much information at once.* Present what is needed for accomplishing the task at hand and let operators access additional information as they need it.

- *Filter information.* Select the relevant information and display only that; do not dump your data base on users unless they request it.

4. MINIMIZE THE OPERATORS' WORK

Computers are machines, and one of the reasons early people invented machines was so that they could come down out of the trees and save themselves some work. Those who fail to recognize this principle and go with the flow in designing a program are not only ignorant of the movement of history, but out of touch with their own basic instincts. After all, why would people buy computers if they were not trying to do something that would be a lot more work without the computer?

In designing a program, there are many points at which programmers must choose between making things easier for themselves or for the operator. If you have any ambitions of success, then you probably expect that you, as a programmer, will be vastly outnumbered by those who will use your program. On this basis alone (i.e., the democratic principle), you should choose in favor of the operator.

Seriously, design objectives can be met in many different ways. For the operator, some of these ways make things easier than others. Often programmers may meet the letter of a specification by providing a certain program capability, but that capability may be so cumbersome to exercise that operators will avoid it. Consider, for example, the various ways that one may provide access to a data base to do editing. At the worst, raw, unformatted information is thrown up on the screen, without title or headers, and operators must decipher it before acting. At the other extreme is a data-base access program that presents data in the same format in which it was first entered — replicating original data-entry forms.

These two extremes reflect different design philosophies. In the first, programmers minimize work for themselves at the expense of operators. In the second, programmers make the trade-off in favor of operators, although this undoubtedly makes the design and coding of the program somewhat more difficult.

In designing user-friendly programs, always make this trade-off in favor of the program user. The work that this principle seeks to minimize is both mental and physical work. Mental work is the work involved in recalling things, performing mental calculations, making decisions, and so forth. Physical work is the work involved in flipping switches, pushing keys, and the like. Often, you can reduce mental work by letting the computer do some of the job. For example, suppose operators must retrieve a file from a directory. Do you require operators to type in the entire file name? You should not. Let them type in the minimum needed — one or two or three characters — and let the computer perform a fast, systematic search to save keyboard entries.

Here are some other illustrations of how mental and physical work can be minimized.

The work the program users must do to enter data can be made easier by minimizing such things as the number, length, and complexity of keyboard entries. If data already exist in the data base, access it instead of requiring operator reentry.

To minimize the effort required to move between programs, use simple program access methods, such as menus or single-character control codes. Organize the structure and relationships among your subprograms so that users can quickly grasp the program's overall structure and how to move from one point to another.

The foregoing specific examples of how the minimum work principle applies are for illustrative purposes only. In these cases, as in the application of the other design principles, you must interpret the principle in light of the particular design problem.

5. KEEP THE PROGRAM SIMPLE

This may be the oldest universal principle. It is universal in the sense that it seems to have found its way into the aesthetic of many different domains, including the arts, sciences, and engineering. Generally, those who practice in these fields find a virtue in simplicity. Equally, a well-composed painting without background clutter, a haiku, a short but elegant scientific proof, and a diesel engine design with fewer parts but greater power and economy than its predecessors are accepted as good things.

Of course, not everyone likes simplicity. A person who is lazy, or who does not know exactly what to say in words or in a particular technology, may find it convenient to work toward some other principle. This mentality is what creates such wonders of our age as automobile tail fins, large bureaucracies, and research projects that go on for years without meaningful results.

You may be thinking, "This is fine as fuzzy philosophy, but what am I supposed to do?" Start with attitude. Application of the simplicity principle requires a certain attitude or frame of mind. As you design the various aspects of your program, ask yourself questions such as these:

• Is there an easier way of doing this?
• Are there any ways in which this might confuse the operator?
• Is this really necessary?
• How could I simplify this for the operator?

After you have asked these questions yourself and designed your program, let others try it out and see if they can find any ways of simplifying things.

Here are some examples of how the simplicity principle can be applied.

First, suppose that you must format information for presentation on a display screen. You have a large amount of information to present. You are faced with the choice of fitting everything onto one screen or distributing the information in blocks across several different screens. If the blocks of information can be separated without destroying context, then present them on separate screens.

Second, suppose that you are designing a menu-driven program. You must make several decisions in designing your menus. You must decide how many choices to present on each menu, the wording and length of each choice, how menu options will be selected, and the format of the menu itself. In these four areas, the simplicity principle tells you to limit the number of alternatives, make each menu option brief and explicit, permit menu selection with a single keystroke, and avoid superfluous information on the menu screens.

Simplicity does not mean simplistic. It is more like economy of means. Usually you will recognize it when you see it, and perhaps you will experience an emotion such as that which accompanies the contemplation of something beautiful.

6. BE CONSISTENT

Consistency, like simplicity, is one of those concepts whose virtue we usually accept, or at least pay lip service to. Once in a while some crank will rebel and ask why it is necessary; this might even remind us that Emerson once said that "A foolish consistency is the hobgoblin of little minds." It is probably well to remember this quotation, which comes in handy when we have some ulterior motive for cutting corners. We probably ought also to remember that Emerson said it in reference to the actions of statesmen and philosophers, not computer programmers.

To a programmer, consistency in a program — in the design of input routines, control structure, and displays — is extra work. Why bother? What is the payoff?

The question can be answered in a number of different ways. The most satisfying answer, from the perspective of this book, is that consistency makes a program easier to learn and results in fewer errors after one has learned it. To illustrate how this works, let us consider a concrete example. Suppose that you are designing a program with several different data-entry routines. These routines are located in different parts of the program and will be used at different times and under different conditions. If all the routines operate in more or less the same way (e.g., a brief and explicit prompt appears on a particular part of the screen identifying the required entry and its format, the information is typed in by the operator, entries are error-checked, and error messages are always given if a data-entry error occurs), then the operator only has to learn how to make data entries one time, in one part of the program. The skill developed from the first data-entry routine can then be transferred to other routines elsewhere in the program.

On the other hand, if every data-entry routine is slightly different from every other one, then the learning task is magnified. The operator must learn each data-entry routine separately. Moreover, since there will be certain similarities, as well as differences, among the routines, he or she is very likely to confuse the routines with one another. This leads to errors.

The consistency principle can be applied just as readily, and is equally important, in other aspects of program design. Consider, for example, program control. Suppose that we are writing a control language, to control the functions a computer performs. We know how important consistency is in "natural" language, i.e., the language we speak. Without consistent rules of syntax, we could communicate in little more than concrete concepts (nouns). The complex syntax of a natural language such as English allows us to convey meanings through variations in word arrangement. Once we learn the word patterns, we are able to apply the rules to create meaningful word patterns. Analogously, in the design of a computer control language, consistency is extremely important. If we have a few well-defined rules of syntax, then the program user can master these quickly. If we have many different rules, or an anarchy of no rules at all, then we nightmarishly compound the difficulty of learning the language. Again, failure to observe rules of consistency will increase difficulty of learning and operator errors.

Consistency also applies in the design of displays. Through experience, operators develop expectancies for certain types of information on certain parts of their display screen. In a given program, scores of different types of information may be presented. Attention to consistency in the design of displays helps the operator find things. If you change the rules from display to display, then it will take operators a certain amount of time to notice the difference, reorient themselves, and sort things out. Moreover, differences, as noted above, increase the likelihood of errors.

7. GIVE ADEQUATE FEEDBACK

Feedback is information that is received by human operators from the computer, indicating that something they have done has had an effect on the computer. It may not be the intended effect — it may even be something awful — but it does show operators that they are engaged in an interactive dialog with the computer. In the absence of such feedback, operators may be unsure. They may, for example, know that they intended to press a particular key, think that they did, but with no overt sign (or "echo") from the computer there is no way of being sure. As a consequence, they may repeat the action, perhaps producing some unintended result.

Human beings live by feedback. Feedback is an essential part of dialog and dialogs are a ubiquitous part of our daily activities. Lack of feedback throws us off balance. A dialog cannot occur if the conversation is one-sided. This is equally true of human-computer dialog and of human-human dialog. In designing a computer program, a reasonable rule to follow is that any action the operator takes should produce some explicit response from the computer that it has acted or is acting upon what the operator has done. Here are some examples of how this rule might be applied.

In a data-entry program, as the operator types in information from the keyboard, that information should be displayed on the screen opposite the prompt. When editing, the operator should be able to back up the cursor, remove what was entered earlier, and type in the correction on the screen. Though this simple requirement is fairly obvious, many programs have been written in which what is typed in at the keyboard never appears on the screen, and in which previous entries must be maintained in the operator's short-term memory.

To illustrate feedback in the realm of program control, suppose that the operator has just selected an option from a menu-driven program. What happens next? A number of things are possible. The first screen for the next display may appear. This certainly provides adequate feedback. There may be a delay as the computer sets up the routines to call the next program. If this delay lasts more than about 5 seconds, a message should appear on the screen telling the operator what is going on: "THERE WILL BE A BRIEF DELAY," "NOW LOADING NEXT PROGRAM," or the like. The menu option selected may be illegal. In this case, you should provide an error message to tell the operator that the entry is illegal.

8. DO NOT OVERSTRESS WORKING MEMORY

You remember short-term, or working, memory. That is your little internal buffer that:

• Has a capacity of about seven items ("magic number 7 ± 2")
• Holds onto information for about 15 seconds
• Has new information displace old information, as in a shift register

The "magic number 7" is important but often misunderstood and misapplied. For example, it has been used as a basis for recommending an upper limit of nine (7 + 2) for a plethora of display parameters that have little to do with working memory: number of menu options, number of items of unique information to display simultaneously, and number of switches on a control panel, to name a few. Such recommendations are ill-founded, at least on this basis.

There are ways in which it does apply, however. We may be able to work with up to nine things in memory at one time, but this is stretching our capacity to its limit. In designing something, we would be smarter to play it safe and work with the lower end of the range — with an assumed capacity of, say, five items. In addition, without rehearsal (and we would be foolish to expect rehearsal to occur), the information in working memory will rapidly decay and probably be lost after about 15 seconds.

Two ways to work these facts into your design are: First, as you design, take into account the operator's task and do not require the processing of more than about five items at one time; second, do not expect retention of anything you present on the screen for more than about 15 seconds.

Let us consider a specific example of how these notions might be applied in designing data-input routines and display screens. Suppose that you are designing a real estate investment program. To use this program, a real estate salesperson enters data concerning purchase price, loans, interest rates, appreciation rates, commissions, how long the investment is held, and so forth to calculate the rate of return on the investment. After the data are entered, a new display screen appears showing the results of the analysis. After reviewing the results, the salesperson will usually want to modify some of the initial entries in order to "fine-tune" the results to achieve the rate of return requested by the customer. Do you see the problem?

The problem here is that data entries are made on a screen that is separate from displayed results. Thus, program users must retain one display in their heads while the other is on the screen. As complex as most investment programs are, users cannot possibly remember all the information from one screen to the next. What they do remember from one screen will be lost shortly after they move to the next.

A better design would be to permit program users to view all information — inputs and results — simultaneously. This is how spreadsheet programs work. Another solution would be to permit paging between screens. Paging is not as good as having all the information up there at once, but it is better than long delays between screens. Note that operators could use paper and pencil to copy information off the screen, and thereby overcome their working memory limitations. However, a program should not require its operator to employ such techniques to overcome an oversight in design. Besides, such a requirement violates the minimum work principle.

9. MINIMIZE DEPENDENCE ON RECALL MEMORY

You remember the difference between recognition and recall memory. Recognition memory is what you use on a multiple-choice test. Several items that are presumably in your memory are presented to you and you select the correct one. Recall memory is what you use on a fill-in test item. There, you must organize and conduct a search of your own memory to come up with the right answer.

Many students prefer multiple-choice tests. One reason is that recall memory often fails, even if we have studied something. This happens less often with recognition memory. Once we have learned something, we can recognize it when it is presented to us with less effort than is required to recall it. With study, we are able to recall things as well as we can recognize them. However, to do so we must work harder to learn the material in the first place.

In designing a program, there are instances in which you make decisions that determine whether operators will employ recall or recognition memory. For example, suppose that you are designing a part of the program that requires operators to specify which of a series of data files should be loaded. Such routines are usually designed in one of two alternative ways:

1. A prompt requests the name or number of the file. Operators then type this in from memory. Many word-processing programs work this way. If users cannot recall the name of the file exactly, the file cannot be read, and there will be a delay until they figure out a way to get a look at the file directory as a memory jog.

2. A directory is presented on the screen that lists the files from which a selection may be made. Operators then select the one they want by typing in its name or number. This option makes use of recognition memory and does not require operators to recall the file name exactly.

The second option is usually preferable for the program user.

The same principle applies to the design of program control techniques. You must decide how a program will be selected. Two of the most common control techniques are as follows:

1. Have program users specify the program they desire by entering its name, number, or some code they must recall from memory.

2. Present a list of program options (i.e., a menu) and let operators select the one they want. This technique makes use of recognition memory.

If one were to follow this design principle consistently, all programs would be menu-driven. In many designs, particularly with complex programs that are used by sophisticated operators, menus are not the best control technique because they sacrifice program flexibility. However, menus do make sense for many microcomputer programs that are used by less sophisticated operators. Regardless of your preferences for or against menu-driven programs, the advantages of recognition over recall memory should by now be obvious.

10. HELP THE OPERATORS REMAIN ORIENTED

You will recall from the discussion of cognitive mapping in the last chapter that operators build a sort of mental map of the physical geography they move about in. While we would be misguided to become too literal in thinking about little maps inside of peoples' heads, the mental map is a useful metaphor.

Also, a parallel was drawn between a mental map of physical geography and the control structure of a computer program. For example, the control structure of your run-of-the-mill menu-driven program is typically designed in the form of a tree, with a single node at the top that splits into more nodes at lower levels of the program, and so on, down to the lowest level, where there are the greatest number of nodes. Menu networks can, of course, be designed in many other ways than this, but that is not the point. The point is that a menu network looks a lot like a map, and that operators must learn enough about this "menu map" to find their way about it effectively.

Programs using other types of control techniques — for example, command languages — also require operators to learn and internalize some sort of mental map of the program's control structure. This learning process is aided a great deal if you organize your control structure logically, explain this structure in your documentation, and provide "street signs" within the program to tell operators where they are. These three things are the essence of what is meant here by operator orientation.

What is a "logical structure?" Probably the best answer is *what people expect*. The *hierarchical tree structure* discussed above is certainly logical. Most people who use computers deal with a variety of hierarchies — e.g., linguistic, social, scientific, or economic classification schemes — and anyone who has completed the sixth grade has learned how the outline works. The basic idea is that lower-category items fit into higher-category items, which fit into still-higher-category items, and so on.

A *single-level functional categorization scheme* is also logical. Look at all the subprograms in your program. Group common subprograms on the basis of function (e.g., group subprograms for adding information to, modifying information in, or deleting information from the data base into an "edit" function).

How logical the program structure can be depends, of course, on what your program must do. Some programs do not lend themselves readily to a logical structure. But the more they depart from this, the more they become mazes and the more difficult they are to learn and use.

Obviously, in designing your structure you need to take into account both the type of operators and how often they will use the program. The more sophisticated they are, the more they can put up with, although anticipating sophisticated operators is no excuse for cutting corners in designing the program's control structure. In addition, frequent users of a program will learn its structure more fully and will be able to maintain this skill through practice to a greater degree than infrequent users.

You can help the operator learn your program's structure much more quickly if you explain what that structure is. In program documentation, provide an illustration showing the relationships among programs and how one moves back and forth among them. This is a road map to your program. For some reason, publishers of microcomputer programs seldom provide such road maps. Everyone acknowledges the need for literal road maps in unfamiliar geographic locations. It does not take much of a mental leap to see the need for an analogous road map for the control structure of a computer program.

Finally, provide "street signs" within the program to tell operators where they are. Recognize that they will not necessarily know which program they have selected, what mode they are in, what display is currently on the screen, and so forth. Display this kind of information to them. Operators should never be more than a couple of keystrokes away from a "well-marked intersection."

11. CODE INFORMATION APPROPRIATELY (OR NOT AT ALL)

This design principle will be discussed briefly here in an attempt to raise your consciousness about information coding. It will be covered in greater depth in Chapter 6.

What is information coding? For purposes of this discussion, information coding may be thought of as the form in which the computer presents information to the operator. Information is uncoded when it is presented to the operator in some form that is directly and literally interpretable. (This is an oversimplification, but it will work for this discussion if it is not examined too closely.) An example of uncoded information is an error message such as the following:

```
DOOR OF DRIVE #1 IS OPEN. CLOSE DRIVE DOOR.
```

A coded form of this information would be a particular sequence of speaker beeps, a flashing symbol, or some other form of information that the operator would have to interpret.

Computers permit you to code information in many different ways. On a video display, for example, you can present information in the form of words and use such graphic techniques as shape, size, intensity, color, location, or flash rate coding. Similarly, sound may be used to present information in the form of words, or coded in terms of frequency, volume, repetition rate, or other acoustic variables.

Conventions are attached to some codes. For example, sound is often used to alert the operator to a condition that requires immediate attention. Different types of codes vary in effectiveness for conveying information. Graphics, for example, are highly effective for presenting numeric information such that trends are obvious.

Through experience, we have internalized many coding rules. Certain codes — such as the difference between red and green color coding — carry historical baggage with them that we cannot ignore as we design.

In summary, information can be coded in many different ways. Some coding techniques work better than others for conveying certain types of information. And many codes have been used historically in certain ways. We must take these factors into account. How we do this will be discussed in Chapter 6.

12. FOLLOW PREVAILING DESIGN CONVENTIONS

If you were a highway engineer in North America, you would be unwise to plan highways in which vehicles were required to drive on the left side of the road, or to use blue and white in traffic lights. Regardless of the rationale underlying your design — which might be very sound — it would cause no end of problems if it were adopted. Too many North Americans have learned and become used to driving on the right side of the road and responding to red and green traffic lights. You could not expect them to change the way they do things on your account.

There is an obvious parallel in the design of computer programs. There are many conventions concerning the way operators are supposed to interact with computers. Because of these conventions, operators have certain expectations. If your program does not conform to these, you will make learning more difficult and increase the number of errors made by operators.

Conventions have become conventions through their wide acceptance. Usually, though not always, such acceptance reflects the fact that the convention has passed the test of working successfully in the real world. One such convention is that of displaying columns of numerical information aligned on the decimal point. It would probably take very little to convince you that this makes the information easier to read.

Some conventions have very little more going for them than history. They may have been the best way of doing something back in the old days, but are no longer. Yet they still dog us today. An example is the use of abbreviations for the terms composing the vocabularies used on computer displays. In the past, when memory was dear, it was helpful to use abbreviations and save core. These days memory is cheap, but abbreviations still abound. Never mind that abbreviations must be memorized, that they are a code that must be translated to derive meaning, that this is extra work, that it increases the probability of errors, etc. Obviously, not all conventions are good. But most are. And unless you have a better idea, that you can sell to your audience, you had better stick with them.

Notice that this principle could conceivably put you in a position during program design of having to choose between a design alternative that is the best based on human factors principles and another that is based on standard design practice. What should you do then? Basically, you should decide how strong the convention is and how much of an improvement you can get by dumping it and applying the human factors principle. If the payoff is great enough, proceed. If it is a toss-up or less, stick with the convention. Human factors purists should not be outraged by this advice. There is strong human factors logic in following conventions, for these are what people expect, and by going along with their expectations, you make learning easier.

Four

The Program
Development Process

This chapter will take a close look at the program development process. It starts with some of the basic issues involved in program design and development, and then presents an eleven-step program development strategy.

Program development is the process by which a program concept is transformed, in stages, into a fully operational and error-free program. In its early stages, it demands a high degree of creativity, as the designer builds a design plan. In its latter stages, it demands hard work, compulsive attention to detail, and patience, as the program is coded, documented, and then tested. The creative skills required to design a good program are not the same as those required to perfect it, and there is no reason to expect that they should reside equally in the same person. In fact, the program development process requires perhaps a half-dozen unique skills during its various stages, if a program is to be developed properly.

You have probably heard of "top-down" design and "bottom-up" design. Top-down design starts with a definition of high-level system *objectives*. These might be quite abstract and removed from everyday experience. The objectives are broken down into *functions* which must be performed (e.g., data input, report generation, etc.). Program *modules* are designed to perform each function. Later, the *control* structure, which links the modules together, is designed. *Data structures* (i.e., types of variables and what they are used for) are designed last. The systems approach to design, presented in Chapter 1, is another top-down approach.

In bottom-up design, the top-down process is not totally reversed but occurs differently. Designers will start with *system objectives*. But then they may design a particular *module* and its *data structures, link* it to the next module, design the next module, and so on, in an iterative fashion. In general, bottom-up design is less formal and systematic than top-down design.

It is doubtful that any designer actually practices pure top-down or bottom-up design, as such, although an individual may tend more toward one approach than the other. These are more design philosophies than well-defined procedures. However, they do help us structure our thought about the design process.

Neither of these design approaches, in its simple form, does much for the human operator, although the top-down approach is preferred by human factors specialists. Both are *inside-out* design approaches — they focus first on the inside of the program and only later on the outside, i.e., the human-computer interface. In both approaches, the operator is more or less incidental, a sort of obscure footnote. Researchers have pointed out that programs have failed for not being properly oriented to their users. It is not difficult to imagine how this can happen with a large team of designers who are attempting to solve a complex problem. However, it can also happen in designing a program for your microcomputer — when the entire design and development team consists of you alone.

One way to avoid the danger of overlooking users is to employ a program development strategy that expressly takes them into account. There is such a strategy, and it is presented later in this chapter. It is referred to (no joke) as the *outside-in* approach. The approach focuses first on the design of the human-computer interface and later on the design of the program that it takes to produce that interface. To illustrate, if you were designing a management information system using the outside-in strategy, one of the earliest things you would do is to design the reports that the program would produce. From there you would work your way backward, so to speak, to decide what program modules, control structure, and data structures were required to produce the reports. With the inside-out approach, program outputs might be among the very last things designed.

The design strategy presented in this chapter will use the top-down, outside-in approach. It is, more or less, the approach that human factors specialists use when they design something. However, it is doubtful that this design strategy has ever been presented in a form that can be used by the designer of software for a microcomputer. The following is an attempt at this translation.

The sequence of steps in the design strategy is shown in Figure 4-1. As noted earlier, no designer will follow *any* procedure — top-down, bottom-up, or whatever — *exactly,* and this procedure is no exception. Do not regard it as a rigid formula that you must follow without variation. Rather, look upon it as an ideal. You must adapt it to fit your working style and the design problem that you are attempting to solve.

In the sections that follow, each step of the design strategy is described. Concrete examples are given to illustrate its application in three specific design problems: (1) a computer game, (2) a program to automate a local branch of the public library, and (3) a financial management information system for a medium-sized corporation. In these examples, consider yourself to be playing the role of an ace freelance programmer who must design each of these programs.

STEP 1. DEFINE THE SYSTEM OBJECTIVES

Decide what your system must be able to do.

In designing your game, the goal is to entertain the operator for a

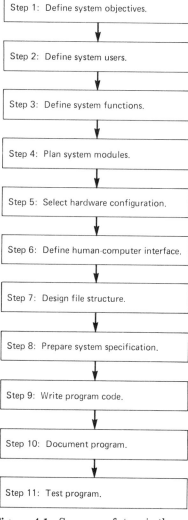

Figure 4-1 Sequence of steps in the outside-in design approach.

particular amount of time. This time must be at least 30 seconds or the operator will feel cheated. If the game goes on too long (i.e., is too easy), the operator will get bored.

The public library has hired you to design a system to put their card files on computer, and their system must meet two objectives: (1) provide a comprehensive record-keeping system that is indexed by author, title, subject, and accession number, and (2) permit inexperienced and experienced operators to query the data base in order to locate references.

When you discussed the financial management system with the corporate leaders, they were a bit vague about what they wanted. They said something about wanting to be able to "put a finger on the pulse of the company." Being more analytical than they are, you translate this into the following objective: "Provide summary financial information concerning past, current, and projected future financial performance that will permit managers to make policy and marketing decisions." Still a bit vague, but it will do as a starting point.

It may seem silly to state such obvious objectives. It is not. You realize this when you witness the end result of an 18-month system development that yields a program that works wonderfully but that does not do what it was supposed to do. This happens when people fail to state the obvious at the outset and move on into detailed design based on incorrect assumptions.

STEP 2. DEFINE THE SYSTEM USERS

Decide who will be using your system. Take all users into account, if you can. Decide what *roles* users will be required to play to use your system.

In the game program, there is only one role — that of game player.

The library system has a minimum of two roles, and probably more: librarians, who will use the system for several hours each day and become very familiar with it; and book borrowers, who will use it infrequently and have little opportunity to learn its intricacies.

The financial management system will have at least two user roles: top-level managers and data-entry clerks, who will punch in the data composing the financial data base.

For each user role, consider the probable operator characteristics in terms of such factors as the following:

• Frequency of use of system

• Computer sophistication

• Education, intelligence, subject matter expertise

• Motivation

• Patience

• Computerphobia

The characteristics of program users are discussed in greater detail in Chapter 2.

STEP 3. DEFINE THE SYSTEM FUNCTIONS

"Function" is one of those vague terms that is both ubiquitous and impossible to define. For the purposes of this discussion, let us think of a function as a class of things that a program must do. To illustrate, some examples follow.

Here are some functions the computer game must perform:

• Present exciting action on a screen display with accompanying sound
• Permit an interactive dialog with the user to control the action
• Keep score

Here are some functions the library system must perform:

• Store data (e.g., 5 million library references)
• Permit additions to, modifications of, or deletions from the data base
• Permit an interactive dialog to find records in the data base by logical rules

Here are some functions the financial system must perform:

• Provide a data base (income, expenses, sales, returns, individual salesperson performance, product performance, etc.)
• Calculate and display performance indicators that permit a comparison of past, present, and projected future financial performance
• Permit an interactive dialog with the user to obtain performance data

Note that in each of these examples, a particular user is assumed. You cannot design a program properly without having a particular user, or set of users, in mind. Heed step 2.

STEP 4. PLAN THE SYSTEM MODULES

This step concerns actual software design. System objectives, operators, and functions are taken into account so that you can decide what modules are required to build your program. In some cases, program modules will derive directly from the program functions defined during step 3. However, a program function is still an abstract animal and does not always map over directly into a particular chunk of software code. It is true that every program function requires at least one program module. Often, a function will be so complex that it will require several.

There are several purposes in dividing your program up into modules. First, you reduce one large problem into several smaller ones. This makes design simpler. Second, a modular design will be easier to maintain. Most complex systems — and particularly electronics systems — are modularized for this reason. If something goes wrong somewhere, you can trace the problem to its source if the system has a modular design structure.

Modules are real things. They are not abstractions like objectives or functions. To decide what modules you need, you must fully understand your design problem and translate the abstractions into something tangible. The following examples illustrate one way of modularizing each of the three programs you are developing.

Here is how you might modularize the game program:

• Game control (i.e., user dialog)
• Display generation
• Score keeping

Here are the modules you might use in both the library and financial programs:

• Data-base entry and editing
• Report generation
• File maintenance utilities

Defining program modules is the first step in breaking down your design problem. In each of the examples, the program was broken into three modules. (There is nothing magic about this number.)

After program modules have been defined, shift your attention to each module itself. Break each module down into submodules. In principle, you can continue in this manner, level by level, until you have reached the level of the subroutine and individual code statement.

How far down should modularization go? Break down the program to the point where you can state a requirement for each human-computer interface routine. For example, in the library and financial programs, a module was defined for "data-base entry and editing." This module is at too high a level to be useful for planning screen displays or

data entry routines. You must break it down into specific submodules
such as the following:

* File display and input routine
* File display and edit routine
* Data-base printout routine
* Data-base search

At the conclusion of this step (Figure 4-2), you should have the
following:

* List of program modules — somewhere between two and six, and well
  short of a dozen
* List of submodules comprising each module
* List of human-computer interface requirements for each submodule
  — input routines and displays

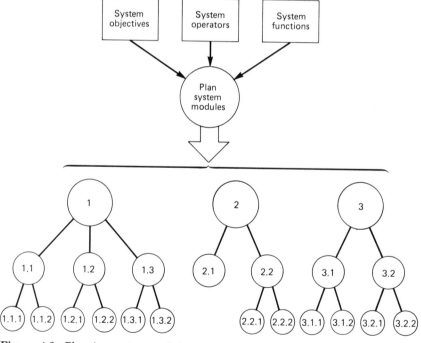

Figure 4-2 Planning system modules. Modules are planned based on system objectives, operators, and the functions that must be performed. Each module is divided into submodules, down to the level necessary for actual design.

As you can see, this step epitomizes top-down design. You started it with a few high-level objectives and program functions. From these you derived program modules and submodules. You finished the step with several specific human-computer interface requirements. We are not yet ready to design our human-computer interface, however. First, we must contend with the matter of hardware. We will do this in the next step.

STEP 5. SELECT THE HARDWARE CONFIGURATION

Logically, hardware should not drive or constrain system design during preliminary steps in the design process. Hardware is not an end, but a means for implementing our system. Thus, hardware is not selected until the current step of the design process.

All of us know folks who are in love with particular machines or programming languages and who will attempt to use them, no matter how awkwardly, to solve every design problem. To them, the hardware or language has become the end, rather than the means. There are reasons for such arrested development, and though they are interesting, it is not productive to explore them further here. Let us move on, rather, to the mechanics of how this step is performed.

The previous step defined program modules, submodules, and human-computer interface requirements. These have hardware implications.

For example, your game program will require a fast display and probably a joystick for operator input. Program size and any supporting data files imply random access memory (RAM) and disk storage requirements. The game will probably be played by one individual on one microcomputer.

Your library system must have a large permanent storage device and be capable of driving several terminals in a multitasking environment. This would take a powerful microcomputer or perhaps a minicomputer.

The scale of the financial system is less clear than that of the game (games are typically played by one individual on one computer) or library system, which, because of its scale, requires large storage capacity and multiple terminals. The financial program could be put on a single, small microcomputer or on a multiterminal system. Which computer to use is a function of what the corporate leaders want and what the budget allows, rather than technical factors.

As these examples illustrate, choosing hardware, when you have a choice, hinges on such factors as:

• Storage capacity required
• Processing speed
• Number of people who must operate the system at the same time
• Hard-copy requirements
• Budget

An additional factor that becomes very important if you are producing programs that you intend to market is the installed base of computers of different types. Other factors held constant, you are well advised to develop your program for the computer that represents the greatest sales potential for the program. Hardware factors relating to system design are discussed in greater detail in Chapter 5.

STEP 6. DESIGN THE HUMAN-COMPUTER INTERFACE

The human-computer interface is the manner in which the operator interacts with the computer, using the program. For purposes of design, this interface has three aspects:

1. *System outputs.* How the computer displays information to the operator
2. *System inputs.* How the operator enters data into the computer
3. *Program control.* How the operator controls what the computer does, using the program

It is important to design the interface — system outputs, user inputs, program control — before designing the files or other technical aspects of the program. This interface should drive the technical aspects of program design, not vice versa.

An important part of the present step is to design the interface on paper and to have the operator audience review the design in its preliminary form. Following review, the design is modified, as necessary, to assure its compatibility with users.

Design output and input displays. Lay them out on paper in as much detail as possible. Your design should convey the information content and display format in sufficient detail for review by others.

Present the displays for review to the types of people who will eventually use your program. This review is to assure that your design will appeal to and be usable by the people it is aimed at.

The design of the human-computer interface is covered in detail in three chapters in this book. Chapter 6 covers data output (i.e., displays), Chapter 7 covers data input, and Chapter 9 covers program control. Chapter 8 covers the design of utility programs which are important in programs that employ a data base. Following this review, modify the displays as necessary.

Design the program control. There are two aspects to designing program control: (1) defining the manner of program control (menu, control language, etc.), and (2) specifying the control structure, i.e., the relationships among the subprograms.

The preferred method of program control for most microcomputer programs is the menu. For some applications, the menu is impractical or undesirable and other methods should be used. (Program control is discussed in Chapter 9.) The second aspect of program control is designing the control structure. If the design strategy presented in this chapter has been followed up to now, the relationships among subprograms will emerge naturally from the program modules and submodules. For example, the highest-level modules will be options on the program's main menu, submodules will be options on the menus for each module, and so on.

If feasible, lay out the control menus and structure on paper, present them to the user audience, and obtain reactions. Modify the control techniques and structure, as necessary, to assure compatibility with the user audience.

STEP 7. DESIGN THE DATA STRUCTURES AND FILES

Decide what data structures your program will require and what the variable assignments will be. Design your files. File design can profoundly affect the way your program works. Files influence such factors as the speed at which you can access file data, how readily file data can be modified, and the probability of certain types of disastrous occurrences. These are human factors considerations. The human factors ideals for your files are the following:

• Instantaneous access to file data
• Access to any file data that have been entered
• Ability to modify any file data

• No possibility of disasters such as overwriting or accidentally deleting files

STEP 8. PREPARE THE SYSTEM SPECIFICATION

A specification is a document that describes, in as much detail as possible, what the program will consist of and how it will work. Writing the specification is an act of design. It is a formal exercise that forces the designer to face design decisions and make them explicit. It thereby reduces the options left open to the programmer and leaves less to chance. If the designer has done the job properly, then the programmer's job is much easier. It becomes an activity analogous to translating from one language (English) to another (the programming language).

The specification is a compilation of all the design information that has been developed up to this step in the design process. Here is what the specification should contain:

• *Statement of system objectives.* What the program should be able to do, as determined during step 1 of the design process.

• *Definition of system users.* Who will use the program, in terms of the characteristics determined during step 2 of the design process.

• *Description of program modules and submodules.* How the program is structured, as determined during steps 3 and 4 of the design process.

• *System hardware.* Equipment that will be used for running the program, i.e., types of displays, random access and permanent storage characteristics, programming languages used, and other hardware features. These were defined during step 5 of the design process.

• *Human-computer interface requirements.* Description of system outputs, inputs, and program control, as determined during step 6 of the design process.

• *Data structures and files.* Descriptions of data structures and files, as determined during step 7 of the design process.

Use these items as a checklist in writing your specification.

The design specification is a complete description of the system and can be used for final review of design before the program is developed or hardware acquired. The larger and more complex the system being developed, the more important it is to prepare a specification. This may seem to be extra work, but it is not. When a good specification has been written, the effort required to get the program up and running is considerably reduced, and the net result is a savings in time and money. If a program is being developed by one or two people, a formal specification is not as critical. Still, careful planning and complete documentation are the best way of assuring that the final product turns out as intended.

STEP 9. WRITE THE PROGRAM CODE

With specification in hand, acquire the necessary hardware and start writing the program. Work on one module at a time and complete each module before moving on to the next. Start with a module that is central to the program. Let us consider the three examples used earlier. First, in the game program, the first module to code would probably be the display generator. In the library and financial programs, the first would be that for data-base entry and editing.

After the first module has been completed, develop the next logical module, link it to the first, and then continue in this manner, until all modules have been completed and linked together. This is a simple, commonsense strategy that allows the program to be developed and tested in stages.

An alternative strategy is to develop several modules simultaneously and then link them together later. This strategy is often used with large and complex systems that are being developed by teams of programmers who are operating under a short time schedule. Careful coordination among teams is required to assure that the pieces fit together properly at the end.

Choose the strategy that makes sense for the type of program you are developing and the constraints you must work under. For the three programs used in the running example, one programmer would be involved, working at his or her own pace, and the first strategy — developing one module at a time and linking each new module into those already there — would be recommended.

STEP 10. DOCUMENT THE PROGRAM

There are two general types of program documentation. The first is *systems* documentation. This is technical documentation that is aimed at the programmer who must maintain the program. Systems documentation should be developed concurrently with the program. The second type of documentation is *user* documentation. User documentation tells the program users what they need to know to make the program work properly. The program user's guide is the most familiar example of this type of documentation. In addition, user documentation may be contained within the program in the form of help screens, directions, detailed prompts, and other user-aiding features. User documentation should be developed as soon after the program is completed as is possible. It is desirable to develop user documentation concurrently with the program, if possible.

Adequate documentation is essential, both to the programmer who must maintain a program and to program users. The quality of documentation is just as important as the quality of the program itself in determining whether or not the program can be maintained and used. Systems and user documentation are described in detail in Chapter 10.

STEP 11. TEST THE PROGRAM

Thoroughly test your program before releasing it for general use. In developing a program, testing occurs at many different stages. The programmer will test the routines used in each module, then test the module, and eventually test several modules together. Such testing, though done consciously, is often haphazard and idiosyncratic. Programmers can develop an entire program, test it to their satisfaction, and leave gaping holes with errors that it never occurred to them to test for.

Beyond such informal testing, the individual modules and completed program should also be subjected to more formal testing by "expert users," i.e., other programmers. These technically sophisticated users will uncover errors that the original programmers overlooked.

Next, the program should be subjected to rigorous and controlled testing by the type of operators who will be expected to use it when it is delivered. Those program users should be provided with the program and user documentation, and they should be required to perform the tasks the program was designed to accomplish.

While testing is shown here as the final step of the program development process, testing should start as soon as you have a complete program module. Ideally, testers should work with different modules of the program as they are developed and should eventually test the entire program.

The important point is that formal testing must occur. Programmers who rely on themselves alone to test programs are rather like the individual who acts as his or her own lawyer and has only a fool for a client. Each of us has blind spots, and it takes a new user little time to find them and help us recall the meaning of humility. Program testing is covered in detail in Chapter 11.

Five

Hardware Considerations

This chapter provides a brief overview of the hardware considerations that are important to the system designer. It begins with a discussion of computer output devices and focuses in closely on the CRT display, hard-copy printer, and sound and natural language output. The second section covers computer input devices, including keyboard, mouse, touch-sensitive screen, joystick, track ball, stylus, and voice interface. The final section deals with operator ergonomics, i.e., fitting the hardware configuration to its operator.

As a designer, you will often be required to decide what hardware to use in a particular system. Even if your forte is computer games, you must decide whether to use a color or a monochrome CRT, and whether to use keyboard, joystick, or track ball input. How do you decide? The best way is to be knowledgeable about each of the devices — its characteristics, and its advantages and disadvantages — and to make the choice based on this knowledge.

Hardware is a key part of the human-computer interface. It is the CRT display we view, the printer whose hard-copy report we review, the keyboard through which we enter data into the computer. Ignoring the hardware that will manifest our computer program is like ignoring the instrument on which a musical composition is played.

Computer professionals are inundated with information and misinformation on the supposed human factors advantages of different types of computer hardware. As this book is written, hot items are CRTs with amber screens and correspondence-quality matrix printers. Advertisers proclaim their advantages. Are they really that good? Read on, and you will find out.

You cannot decide which hardware is best without knowing exactly how it will be used. If you are writing a program that an operator must use for several hours each day, then make sure that operator gets the best in terms of both hardware and software. Do not require a data-entry operator to punch data in at a membrane keyboard and view computer output on a fuzzy, 9-inch television set.

With a less demanding application, you can cut corners. You do not need an expensive red, green, blue (RGB) color monitor for playing computer games. In the end, hardware selection reduces to a question of cost effectiveness — hardware cost, and operator effectiveness. The cost part of this formula is easy to sort out. For the purchaser, cheap is better than expensive. The effectiveness part of the formula is more difficult. As noted in Chapter 2, human beings are adaptable and can, with practice, become quite good at using bad programs. The same is true of using bad hardware; but there are hidden costs in terms of fatigue, efficiency, and attitude. Keep these factors in mind when you weigh the effectiveness part of the cost-effectiveness equation.

OUTPUT DEVICES

This section discusses computer output devices — CRT, printers, and sound and natural language output.

CRT Displays

Color versus Monochrome CRTs. The CRT is the most common computer output device. CRTs may be single-color (monochrome) or color. In general, monochrome displays have better resolution and cost less than color displays. Unless a program requires color, a monochrome display should be used.

When the computer's video signal drives the CRT directly, the CRT is referred to as a monitor. Television sets may be connected to computers by using a device referred to as a radio frequency (RF) modulator. RF modulators translate the computer's video signal into a form that will drive the TV set. Certain high-quality television sets (such as are used in the broadcasting industry) have circuitry that permits them to be used as either monitors or television receivers. The modulator-driven TV set produces a picture of lower resolution and poorer quality than a monitor that is driven directly by a video signal. TV sets are adequate for limited home or hobbyist use but should be avoided for serious applications. They produce inferior displays and are fatiguing to the operator.

There are two basic types of color monitors: (1) composite color and (2) RGB. Composite color monitors connect directly to the computer and produce video that is superior to that of an RF modulator–driven TV set but inferior to that of a monochrome monitor. In general, the quality of a composite color monitor is inadequate for word processing or other text-dependent applications. The RGB monitor requires a special interface which separates the color signal into red, green, and blue signals before they drive the monitor. The resultant color image is superior to that of a composite monitor and approaches the quality of a monochrome monitor. As you might expect, the RGB monitor is more expensive than the composite color monitor. However, an RGB monitor should be considered a requirement for any color application which makes heavy use of text or requires the operator to make other fine distinctions.

Do not use color unless you really need it. These days, color is more or less required to make game or entertainment programs commercially viable. It is being used increasingly in more serious applications such as business programs. Its utility in many such applications is questionable.

Color has two key, legitimate uses:

1. *To code information.* Different colors represent different information dimensions (e.g., product lines, months of year, topographic features, etc.).

2. *To divide a display screen.* Different colors are used in different areas, based on the type of information presented.

The eye can perceive more different colors on a color display than it can shades of gray on a monochrome display. Therefore, color has advantages over monochrome when it is used in either of these two ways. Human brightness and color perception were discussed in Chapter 2, and color coding is discussed in more detail in Chapter 6.

CRT Size. A key issue in selecting a CRT is the size of the information that is displayed to the operator. This in turn is a function of CRT size, viewing distance, the type of information displayed, and the manner in which the information is generated. The recommendations that follow are based on the assumption that the operator will be seated at a normal viewing distance from the CRT (20 to 28 inches) and will be viewing alphanumeric information (letters, numbers, or other common typewriter symbols) produced by a character generator on a raster scan CRT display. Most microcomputers produce rows of information consisting of between 40 and 80 characters. The more characters produced per line, the smaller the characters must be and the more difficult they are to read. Thus, larger screen sizes should be used as the number of characters per line increases.

The television industry established the convention of measuring screen size based on the screen diagonal. CRT monitors are also measured in this way. The ratio of height to width of a CRT screen is typically 4 to 5, and so the width of a CRT screen can be calculated based on the diagonal using elementary geometry: screen width = screen diagonal × 0.78.

Given the choice of several good-quality monochrome monitors, the minimum screen size that should be considered is 9 inches. Such a screen will be adequate for displaying rows up to 40 characters wide. The de facto standard for most microcomputers today is the 12-inch CRT. This is recommended for all-around usage in at least one design standard. A 12-inch monitor is preferable to a 9-inch monitor for most applications. If a 12-inch monitor is used, the maximum number of characters per row should not exceed 80.

If more than 80 characters per row must be displayed, a 15-inch or larger CRT should be used. In general, a larger CRT is better, particularly if the CRT is of average or poorer quality or if color is being used.

Many of the so-called portable computers use 5- to 9-inch screens, and virtually all fail to meet the above screen-size recommendations. Anyone who has used a small screen for an extended length of time knows how hard it can be on the eyes. You can adapt to it, but it is fatiguing.

Phosphor Color and Screen Contrast. The two most common phosphor colors for the types of monochrome displays used on microcomputers are *white* and *green*. Green phosphors appear to be gaining in popularity, particularly with the more expensive microcomputers. A less common but increasingly popular phosphor is *amber*. Amber phosphors are quite common in Europe and seem to be catching on in the United States now as well.

The advertising claims about the virtues of one phosphor or another are mostly meaningless rhetoric. Green phosphors are reputed to be restful for the eyes, which may be true, but there is little if any hard evidence to back this claim up. The pitches for amber phosphors seem to be based on the same snob appeal as those for European automobiles. While it is true that amber is widely used abroad, there is insufficient evidence at present to back up any claims about its superiority.

The dark-adapted eye is somewhat more sensitive to green than the light-adapted eye. As brightness increases, eye sensitivity shifts toward the yellow and white. On this basis, it may be argued that a green phosphor monitor is preferable if the working area will have low ambient illumination, while white or yellow phosphors are better in brighter surroundings.

Other things held constant, a CRT with green phosphor will have less *contrast* than one with white or amber phosphor. This assumes that the background field is identically black in all three cases. The blacker the background, the better the contrast, and the brighter the background, the lower the contrast. CRT contrast is an important selection factor in its own right, apart from its tie in to phosphor color. The brighter the working environment, the more contrast you need to make a display legible. If you work in the dark, you can get by with a low-contrast display. If you work in a brightly lighted office, or outside in the sunlight, you need a more contrasty display.

In sum, forget the advertising claims and pick what you like. It is probably much more important to worry about CRT *resolution* and *contrast* than about phosphor color, per se. Higher resolution translates into increased sharpness.

Resolution. Finally, we come to the issue of display resolution, or sharpness. Good monochrome monitors have far better resolution than

TV sets and are less subject to pincushion or barrel distortion. A reasonably good monitor has a resolution of 600 lines and is capable of projecting characters of consistent sharpness across its entire display surface. Image degradation will generally be greatest at the edges of the display. If you can, test the monitor for sharpness and distortion before you purchase it. To do this, fill the screen with a symmetric character (the numeral 8 is suggested), and then compare the appearance of the character across different portions of the screen. Generally, the character will be sharpest at the center and poorer at the edges. On a good monitor, there will be little difference in the way the character looks, regardless of where it is checked.

To check the display for distortion, look for obvious curvature in the rows and columns on the screen. If the display is very distorted, this may be obvious to the unaided eye. Do not rely on your eyes alone, however. Put a straightedge on the screen and see if the rows and columns line up consistently everywhere. A good-quality monitor should show no distortion.

Printers

The printer is an essential part of most computer systems. Printers and CRTs are, in a sense, analogous devices. Both present computer output to the operator, the difference being that with the CRT, presentation is temporary, and with the printer, it is permanent.

In designing some programs, the programmer applies a principle of parallelism or redundancy between CRT and hard-copy displays. That is, the program permits the operator to select whether the computer's output should be sent to CRT, printer, or both. Whether or not this capability is required in the program you are designing, keep it in mind, for it often comes into play. It has implications during the selection of a printer — your printer should be able to display whatever you can show on your CRT. If you have an eighty-column CRT, then your printer should be able to print at least 80 columns. If graphics are important in screen displays, then you should be able to present these on your printer. The same goes for color and for other CRT dimensions that can be translated into printer terms.

The permanence of a printer record is only one part of what makes printers important. Equally or more important in many applications is that the printed record has no length limitation. A CRT display can look only at a small window of data, typically 80 by 25 characters in size. To look up, down, left, or right, you must move the window and displace the display that is on the screen. The printer can show everything at once, and provides the user with instantaneous, random access to information anywhere in the display field. This is why many computer programs are printer- rather than CRT-oriented. Management information systems (MIS), for example, often provide only hardcopy reports of the information they produce and have no CRT equivalents. Often this is because it is impractical to fit the information produced by the MIS into CRT-sized windows.

Printing Technologies. There are perhaps a dozen or more printing technologies. These are divided into two general categories: nonimpact and impact.

Most *non-impact* printers employ specially treated papers which produce dot matrix characters when they are exposed to heat or an electric current. Fully formed characters cannot be generated using these techniques. The papers are expensive, and so nonimpact printers are not practical for high-volume output.

An important and emerging nonimpact technology is the ink jet (Figure 5-1). Ink-jet printers produce images by electronically guiding and depositing a stream of dry ink particles on normal paper. Such printers produce good-quality images at high speed. Ink-jet printers are expensive at present and impractical for most microcomputer applications. However, their prices are dropping, and they should be considered.

Nonimpact printers are fairly quiet. In some applications, this may be an overriding consideration. If you are designing a program that

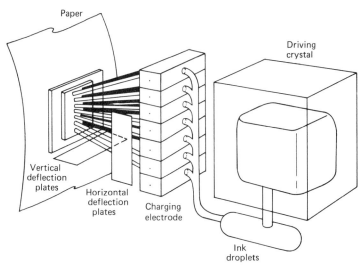

Figure 5-1 Ink-jet printer mechanism. Ink particles are "fired" by a nozzle and guided by electrical plates to form characters on paper.

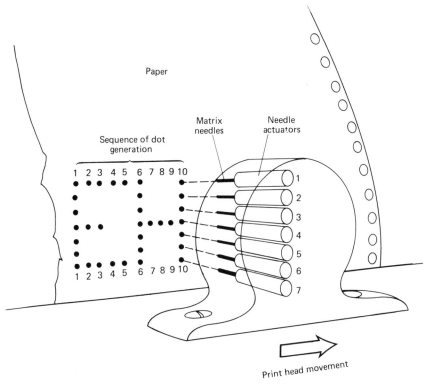

Figure 5-2 Dot matrix printer mechanism. Characters are formed by a moving array of electromagnetically driven print wires.

will be used in a quiet office environment and that will produce a limited volume of hard-copy output, one of the nonimpact technologies should be seriously considered. For high-volume applications, they usually do not make sense.

Impact printers have found greater acceptance and are much more widely used than nonimpact printers. There are many different impact printing technologies — dot matrix, daisy wheel, golf ball (i.e., Selectric), rotating drum, belt, chain, train, etc. Of these, the most widely used in microcomputer applications is the dot matrix printer (Figure 5-2); it is flexible and inexpensive. Where a higher-quality printed output is required, fully formed character printers such as the daisy wheel are used. The golf-ball printing mechanism (Figure 5-3) is used less and less in computer applications these days due to the combination of the higher speed and reliability of daisy-wheel printers. Today, the daisy-wheel printer (Figure 5-4) is preeminent in microcomputer applications requiring letter-quality output.

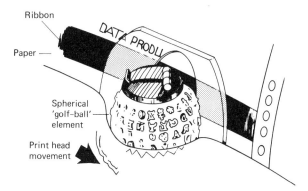

Figure 5-3 Golf-ball printer mechanism. The print ball is rotated and tilted to position the appropriate character and then driven against the ribbon to print the character on paper. The best example of this mechanism is the familiar IBM Selectric (TM) typewriter.

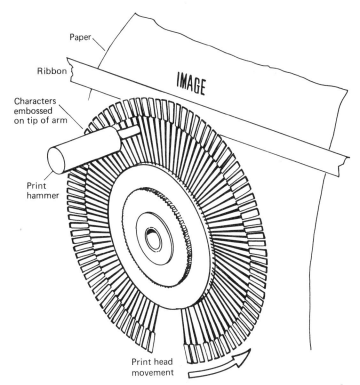

Figure 5-4 Daisy-wheel printer mechanism. A plastic or metal printwheel is rotated into position and a hammer strikes the appropriate "petal" to print the character on paper.

The remaining impact printing technologies — drum, belt, chain, train, etc. — are reserved for high-speed line printer applications and are seldom used with microcomputers.

The following discussion will focus on the dot matrix and daisy-wheel printers, as these are the most logical candidates for use and can fulfill most printing requirements.

Dot Matrix Printers.   The print head of a dot matrix printer consists of a series of print wires (usually seven or more), arranged one above the other, each with its own driving electromagnet. As the print head moves horizontally across the page, the computer's character generator instructs each of the print wires' magnets when to pull its print wire forward, pushing a ribbon against paper that is held against a platen. Characters are formed out of separate dots from separate print wires. The more wires used to form a character, the more fully formed it will be. The minimum acceptable matrix size is 5 (horizontal) by 7 (vertical) dots. Research has shown that a larger matrix (7 by 9 or greater) is preferred by operators and improves their performance.

Forming characters with a dot matrix printer is rather like spelling your name on a blank wall with a tommy gun. The more complete you want the character to look, the more time and bullets it takes. Thus, there is an obvious quality-speed trade-off to be made.

In comparison to daisy-wheel or other letter-quality printers, dot matrix printers are relatively inexpensive. They usually have a single moving head, some stepper motors, and a few other moving parts. They do not require special paper. Their prime drawback is that they do not produce fully formed characters.

Dot matrix printing technology has advanced to the point that some printers are capable of rivaling the print quality of fully formed character printers. They do this by firing a lot of bullets into the wall — using print heads with more than the usual number of wires (up to fifteen) and/or running the print head over the page more than once. Some dot matrix printers can print in either a normal- or "correspondence"-quality print mode. If a dot matrix printer could retain its combination of high speed, reliability, low cost, and produce the print quality of fully formed character printers, it would certainly be the printer of choice. Unfortunately, the print speed of a dot matrix printer used in correspondence mode is usually slower than that of a fully formed character printer, and the print quality is not as good. You can examine the print quality of the daisy-wheel printer in Figure 5-5.

A typical dot matrix printer of the type that would be used with a microcomputer prints at a speed of 100 characters per second (cps) and produces eighty-column output. This is about the minimum that

This is typical output from a daisy-wheel printer. Characters are fully-formed and generally more legible than those produced by a dot-matrix printer. Daisy wheel printers use a plastic or metal print wheel and typically have a print speed of about 30 characters per second. This is the printer of choice for serious word processing applications. (Proportional spacing, Bold type style)

This is typical output from a daisy-wheel printer. Characters are fully-formed and generally more legible than those produced by a dot-matrix printer. Daisy wheel printers use a plastic or metal print wheel and typically have a print speed of about 30 characters per second. This is the printer of choice for serious word processing applications. (10-Pitch spacing, Titan type style)

This is typical output from a daisy-wheel printer. Characters are fully-formed and generally more legible than those produced by a dot-matrix printer. Daisy wheel printers use a plastic or metal print wheel and typically have a print speed of about 30 characters per second. This is the printer of choice for serious word processing applications. (12-Pitch spacing, Letter Gothic type style)

Figure 5-5 Typical daisy-wheel printer outputs. Daisy-wheel printers produce excellent output at fairly high speed and set the standard for word-processing applications.

should be considered for serious computer applications. Many printers are capable of printing more columns and at higher speeds than this. When used in correspondence mode, a dot matrix printer will typically print at a speed of 30 cps or less.

How good is the correspondence-quality print produced by a dot matrix printer? This question cannot be answered in an absolute sense. You must decide for yourself. Dot matrix printers are becoming increasingly common and acceptable for use in word processing. This trend is occurring partly because of the improved print quality of dot matrix printers in recent years, but also because of a change in peoples' attitudes.

Daisy-Wheel Printers. When the highest-quality print is absolutely required, the best choice is a daisy-wheel printer. Typical output from a daisy-wheel printer is shown in Figure 5-5. These printers are so named because the printing element is of plastic or metal, shaped like a daisy (or in some cases a thimble), with a character at the end of each "petal." As the print head moves across the page, the petal rotates and a precisely timed hammer blow presses the print element against a ribbon and page. The entire character is thus produced in an instant, just as in a typewriter.

Daisy-wheel printers are superior to typewriters, however. They have fewer moving parts, are primarily electronic, and are much less subject to mechanical breakdown than typewriters. Print speed is typically 30 cps, although the least and most expensive daisy-wheel printers have a print speed of about half and twice this much, respectively. This is considerably slower than dot matrix printers, the slowest of which typically operate at around 50 cps, and many of which print at several times this speed. Virtually all packaged word-processing systems employ daisy-wheel printers.

Printer Noise. Unnecessary printer noise will have negative effects on an operator's performance and should not be ignored. The noise output of the printer will vary with the model and how the printer is used. Consider these factors before selecting a printer. If the printer will be used heavily in a small area where the operator will be constantly exposed to its noise, then select the quietest printer that you can, consistent with other requirements. Consider getting a sound-deadening enclosure for it.

In word-processing applications, it is important for the typist to have convenient access to the printer, and so it is not practical to run long cables from computer to printer or to put the printer in, for example, another room behind a closed door. The typist must monitor the printout to make sure that nothing goes wrong.

The Ideal Printer. What we want in a printer is an impossible combination of properties: high speed, low cost, excellent print quality, the ability to print on any type of paper, low noise, and high reliability. Since we cannot get all these properties in one machine, we must make a trade-off. Most often, the choice will reduce to one between a dot matrix and a daisy-wheel printer.

Graphics and Color. Before we leave the subject of printers, a footnote should be added concerning two optional but increasingly common features found on some dot matrix printers — the abilities to print graphics and color.

Many dot matrix printers are capable of printing graphics — that is, addressing individual print wires on the print head such that a graphic image can be generated on the printer. This is becoming less an expensive option, and more a standard feature. A number of inexpensive dot matrix printers have appeared recently that are capable of printing in color. The designer should keep this in mind and consider them, if the particular application can capitalize on the legitimate uses of color.

Sound and Natural Language Output

Microcomputers vary in their ability to produce different types of sound. This section will explore three different types of sound output, each of which calls for somewhat different hardware configurations.

Warning Signals. The first and most common use of sound is as a warning signal. Most microcomputers are equipped with audio circuitry which can be controlled with software. This gives the programmer the ability to produce tones of controllable length and frequency. Such tones are commonly used to warn the operator of an error condition or other problem. Unless deaf, the operator cannot ignore the tone and does not have to monitor a visual display to sense it.

Computer-Generated Music. Some microcomputers come or can be equipped with peripherals that permit software control of music generation. Herbie Hancock, Chick Corea, George Duke, and other jazz musicians are very checked out on the subject. If you want to compose or produce music, these capabilities can be very useful to you.

Even if this does not interest you, the ability to control such a powerful sound-producing apparatus can be useful in programs that have nothing to do with music at all. You can use different sound patterns, for example, to signal the onset of a program state or to code information. Used in this way, sound is an extension of the simple warning signal and becomes multidimensional. For example, you can have several different types of "warning" signals, not all of which mean that something bad has happened or is about to happen.

Computer-Generated Speech. Finally, we come to the issue of computer-generated speech. As everyone who has read Arthur C. Clarke's novel *2001, A Space Odyssey* (see the Bibliography) or seen Stanley Kubrick's movie of the same name knows, computers will someday speak to us, and we to them. For us, this is the most natural way for a dialog to occur. To date, the most widespread general use of computer-generated speech in microcomputers has been in games. Not much has been done beyond this limited realm, except in the laboratory. Designers are only now beginning to explore some of the real possibilities of computer-generated speech. It is possible to generate comprehensible if somewhat spacey-sounding speech with many microcomputers.

One promising application is in programs whose users lack reading skills or cannot see. The sightless and many other handicapped people cannot respond to the written menus, instructions, and so forth that are required to use most computer programs. Substitution of spoken messages can, in many cases, make the computer accessible to them.

More generally, we ought to give serious consideration to the use of voice in any aspect of a human-computer dialog that would otherwise involve a CRT display. Here are some possible ways that spoken output could be used:

* To provide warning messages
* To give directions
* To request that certain data be entered
* To give the operator prompts
* To report the result of a mathematical calculation (as in a speaking calculator)

Speech-generating capabilities are still limited, and they have a substantial overhead cost in terms of software and memory. Moreover, the industry has insufficient experience to know when and where it is most cost-effective to use such speech — beyond the obvious application in games. However, speech-generating capabilities are improving, and adventurous programmers may want to experiment and get the ball rolling now.

INPUT DEVICES

This section discusses eight computer input devices in the approximate order of their popularity: the keyboard, light pen, mouse, touch-sensitive screen, joystick, track ball, stylus, and voice interface. This section will give you an overview of the most common input devices and techniques and will permit you to make analogies to those not covered.

You are probably familiar, to some degree, with these eight input devices. Most computer users have encountered them in one program or another. When we see an input device being used, we usually take it for granted. We rarely ask why it was used in a particular application or whether some other device would have been better. The selection criteria are often obscure. They should not be — nor should the selection of an input device be based on instinct, habit, or standard practice alone. We should analyze the requirements of the input task and then pick the device that best meets those requirements. This section will give you the information you need to make an intelligent selection.

These devices will be put in perspective before they are discussed in more detail individually. First, the keyboard is by far the most common input device. Its use assumes typing skills (although attempts have been made to develop keyboards that do not require these skills). It also gives the operator access to the greatest range of discrete input possibilities. Use of a keyboard gives operators control of language — their own or the computer's. Used this way, the keyboard is a very powerful tool.

The remaining input devices, excepting voice interface, give the program user less control of language, trading it off for convenience or for the ability to make a direct analog input. The light pen, mouse, and touch-sensitive screen are most often used as pointing devices to select menu options in highly structured programs. The joystick, track ball, and stylus are most often used to provide direct analog input to the computer for graphics or tracking tasks. Direct voice input permits the user to speak to the computer in natural language — however, voice recognition by most microcomputers is limited to a vocabulary of a few dozen words.

In selecting in input device we ought to look for the one that is most "natural" for the application. Often this will be a device which is similar or analogous to something the computer is representing. This idea is perhaps best illustrated in concrete terms. If we were attempting to simulate flight with a computer — showing the effect of control motions upon the horizon and aircraft instruments — it would be quite natural to use a joystick as the input device, since it is similar to the control stick of an aircraft. Here we have a direct physical analog between the two devices (Figure 5-6). In another program, we might be generating three-dimensional computer graphic figures. One important function of this program would be to rotate the figures about their

Figure 5-6   A joystick such as this can be used for cursor control, pointing, and other functions, and it is a natural for controlling the movement of a graphic, such as an aircraft, where its movement can be programmed to have the same effect on the figure as the control stick of an actual aircraft.

axes. In this application, the most natural input device would be a track ball, whose physical movement would produce analogous movement of the figure on the screen (Figure 5-7). Here the analogy is between the input device and what is displayed on the screen. In developing a program that would permit the user to draw figures, the most natural input device would be one that was like a drawing instrument — a light pen or a stylus used with a graphics tablet (Figure 5-8). These examples illustrate what is meant by "analogs." This is an important notion to keep in mind when you are selecting an input device.

Note that each input device carries with it certain software requirements. For example, to use a mouse, you must obtain the appropriate hardware interface and then create the software that will permit the mouse to work — the menus or graphics that appear on your screen and the software interpreter that translates mouse movements into a form that is meaningful to your computer. Each input device is discussed in greater detail below.

Keyboard

History.   The keyboard is by far the most common computer input device. The modern computer keyboard (Figure 5-9) is a direct descen-

Figure 5-7 Use of track ball to control figure movement. The track ball is a natural in three-dimensional graphics, where the operator can use it to reach into the display to rotate the displayed graphic.

dant of the typewriter keyboard of the nineteenth century. The resemblance between what your great-great-grandparent may have been typing on in 1872 and the slick keyboard on your computer is more than superficial. Key sizes are about the same, and in most cases the locations of the alphabet and number keys are identical. Most computers are shipped with the "QWERTY" keyboard, so named because of the sequence of the top row of its letter keys. This keyboard was originally developed in the 1860s.

The arrangement of keys is not optimal. Only one vowel (A) is on the keyboard's middle, or "resting," row, and the remaining vowels are on the upper row. Logically, the keyboard should have its vowel keys where they can be reached with the least finger movement, close to the strongest fingers of the hand. Keys should be arranged based on their frequency of use. The QWERTY keyboard fails this test. Some historians believe the keyboard was designed this way to slow down typing speed in order to avoid jammed keys on the early mechanical typewriters.

Figure 5-8 The stylus and graphics tablet, or the light pen, are naturals for drawing since they bear a strong similarity to a drawing instrument such as a pencil.

Alternative Key Arrangements. Are there better keyboard layouts? Yes and no. One can, on logical grounds, design a keyboard better than the QWERTY. A number of people have done just that. The most well known "improved" keyboard is probably the Dvorak keyboard (Figure 5-10); all the vowels are on the middle row, and its other keys are located based on their frequency of use. Typing performance using the Dvorak layout has been studied and results have been mixed. There is no overwhelming evidence of its superiority. Moreover, since most keyboards in existence use QWERTY arrangement, and most typists have mastered it, it is unrealistic to expect a changeover to the Dvorak or other alternatives at this point. Still, the Dvorak keyboard is available, and some users prefer it, even though it is unconventional. Consider it — if your target audience states a preference for it.

The touch typist, programmer, or other person who is skilled with the QWERTY keyboard should never be forced to use some other key arrangement. However, if the user audience consists of nontypists, certain nonstandard key arrangements may make sense. The *alphabetic* keyboard is one possibility — if user inputs are short. The alphabetic keyboard in the hands of a nontypist is not the same as a QWERTY keyboard in the hands of someone who types. For some programs, it may make sense to use a small, special-purpose keyboard.

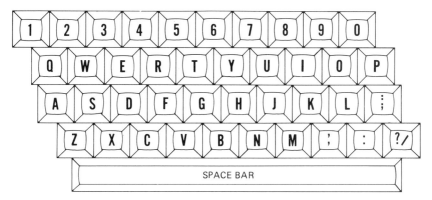

Figure 5-9 QWERTY keyboard arrangement. This keyboard has its origin in the nineteenth century, but it is the industry standard today.

The Numeric Keypad. A numeric keypad is advisable if the operator will make frequent numeric inputs. The numeric keypad is a standard item on many microcomputer keyboards these days. Thus, the keyboard you use should probably have one unless you have good reason to choose another. The experienced operator will expect it, and the inexperienced operator will find it easier for entering numeric information than the top row of the alphabetic keyboard.

Function Keys. Function keys, like the numeric keypad, are becoming standard items. It is only a matter of time before they will be found on all microcomputers. These programmable keys are used to perform functions that would otherwise require the operator to make several keystrokes. If programmed properly, they make the program easier to

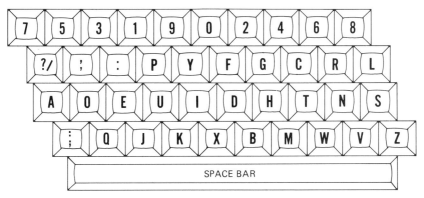

Figure 5-10 Dvorak keyboard arrangement. This "improved" keyboard, with its sensible arrangement of keys (e.g., all the vowels on the middle row) has never really caught on because of the widespread use of the QWERTY keyboard.

use and save the operator work. They are valuable in word processing, spreadsheet programs, and in other applications that perform repetitive functions.

Other Desirable Keyboard Features. Here are several keyboard features which are desirable:

* *Typewriterlike keyboard layout.* As much as possible, the keyboard should resemble the industry standard, which is the IBM Selectric typewriter. (It is an interesting historical footnote that the company that originated this keyboard chose not to use it in its personal computer — and has been widely criticized for its new keyboard design.)
* *Tactile and auditory key feedback.* As a key is depressed, the user should feel it yield and hear a faint "click" to indicate that the key has been successfully pressed. Without such feedback, the user will often be unsure.
* *Sculptured keytops.* The keys should be curved slightly inward, in conformity with the fingertip, to provide a comfortable finger rest.
* *Tactile index points (bumps) on strategic keys.* To help the fingers find their "home" positions on the keyboard, without the user actually looking at the keys (remember how much typing teachers hate this), strategic keys should have small bumps. These are usually placed on the D and K keys on the letter keyboard and on the 5 key of the numeric keypad.
* *Cursor keys that permit the cursor to be moved left, right, up, and down.* Preferably these should be set in a "compass" arrangement (Figure 5-11).
* *Built-in "repeat" of all keys after they have been depressed for about 1 second.*

One basic principle of human factors is to give operators flexibility in using what you design for them. Consider this principle when you select a keyboard. The low-profile, detachable keyboard is by far more flexible than one that is built into a computer or a terminal. It permits operators to arrange the keyboard in the way that suits them best — on the lap, on the corner of the desk, or whatever. Most of the current generation of microcomputers is equipped with low-profile detachable keyboards. These have become the industry standard not only for microcomputers, but for CRT terminals and word processors as well.

The keyboard should be fairly thin and its slope should be adjustable. Most users will not want a flat keyboard; they will want the top row of keys to be higher off the table than the lower keys. Current

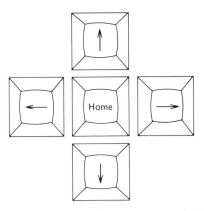

Figure 5-11   The best arrangement of
cursor keys is like a compass, with a cursor home key at the center.

ergonomic standards call for a maximum keyboard slope of 15°; this is
probably higher than most users will want. The slope should not exceed this, and it should be adjustable.

Light Pen

The light pen (Figure 5-12) is a light-sensing device, combined with a
switch and timing circuitry, that permits the computer to calculate the
X and Y coordinates of a point on the CRT screen that the light pen has
been placed over. Light pens are typically used as pointing devices.
They are commonly used for menu selection, tracking, and graphics
input.

Menu selection is probably the most common application with microcomputers. Tracking tasks are rare in microcomputer applications
but are common elsewhere, e.g., when entering geographic coordinates
of an object shown on a radar screen as in air traffic control. Graphics
input is more common. Here a light pen might be used to enter selected
X and Y coordinates on a computer-generated display. For example,
the light pen would be used to mark the point on the screen that was to
become the new right edge of the display, to pick the points on a graph
to use in computing the factors in an equation, or to point to where the
Knight should be moved on a game board.

When designing programs for people who lack typing skills, consider the light pen. Its use is obvious and easy to learn. If the program
is menu-driven, and all or most entries can be made by pointing the
light pen at information displayed on the screen, it may be possible to
dispense with the keyboard altogether. Used in this manner, the light

Figure 5-12 A light pen such as this is excellent for locating
a point on the screen, as in menu selection. It is also commonly
used for tracking or graphics input.

pen is a simple substitute for the keyboard. Obviously, there are limits
to what you can do with a light pen, but many programs can be built
within these limits.

The following are desirable features to look for in a light pen:

• It should be rugged and able to tolerate the wear and tear of likely
users.

• It should have an activating switch, such as a push button, at its tip.

• It should project a circle on the screen so that you can see what it is
pointed at.

• It should be at least 5 inches long.

In designing software that requires a light pen, the ideal is to have
the light pen control everything and to avoid a mixture of keyboard
and light pen inputs. This ideal will be unachievable in most cases but
should be kept in mind anyway. At the very least, use one input device
at a time and avoid switching back and forth between them.

Mouse

The mouse (Figure 5-13) is so named because of its shape — small,
contoured, fitting neatly in the palm of the hand — and perhaps be-

Figure 5-13 The mouse is probably the most rapid and accurate pointing device, but takes training and practice to master. It is being used increasingly in newer computer systems, such as the Xerox Star, as shown in this figure. *(Photograph courtesy of Xerox Corporation.)*

cause of someone's sense of humor. The mouse is gripped and then moved over a flat surface. As it moves, X- and Y-coordinate signals are generated in proportion to the amount of physical movement of the mouse. These displacement signals can be translated into cursor movement on the screen. Some mouses have two perpendicular wheels at the bottom which generate the X- and Y-coordinate signals. Others have a roller or an optical sensor that must be moved over a special surface. If it is not well designed, rapid movement of the mouse can produce slippage, resulting in inconsistent output.

The mouse is most often used for positioning the cursor on the screen to point at things; it is fast and accurate. The mouse is rarely used for graphic input — that is, for drawing things on the screen — as it is awkward for this application.

The mouse has been around since the 1960s but has not made a significant impact on the computer world. Recently, its impact has been stronger. It is used both with the Xerox Star work station and with Apple's Lisa computer system. Both systems have achieved notoriety on the basis of their advanced human factors, and for this reason the mouse may seem to be the logical choice in new designs. It is probably the most rapid and accurate pointing device there is, but takes training and practice to use properly, requires a flat work surface, and — as noted above — is not particularly good for graphic input.

Here are some features to look for in a mouse:

• It should fit comfortably in the palm of the hand and should be smoothly contoured without sharp edges.

• The input buttons (there are usually two) should be located so that they can be depressed without readjusting the hand.

• The mouse should move smoothly and should track without wheel slippage as it is moved across the surface.

• It should be between 3 and 5 inches long, between 1½ and 3 inches wide, and between 1 and 1½ inches high.

Touch-Sensitive Screen

The touch-sensitive screen (Figure 5-14) employs infrared sensors or is a transparent overlay that attaches to the surface of a CRT. It can be used to identify the approximate X and Y coordinates of a point on its surface which has been touched by an object such as a human fingertip. Its resolution is more limited than that of a light pen.

These screens are primarily of value for programs operated by naive users who will perform highly structured tasks that can be controlled with menus. One common application is in after-hours bank deposit and withdrawal terminals. In this and similar applications, users are prompted to touch the screen to select the option they want. The touch-sensitive screen should not be used in programs designed for experienced users. It is best limited to programs for naive users who must interact with a computer without receiving any training.

Joystick

The joystick consists of a rod attached to a joint that permits movement in two or more directions. The operator grips the shaft in the palm or between thumb and forefinger. Rod movement is translated by the computer into cursor displacement on the CRT. By moving the shaft, the operator can move the cursor around the screen to locate stationary or to track moving targets.

Figure 5-14   The touch-sensitive screen has limited resolution, but it may be valuable for programs that will be operated by naive users performing simple tasks that can be controlled with menus.

In microcomputer applications, the joystick is most often used in action-oriented games, either to track something on the screen or to control the movement of a computer graphic such as an aircraft or helicopter.

The joystick is not difficult to master but does take practice to use properly. It is best used as a tracking device. Though it can be used to position the cursor for menu selection, the light pen or mouse is better for this and for other pointing tasks.

In selecting a joystick, find one that is rugged, comfortable to use, and equipped with one or more push buttons to tell the computer what action to take at a particular screen location — enter data, fire laser, etc.

Track Ball

The track ball consists of a ball mounted in low-friction bearings. The top of the ball is exposed and the operator can rotate it freely. When pressure is removed, the ball will stop but will not return to its "home" position. The ball is not self-zeroing like the joystick.

The track ball is usually used for tracking targets. It can also be used effectively for pointing tasks. For tracking tasks, the ball should be used only in such a way that its movement produces an absolute, linear effect on the display — rotating the ball a given amount moves the cursor a given amount on the CRT. This is required because it does not automatically zero, and the operator has no way of judging how far the ball is displaced from its home position. The track ball should be used only in applications where home does not matter.

The track ball is also effective for rotating three-dimensional graphics. It is a direct analog of the displayed graphic (see Figure 5-7). Using it, the operator can effectively reach into the display to move the graphic in a way that seems very natural.

Stylus

The stylus is one part of the familiar graphics tablet. The tablet itself consists of a flat surface on which a matrix has been etched or printed. The operator locates X and Y coordinates by placing the stylus on the matrix. Using the stylus, the operator can locate points, draw lines, or draw complete figures.

The stylus bears a superficial similarity to the light pen. However, while the light pen is primarily used for locating objects that are displayed on the screen, the stylus more often is used for creating a graphic which is transmitted to the screen for display.

The stylus also has a certain similarity to the mouse, since both require flat surfaces. However, while the mouse is somewhat awkward for generating graphics, the stylus has nearly the flexibility of a pencil. The stylus is not recommended for locating points on a CRT or for tracking targets. It is best used for creating graphics on the CRT.

Voice Interface

Sound and natural language output were discussed earlier in the present chapter. It is possible to obtain inexpensive voice interfaces that permit you to teach your computer to recognize a vocabulary of several dozen words. Microcomputers are a long way from beginning to handle the complexities of natural language, but you can program them to react to simple commands.

Voice input should be considered when a quick response is required from the computer, operator input is limited to numbers or to a few discrete commands, or the hands are otherwise occupied or cannot be used. Voice input is becoming increasingly important in programs developed for the handicapped, in industrial or business tasks where the hands cannot readily enter information into a computer, and in fast-action computer games.

Researchers have achieved impressive results with speech input systems. So far, however, the effective use of speech requires either a small vocabulary of words, which most people speak in the same way, or careful training of the operators and calibration of the computer to assure that errors are minimized. Extensive testing is required to assure that error rates are kept within acceptable limits.

OPERATOR ERGONOMICS

"Ergonomics" is a popular word these days, and much of the computer industry has climbed onto the bandwagon. Manufacturers of CRTs, keyboards, printers, tables, chairs, and other computer-related equipment loudly proclaim the ergonomic virtues of what they sell. Much of what is claimed is advertising hype. However, the underlying interest in improved ergonomics, which drives the ad agencies, is a good thing.

Most of the interest is in people who work at computer terminals for long stretches of time. These include secretaries who use word processors, data-entry operators, telephone operators, computer operators, and various other folks whose occupations bring them into prolonged contact with a CRT, a keyboard, and perhaps a printer. An enormous amount of research has been and continues to be conducted concerning the design of video display terminal (VDT) work stations. This research has been motivated by the symptoms widely reported by such operators. The following is a sampling of these symptoms:

• Eyestrain

• Lower back pain

• Pain in the shoulders, arms, and wrists

• Increased anxiety levels

• Excessive fatigue

Most VDT operators have experienced some or all of these symptoms at one time or another. The symptoms are caused, totally or partly, by the necessity for VDT operators to sit in a more or less stationary position for an extended period of time, performing a repetitive task that requires them to conform their physical anatomy to the requirements of the work station.

If this work station is not physically suitable, the operator must adapt to it, thereby producing a prolonged stress of one kind or another. For example: If the keyboard is too high, the operator must raise both arms and bend both wrists to reach it. If the chair lacks adequate back support, then continuous muscle tension is necessary to compensate. If there is a large distance between CRT, keyboard, and the copy being entered, then the eyes must constantly dart back and forth from one to the other and eyestrain will result. If the CRT is dim, is out of focus, is misaligned, or has poor resolution, eyestrain will result. If the working space is brightly lighted and produces reflections on the terminal, eyestrain will result.

These are a few examples of the ways a work station can oppress its operator. It does not have to be this way. And buying some manufacturer's "ergonomic CRT" or CRT table is only chipping away at the problem, not really solving it. The design of a comfortable work station imposes several requirements, and all of these must be considered together.

The basic requirements for a work station are illustrated in Figure 5-15. The most important principle in designing a work station is *adjustability* — a factor which allows the operator to modify the station to suit his or her unique needs. Except for twins, no two people are exactly alike, and all of us should be able to adjust a work station to suit ourselves. One size does not fit all.

What needs adjustment? Start with the chair. The chair should be fully adjustable, capable of moving backward, forward, left, right, up, and down. Its back should provide adequate lumbar support, and the back rest should be adjustable. Based on current knowledge, the best chair tilt is either level or tilted slightly forward. Most people work comfortably with the chair level. The chair should not tilt freely, once adjusted, but should stay fixed to give the operator firm support. The feet of a seated operator should touch the floor. If they do not, a foot support should be provided to keep them from dangling in the air.

Consider the tabletop. The operator, seated upright, should be able to extend her or his arms straight forward, at an angle of 90° with the torso, and touch the center of the keyboard. If the arms must be raised to do this, then the keyboard is too high. The proper height for the keyboard is several inches lower than the proper height for a desk or worktable. The only satisfactory solution to this problem is to use a table with a recess for the keyboard. The tabletop should be level. The slope of the keyboard, in relation to the tabletop, should be in the range of 10 to 20° and should be adjustable.

The CRT should be 20 to 28 inches from the operator's eyes. Its distance, height, and tilt should be adjustable. The CRT should be close to the keyboard, not placed on a shelf at eye level. The angle between the operator's line of sight and the horizontal should be in the range of 20 to 30°.

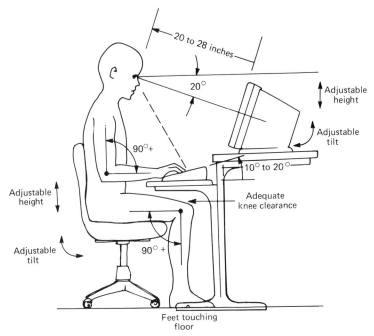

Figure 5-15   The key work station ergonomics requirement is that of *adjustability* — in the height, tilt, and relative locations of the operator's chair, keyboard, and display.

If the operator is typing from copy, that copy should be at the same level as the CRT and as close to the CRT as possible. The tabletop should have sufficient free area to allow the operator to arrange working materials without making piles or getting them mixed up.

There should be sufficient ambient light to allow the operator to read any written materials to be worked on. However, the lights should be arranged, or adjustable, so that they do not reflect from the CRT, keyboard, or other computer equipment. Light shields or CRT filters may be required, to eliminate reflections.

The printer, if there is one, should be conveniently located for operator use. If hard copies are run frequently and the operator must be in attendance, then a sound-deadening enclosure should be used.

Six

Data Output

This chapter covers data output — the presentation of information on computer displays to program users. The focus is on how to present information on CRT displays, although most of what is covered also applies to printed reports. These are not the only output devices that people use, but they are the most common. Moreover, a large amount of research has been conducted concerning how to present information on these displays.

The displays discussed are information displays; they present operators with the numbers, words, and graphics they need to analyze information, draw conclusions, and make decisions. These displays are found in programs such as management information systems, statistical analysis packages, data-base management programs, and electronic bulletin boards.

The chapter begins with a discussion of the trade-offs between CRT and hard-copy displays. The second section covers the design of CRT screens. The final section covers information coding.

CRT VERSUS PRINTER

Given that your computer has something interesting to tell people, when should you present it on a CRT and when on a printer? First, and obviously, if there is only one type of display, that is what you must use. This is the least defensible basis for choosing the display. It has nothing to do with the relative merits of one display versus the other. In some cases this will mean using the inappropriate display. And in some of these cases, the display used will be detrimental to operator performance.

When is a printed report needed? The most common reason for choosing a printed report is the need for a permanent record. This in turn reflects more basic, underlying needs, such as one (or more) of the following:

• The report must be seen by more than one person, and not all users will have access to a computer.

• A permanent history must be kept and filed.

• Generating the report is time-consuming and impractical to do on-line.

• The report is too big to fit onto a CRT display.

• It is important to cross-correlate different parts of the information "geography," and this is impractical with the narrow window of a CRT display.

When is a CRT better than a printer? A CRT is usually preferred when speed is important and hard copy is unnecessary. CRT displays are faster than printers and do not use up paper. In addition, CRTs can do some things that printers cannot — flash on and off, for example — or that most printers are not equipped to do — print graphics or color.

Realistically, the CRT versus printer question is not an all or nothing proposition. Often, you can have both. When you can, it is not a matter of deciding which device to use for everything, but of which information to present on which device. The decision rule given above still applies: When speed is important and the reasons for using a printer are not present, a CRT should be used; otherwise, a printed report is required.

There are cases in which you must make output selectively available on both CRT and printer. If some program users will have a printer and others will not, then you must provide display redundancy. If you do not, program users with the wrong equipment configuration will not be able to gain access to important information.

CRT SCREEN DESIGN

This section contains a compendium of design recommendations which are loosely organized under the following headings: screen access, screen content, use of language, screen layout, presentation of numeric information, tabular versus graphic presentation, presentation of lists and directories, and conventions for presentation of dates, times, and telephone numbers. Though the focus is on CRT displays, much of what is covered applies also to printed reports. Use your common sense to sort things out.

Screen Access

The CRT may be thought of as a window onto the landscape of information your program can produce. This window can look onto many different scenes in the information landscape. In some programs, the landscape is a continuous one, consisting of a matrix of information over which the window moves (Figure 6-1). In other programs, the landscape is not continuous, but consists of a series of discrete scenes, more like a slide show (Figure 6-2).

In general, it is better to access screens by paging than by scrolling. That is, clear the screen completely before putting up the next display. When a display scrolls, its information moves, producing a needless distraction and causing eyestrain. It is particularly important to use

```
                PROJECTED PROFITS BY MONTH AND YEAR
PRODUCT LINE              Jan 81    Feb 81 ...               ...March 86

Men's wear                17456     30912                          2109432
Ladies fashions           40516     38720                          3271955
Junior fashions           18737     16544                          1825697
Shoes                      8212      7995                           621633
Sporting goods             6770      8527                           457832
Toys                       9339      5210    6375    11298          875590
Housewares                 6554      7321    8329     9753          502717
Automotive products        6883      4460    7501     6260          426624
Hardware                   4572      4222    5997     3775          377188
  .                          .         .       .        .             .
  .                          .         .       .        .             .
  .                          .         .       .        .             .
========================  =======   =======  =====   ======       =======
Total                    322160    319757   367220  427703        21172260
```

Figure 6-1   Some programs, such as Visicalc, produce an output landscape that is continuous and that cannot be fitted onto a single screen. To view the information, the operator must move his CRT window around on the landscape.

the paging technique on programs of the "discrete scene" type. Since each of the scenes in these programs is separate, it should not be linked to others on the display. Paging makes a clean break between scenes.

A modified form of scrolling, called "windowing," is sometimes desirable in programs of the "continuous landscape" type. In such programs, operators may want to move the window around on the landscape much as they would a telescope in the night sky. They should be able to do this as desired, moving the window up, down, left, or right. Windowing is different from scrolling. In windowing, the scene is fixed, and program users move the window over it. When they give the "window-up" command (using a function key or whatever), the displayed information moves downward on the screen. In scrolling, the window is fixed and the information field moves. This is like looking through a microscope at a specimen. In this case, when the "scroll-up" command is given, the information on the screen moves upward. Research has shown that operators prefer windowing to scrolling, and that they perform better using it.

Screen Content

A display screen is meant to be used by an operator to perform a specific task. Know what this task is before you design the screen. Then design the screen to help the operator perform the task efficiently — and do nothing more. Limit the display screen to what is needed. Eliminate the superfluous. Design the screen, and then examine it element by element and remove what is not needed. Some designers have recommended the rule "one logically connected thought or idea

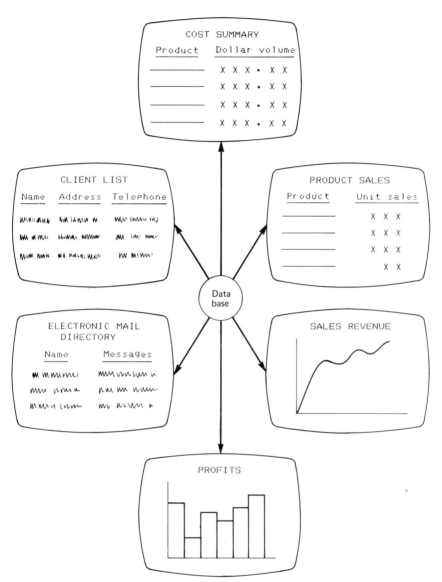

Figure 6-2 Some programs produce an output that consists of a series of discrete scenes, which do not flow naturally into each other. Using such a program is more like viewing a slide show than like moving a window around on a larger scene.

per screen." This is like limiting a paragraph to a single idea. It is probably a good rule to keep in mind, although you should not follow it slavishly.

Along these lines, some programmers seem challenged by the act of screen design and take a certain satisfaction in seeing how much information they can put on each display. They may gain a degree of satisfaction from this, but they do it at the expense of the operator.

It is also possible to provide too little information. If operators must work with certain related pieces of information to accomplish their objectives, then these should be presented on the same display, if possible. Do not expect operators to work with one display and then carry its contents in their memories to the next. Technically, the rule is that operators can carry about five pieces of information in their heads from display to display (approximately the capacity of short-term memory), but it is better to avoid dependence on operators' memory, if possible.

Use of Language

Computer programs have not been distinguished by their effective use of language. The following is a brief catalog of common but undesirable practices, along with suggested alternatives:

- *Printing everything in capital letters.* Solution: Use uppercase and lowercase. It is easier to read and what we are used to.
- *Using abbreviations.* An abbreviation is a code that must be translated. In order to translate it, operators must first learn it. If they have not done this, the code remains a mystery. Even if they have memorized it, translating it takes time. Solution: Do not use abbreviations.
- *Using jargon.* Jargon is a specialized vocabulary, like a foreign language. Again, if operators do not know it, you leave them out in the cold. Solution: Avoid using jargon.
- *Not labeling things.* There is the display, and that is information on it, all right, but what is it? If you cannot tell what it is without a manual, then it is not properly labeled. It is like a table without a title or a figure without a caption. Solution: Put titles on screens and over the different blocks of information they contain.
- *Giving cryptic prompts, messages, and directions.* What do you do when the computer gives you a choice between "RESET THE FACILITATOR" and "BLOCK THE UNITIZER"? What do you do when this message appears: "SYSTEM ERROR 593"? For many operators, the response is a rise in blood pressure and the desire to wring the programmer's neck. Solution: Put the prompts in plain

English and the error message in a form that does not require program users, as a sort of penance, to look up their sins in the reference manual's catalog of errors.

Here are some general guidelines for the use of written language in your program:

• *Begin each sentence with its subject or main topic.*

• *Use short, simple sentences.* Long sentences — especially those with multiple clauses — are more difficult to understand.

• *Use simple, commonplace words.* Avoid complex words where simple ones will do. Use concrete rather than abstract language. Avoid abbreviations and jargon.

• *Make statements in a positive rather than a negative way.* For example, here are two ways to tell the operator how to prepare to print reports:

```
(Positive) Load the file before printing reports.
(Negative) Do not attempt to print reports until the file is
loaded.
```

• *Make statements in the active rather than passive voice.* For example:

```
(Active) Load the file before printing reports.
(Passive) The file must be loaded before reports can be
printed.
```

• *State actions in the order they must be performed.* For example:

```
(Correct order) Load the file before printing reports.
(Incorrect order) Before printing reports, load the file.
```

• *When listing multiple items or giving a set of directions, list each point on a separate line.* This makes the points easier to separate. For example:

```
(List sequence): To load file,
   Call file directory
   Select file
   Type in file number
   Press Return key
(Nonlist sequence): To load file, call file directory, select
file, type in number, press Return key.
```

If anything, proper use of language is more critical within computer programs than in normal written communication. Economy of communication in computer programs is desirable, since there is a memory penalty in being too verbose. But if we are too concise, we become cryptic and incoherent. Programmers must be better than average writers and editors in order to communicate concisely what they want.

Perhaps the bottom line on this is that we need to redefine the standard for what is considered acceptable language usage in computer programs. The standard must be raised at least to that of normal written communication, and it must expand beyond the conventions established in the past with computers of limited memory.

Screen Layout

There are four general rules for laying out a display screen:

1. Label or title it.
2. Center the information.
3. Be consistent in the way you present information.
4. Separate the different types of information.

Labeling or Titling.   Title the display so that operators know what it is (Figure 6-3). Without a title, the display has no name and operators must make up one of their own. It is better if you do this for them. In addition, you cannot really talk about or deal with something that does not have a name, as you find out when documentation is being prepared. For example, it is awkward to talk about the "screen that appears when you page from the display selected with the third option of the main menu." Much better to talk about the "file definition" screen.

Display screens will usually contain different types of information. Provide labels to make these stand out to operators. Do not make them decipher a display. Using your program should not be a test of their intelligence or ingenuity. Make it easy on them. Label things.

Centering.   Center information. Think of the display screen as the page of a book. The information on a printed page does not start at the left edge of the paper. Rather, left and right margins are set, and then the information is centered. Figures and tables are centered as well. For partial pages, information is centered vertically. When a line of text is long, or the print is small, text is divided into two or more columns.

These conventions are followed by typographers because they make a page easier to read and more symmetric and pleasing to the eye.

```
                    FILE STATUS DISPLAY

           Form        On file        Max
           ------      ----------     ------
             1           229          3500
             2           107          3500
             3            69          3500
             4           107          5000
             5            22           376
             6            52           100
             7            60           250
             8            34           250
             9            11           128
            11             7          1000
            12             6            64
            13             0           128
            14             0           384
```

Figure 6-3 A properly titled and labeled display. Each display should have a title at the top, and the different types of information it contains should be labeled separately.

They are also the conventions that every one of us has learned and gotten used to. It is natural for operators to expect text conventions to be followed within computer programs.

Consistency. Display screens often contain different types of information, such as a title, directions, prompt line, error-message line, operating mode indicator, and so forth. A given type of information — prompt line, for example — may appear on several different displays. Determine what types of information you will present and then present this information consistently from screen to screen. Assign an area to each type of information. Assure that each type of information always appears in the same place, regardless of screen.

By being consistent, you make it easier for the operator to learn your rules for displaying information. If you follow the same rules for all displays, then operators can learn them quickly. If you change the rules on every display, then they have more to learn and you make it more difficult for them. In addition, if you are not consistent, operators may mistake information appearing on a particular part of the screen for something that it is not. For example, if you present error messages on the second line of one screen and the operating mode indicator there on another screen, operators might confuse one for the other.

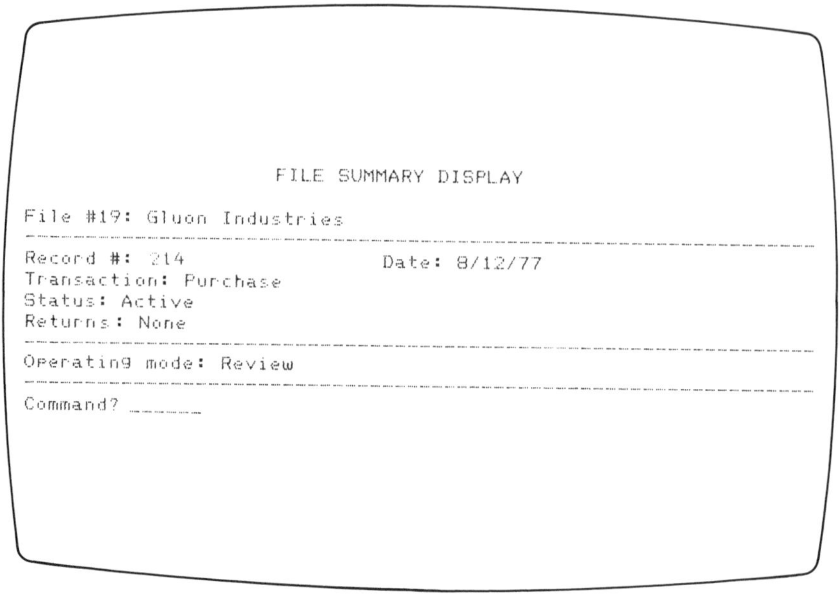

```

                         FILE SUMMARY DISPLAY

      File #19: Gluon Industries
      ────────────────────────────────────────────────────────────
      Record #:  214                    Date: 8/12/77
      Transaction: Purchase
      Status: Active
      Returns: None
      ────────────────────────────────────────────────────────────
      Operating mode: Review
      ────────────────────────────────────────────────────────────
      Command? _____

```

Figure 6-4 The different categories of information on a display screen should be separated graphically with rows or columns of blank spaces, with lines (shown), or by color-coding different screen areas.

Consistency is obviously an ideal and can rarely be accomplished fully. By necessity, some parts of the display must be used for many different things. The bottom line of the screen is often used for prompts, error messages, and as an input line. Using it for more than one thing does not pose a serious problem. The serious problem arises when we do something one way in one place and differently somewhere else. Here the rule apparently changes and may confuse operators.

Separation of Information. Format the display screen so that the different types of information are clearly separated from one another. If one thing runs into another, the implication is that both are parts of the same thing. Following the rule of consistency (noted above) will help the operator sort things out, but you should go a step further. Separate the screen areas graphically (Figure 6-4). That is, divide the screen up into different blocks, and separate the blocks by rows or columns of blank spaces, lines, or by color-coding the blocks themselves. Color coding is the most effective way to separate screen areas, but it is tricky to find acceptable color combinations. Both Chapter 2 and the section on coding later in this chapter offer some guidance. The next best technique for separating screen areas is to use lines. Blank

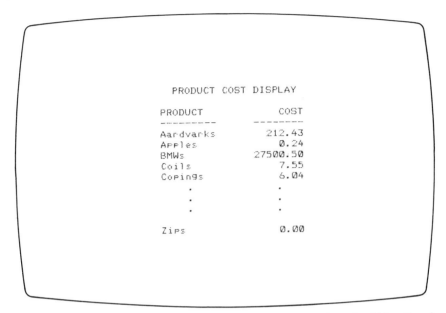

PRODUCT COST DISPLAY

PRODUCT	COST
Aardvarks	212.43
Apples	0.24
BMWs	27500.50
Coils	7.55
Copings	6.04
.	.
.	.
.	.
Zips	0.00

Figure 6-5 In displaying columns of numeric information, numbers should be aligned on the decimal point to make them readable.

spaces are not as good as lines, but they are effective if the display is not cluttered.

Presentation of Numeric Information

This section will consider one convention (decimal point alignment of columns of numeric information) and one rule that should be a convention but is not (breaking up long strings).

Presentation of Columns of Numeric Information. Columns of numeric information (such as the deposits and withdrawals shown on the monthly summary sheet from your bank) should be aligned on the decimal point (Figure 6-5). This is a good convention. It permits us to use a graphic cue — how far to the left of the decimal point a number extends — to estimate its magnitude. When numbers are aligned at a common left margin, we cannot use this cue and must read each number and keep score to determine which is biggest, smallest, or whatever.

In presenting monetary amounts, a related convention is followed. This is to show all numbers with the same number of significant digits. That is, twelve dollars would be shown as $12.00, 7.2 dollars would be

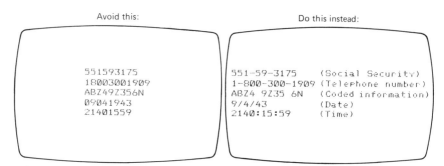

Figure 6-6 Long strings of information should be broken up for display into blocks of no more than 5 characters each.

shown as $7.20, and so on. This convention also makes sense in numeric listings where a specific number of significant digits is expected. For example, stock prices typically move up and down in increments of one-eighth (0.125), which translates to a requirement for three significant digits, if stock prices are displayed in decimal form. This convention does not make sense for displaying unpredictable numeric quantities.

It is customary to limit the number of significant digits displayed to some preset figure and not show more than this.

It is also customary to display all information in the same format, if possible, and not to intermix numerical quantities in, for example, decimal, floating-point, and scientific notation.

Presentation of Strings. A string is a sequence of alphanumeric characters, such as this combination: "14H2GPQ39914X4X4H2." Other strings are telephone numbers, social security numbers, and credit card numbers. Such strings are used in various ways in computer programs — for example, as passwords, codes, or data entries.

A distinguishing feature of the string is that, as a whole, it does not have a meaning that you can associate with a single concept, such as a name or command. To get the string right, you must pay attention to every character. A long string of, say, 15 characters, is very hard to read if all the characters are run together, end to end. Break up such strings for display into blocks of no more than 5 characters each (Figure 6-6). Separate each block by a space or appropriate symbol that will not be confused with a character that could appear in the string. Telephone numbers are usually divided up into three blocks (area code, prefix, number), separated by hyphens. Without such blocking, they would be much more difficult to read.

The use of strings to present coded information should be reviewed

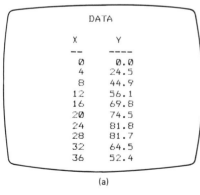

Avoid this: Do this instead:

Figure 6-7   If possible, avoid using strings of numbers or letters to present information to the operator. It is better to present the information in its natural form, with each item separately labeled.

critically. It is better to present the operator with information that is in directly usable form. It takes time and mental effort to translate a string. This increases the operator's work load and causes errors. On the other hand, your computer will not complain if you make it do the translation, will not become fatigued, and will make no more errors than usual. In short, avoid displaying coded strings if you can (Figure 6-7).

Tabular versus Graphic Presentation.   Often one has the choice of printing out numeric information in either tabular or graphic form, using the familiar X-Y plot (Figure 6-8). Which form is best in a particular situation depends on such factors as the nature of the information, the user audience, and what must be done with the information.

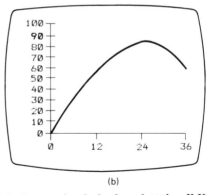

(a)   (b)

Figure 6-8   (a) Two columns of figures and (b) the way they look when plotted on X-Y coordinates. The general significance of the figures can be grasped in an instant by looking at the plot, but the columns of information are necessary to determine values accurately.

Graphic plots are effective for showing trends and relationships among variables. You can look at a graph and see everything in an instant — for example, highest price, lowest price, when the largest price jump occurs. You cannot do this as quickly with a table of numbers. A person can process a graph as a pattern but must process a table of numbers serially, one number at a time. With a table, each number must be stored in short-term memory, in turn, and the information must be dealt with in a conscious and deliberate fashion. Obviously, it is more work to make sense out of a table than out of a graph.

Graphs are not best for everything, however. First, you need to take into account the nature of the information being portrayed. If you are attempting to test a relationship among two or more variables, a graph can be invaluable. If you do not expect such relationships, and are only interested in absolute quantities, there is no point in using a graph.

You need also to take into account users, and what they will do with the information. Some users do not really care about the precise numerical quantities you may display to them; they are interested in trends. Managers are a good example. Often, they are not as concerned with precise amounts as with approximate amounts and direction of movement — sales, productivity, accidents, and the like. They will use the information for decision making, and precise amounts are not required for what they do.

Alternatively, some users do not care so much about trends as they do about specific amounts. They do not make decisions based on approximate data; they perform specific job functions that require specific knowledge. Examples are the accountant who must write a check, the production line worker who must increase productivity by five units per week, and the store owner who must increase the price of granola by 30¢ per pound.

It will often be the case that a number of different user groups will receive program outputs and that their needs will differ. It may make sense to provide graphics to some groups and tabular information to others.

Presentation of Lists and Directories

Many programs contain lists or directories. Examples are a list of documents, a list of part numbers, and a directory of names and telephone numbers. Such lists should be presented in a recognizable order. For example, the list of documents should be presented in alphabetic order, the part numbers in numeric order, and names in alphabetic order (Figure 6-9a,b,c).

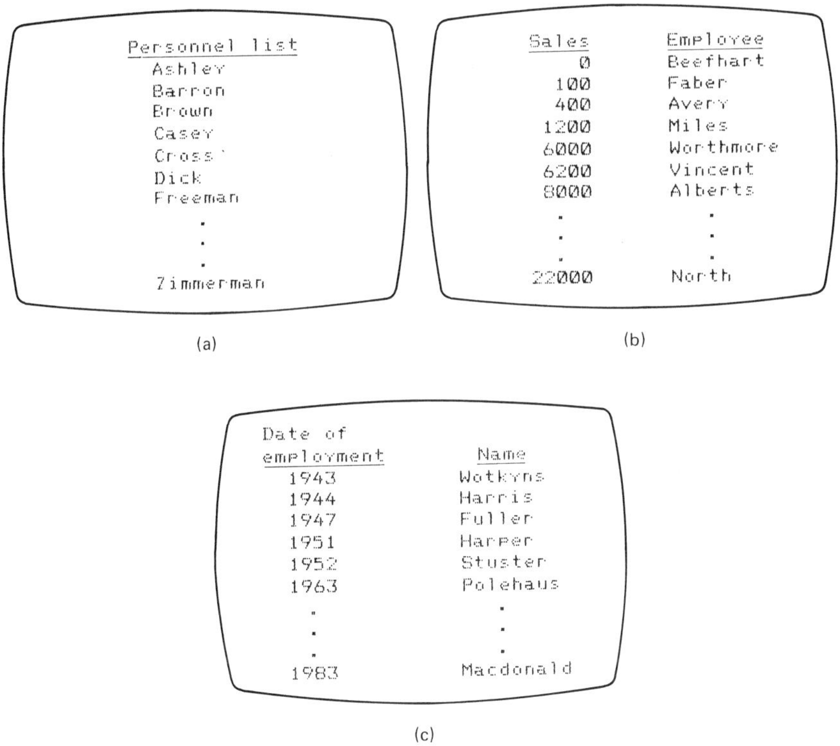

Personnel list
Ashley
Barron
Brown
Casey
Cross'
Dick
Freeman
.
.
.
Zimmerman

(a)

Sales	Employee
0	Beefhart
100	Faber
400	Avery
1200	Miles
6000	Worthmore
6200	Vincent
8000	Alberts
.	.
.	.
.	.
22000	North

(b)

Date of employment	Name
1943	Wotkyns
1944	Harris
1947	Fuller
1951	Harper
1952	Stuster
1963	Polehaus
.	.
.	.
.	.
1983	Macdonald

(c)

Figure 6-9 Three ordered lists: (a) alphabetic, (b) numeric, (c) chronologic. Ordering information in a logical way makes it easier for the operator to find things.

By using an order, we give operators a key that allows them to relate any item on the list or directory to any other. This simplifies search and saves time. They do not have to search the entire list; they can quickly focus in on the part that should, by the ordering rule, contain what they are looking for.

Conventions for Presentation of Dates, Times, and Telephone Numbers

Follow these conventions for presenting dates, times, and telephone numbers:

• *Date:* Month/day/year. For example, 12/5/62, or 3/15/27.
Do not use leading zeros in presenting dates. Avoid such nonsense as 03/05/53. Avoid such other common sins as encoding the date as a

long string (040943), separating the items by commas (3, 15, 41), or ordering the month, day, and year in an uncommon way (reversing month and day is okay in Great Britain, but not in the United States).

It may be good to store the date in nonstandard format as a string to aid the computer in sorting, searching, or storage, but this is to help the computer, not the operators. Operators should deal with data in the form that is most natural to them, and which does not require them to transpose, translate, or transform what is presented.

- *Time:* Hour:minute:second. For example, 12:15:59.

This is the convention used with digital watches and clocks. The hour may run from 0 to 12 or 0 to 24 (military time), depending upon the intended user. Leading zeros should not be used with the hour, but they are acceptable with the minute and second.

- *Telephone numbers:* Area code-prefix-number. For example, 123-456-7890.

Leading and trailing zeros are acceptable in all three number groups, since they are significant to the user.

Use the separators shown: / for date, : for time, - for phone number. This will be significant to the user, since it is one cue to what type of information is being presented. By all means, avoid the temptation to run these numbers together into one long string or put them in front of the operator in the form your computer uses them.

INFORMATION CODING

An information code is a way of conveying a message in an indirect form. We deal with many codes in our daily lives, and we have become so skilled at using some of them that we do not think of them as codes at all. For example, our written language is built on a coding system for sounds; in this system, combinations of symbols have referents in the real world. Most of us would not think of written language as a code since we have become so skilled in using it that it seems as natural as speaking.

We use a number of other codes in daily life as well: a raised eyebrow to express amazement, a finger pointing at a watch to tell a colleague we have to get back to the office, a quickly closed front door to tell the obnoxious salesperson that no, we do not want any today.

Codes can be helpful in many programs and are absolutely essential in programs that use graphics to convey complex information. Codes commonly used on CRT displays are color, alphanumeric, shape, size, brightness, and flash rate.

These codes can be used alone or in combination. For example, flash rate might be used as an alerting technique to draw the operator's attention to a particular message. It might be combined with color such that a red flashing message has a significance different from that of a blue flashing message. Combining codes in this manner is generally more effective than using a single code by itself. In using codes, you need to keep at least three factors in mind:

1. *Be consistent.* When you establish a coding system, you are essentially designing a language. People decipher languages by knowing the rules. If you violate the rules, your language no longer has meaning. If your flashing red message means danger on one display, it must mean the same thing on all other displays as well.

2. *Follow established conventions.* Some codes follow established conventions that people know and expect. Follow these to the extent that you can. Here are some examples: In color coding, red is danger, amber is caution, and green is safe; alternatively, red is hot and blue is cold. A flashing word or symbol is used to attract attention to something — a warning message, the symbol for an approaching target, a pointer (cursor) on part of the display. A longer line represents more of some quantity, as in a bar graph.

3. *Limit the levels according to the code.* The number of different levels you can display using a code depends upon the code. The maximum number has in most cases been established through research. If you exceed the maximum, the operator will confuse different levels and make errors. The maximum number of levels for each code is given in the table below. It is best *not* to use the maximum number of levels, since this is the limiting case. (A good rule of thumb is to divide the values in the table by 2.)

Maximum Number of Coding Levels for Different Types of Codes

Code	Maximum no. levels
Color	12
Alphanumeric	Unlimited
Shape	15
Size	5
Brightness	5
Flash rate	4

Most of these codes may be used in either an absolute or a relative way. Used in an *absolute* way, the operator must memorize and internalize the code and then be able to interpret it when it appears on his display, without reference to a key or other expressions of the code. When used in a *relative* way, a code key may be presented, or the code may be expressed at several different levels. The basic difference is that in the absolute case, the operator must rely on an internal standard and cannot compare the code's expression with anything else on the screen. Obviously, it is more difficult to use a code in the absolute way than in the relative way. You can distinguish more fine differences when you have a basis for comparison — a key or other expression of the code — shown on your display screen.

Each code is discussed briefly below in terms of its characteristics, maximum number of levels, and possible applications. The codes are discussed in the order of their general utility.

Color Coding

Color coding is particularly effective for search tasks. In such tasks, color is often combined with another code such as shape.

One must establish a color alphabet to use a color code. The sensitivity of the human eye to differences in hue varies along the hue spectrum, which makes designing a color alphabet no simple task. In general, the maximum number of colors in the alphabet that can be absolutely identified without extensive training is between eight and twelve hues. However, it is preferable to use fewer than this, if possible. If the program will be used on computers with monochrome screens, then color codes reduce to brightness codes, which have far fewer discriminable levels.

Alphanumeric Coding

Alphanumeric (number and letter) codes offer an almost unlimited number of levels. Often they will be used in combination with other codes, such as color (as background or colored alphanumeric itself), or shape (e.g., an alphanumeric enclosed within a shape). Pure alphanumerics take longer to locate than color alone, and they are not as good for search tasks.

Shape Coding

Shape coding can be quite effective for search tasks and does not require a color display. Researchers recommend that the shape alphabet be limited to a maximum of about fifteen items. In using shape codes, you must design a shape alphabet consisting of the set of symbols you will use. Here are some rules to follow in designing your alphabet:

• Use simple shapes rather than complex ones — people will identify them more quickly and accurately.
• Make the shapes distinct from one another so that they will not be confused.
• If possible, design shapes that relate to something in the real world — a physical object, for example. People will learn these shapes more quickly than they will learn abstract shapes.

Shape coding is often used in combination with other codes — typically color or flash rate coding.

Color, alphanumeric, and shape coding are the most powerful coding methods. They offer the greatest number of coding levels — ten or more. Color and shape coding are the best techniques to use in search tasks, particularly when combined with other coding methods such as flash rate coding.

Size Coding

With size coding, different-sized objects have different meanings. For example, the length of a line may be varied to represent different values. The maximum number of levels that can be absolutely discriminated is about five. If a scale or reference is provided on the display, more coding levels are possible. A problem with size coding is that larger sizes take up more room on the display.

Search time with this code is longer than with color coding or with shape coding.

Brightness Coding

Brightness coding is similar to color coding, but the alphabet consists of a single hue which varies in brightness. Brightness coding is what color coding reduces to when a monochrome display is used. Where absolute judgments of brightness must be made, the maximum number of brightness levels that should be used is about five. If a reference key is shown on the display, this can be stretched to perhaps six levels. It is best to limit the number of brightness levels to about three.

Flash Rate Coding

In flash rate coding, different flash rates have different meanings. Flashing symbols or alphanumerics are very attention-getting and are typically used to attract the operator's attention to a situation that requires immediate action. It is best to limit flash rate coding to these situations rather than to use it as a general coding technique. It has limited utility for general coding purposes, since the maximum number of flash rates that can be absolutely discriminated is about four. As in our other design recommendations, this is an upper limit, and the designer would be well advised to stay below it.

Flashing symbols aid search for target symbols and are often used this way. They are particularly useful when combined with shape codes, and they aid operators working with cluttered displays.

Flash rate coding becomes less effective, of course, with long-persistence phosphors, since flashes are masked.

Coding Recommendation Summary

The first three coding modes — color, alphanumeric, shape — are more flexible and powerful than the last three — size, brightness, flash rate. The first three coding methods also have more levels. Because of the limitations of the latter three coding methods, it would be good, as a general design philosophy, not to use them as coding techniques at all, and to use flash rate coding only in attention-getting situations such as search tasks or alerting messages.

Seven

Data Input

This chapter deals with data input — the entry of data by a program operator into the computer. The operator entries may be permanent — as when they add information to the program's data base — or very temporary — as when the operator selects a display or control option within the program. Designers sometimes distinguish between the inputs required for *data entry* and for *program control*. To be sure, there are differences. However, there are many more similarities and, for the most part, the same design guidelines apply. This chapter does not make a distinction between these two types of inputs; it is left to the reader's common sense to sort things out.

Data input can occur in many different ways, using any of the data-input devices covered in Chapter 5, as well as others. The focus in this chapter is upon inputs from keyboards. Such inputs have received much attention from researchers and designers, and design guidelines are well established. Many of the guidelines for keyboard input apply also to other types of input devices. Here, again, it is left to the reader's common sense to sort things out.

Data output and data input are intimately related. It is not conceivable to have an interactive program with one and not the other. This book covers the two topics in separate chapters, mainly for convenience. In designing a program, it is useful to distinguish between the two and treat them as separate but related design problems. At some point, however, we must abandon this fiction and bring the two together. Along these lines, one of the basic design principles, discussed below, is to assure consistency between the way information is displayed by the computer (output) and the way it is entered into the computer (input).

Since output and input are obviously related, the reader may wonder why output is discussed before input. Logically, it would seem to make more sense to discuss them in their natural order — input first, output last. After all, you cannot display information until you have entered it.

There are two reasons for discussing things in this order. First, it is a logical order to follow based on the top-down program development strategy described in Chapter 4 — in that approach, you design outputs before inputs or control structure. Second, data input is a more complex subject that presupposes a knowledge of how information should be displayed. For example, you cannot write a good input prompt without a basic knowledge of the design principles involved in information display.

In many cases, the distinction between output and input will tend to blur. For example, with full-screen data entry, inputs are typed into a blank form that appears on the screen, but the screen is itself a display.

As you can see, reality tends to highlight the shortcomings of this convenient classification of things into input and output. This chapter is divided into three sections. The first contains a set of general design guidelines for data input. They are ideas you need to bear in mind during the high-level design of your program. The second section describes the input-validation sequence — the actions that occur prior to, during, and following data entry. Data input is not a single action, but a process consisting of several steps. The final section is rather ominously titled "Avoiding Disasters." One pervasive aspect of programmers' lives is the anxiety that attends the use of their programs by others. This anxiety emerges from the mature programmer's awareness of the high probability of human error and the impossibility of writing a perfect program. The program disaster — when a data base is wiped out, the program ceases to function, or some other awful thing happens — is a programmer's nightmare. This section offers some ways to lessen the likelihood of such events.

GENERAL DESIGN GUIDELINES

This section presents five general design guidelines. These follow logically from the design principles presented in Chapter 3. If you have not read Chapter 3, it would be a good idea to do so before going further with this chapter. Each guideline is defined, discussed, and illustrated with one or more concrete examples.

1. Let the Operator Control Data Input

At the end of Chapter 5, we looked at operator ergonomics and the factors that make the difference between operator comfort and fatigue. The importance of letting the operator control the height, tilt, and position of the chair, keyboard, and CRT was noted. The underlying principle is *adjustability*. Since no two operators are alike, it is impossible to design a computer work station that suits everybody.

There is an analogous principle in data input. Just as no two operators will be happy with the same physical arrangement of equipment, no two operators will be exactly alike in terms of what they prefer for data input. The solution to this problem is to give the operator control of the data-entry process. There are a number of specific ways this can be done, but they are all based on the same concept: *Operators should never feel that the computer is controlling them*. Rather, they must be the ones who give the orders, set the pace, and manage things.

Here are some specific ways to give the operator control:

• *Let the operator control what data are entered and when.* Operators should not be forced to go through a long, inflexible data-entry sequence. Rather, they should be able to select what data to enter, and to enter them when they want.

• *Make data entry self-paced.* Operators, not the computer, should set the pace at which inputs are made. This can be managed by requiring operator verification of each field as it is entered, before requesting the next entry. This allows operators to pause, if they want to, or to move ahead as rapidly as they please.

Alternatively, the program should not pause for lengthy delays that will cause the operator to wait. An acceptable data-entry delay is about 1 second. If the computer requires longer than this to process the entries, then they should be buffered so that the operator does not have to wait.

In short, it is all right for the computer to wait for the operator, but not vice versa.

• *Let the operator set the prompting level.* Inexperienced operators need more prompting than experienced ones. New operators appreciate detailed prompts, help screens, and detailed error messages. Detailed prompting slows down the program, but it will help operators master the program more quickly. As they gain experience and skill, they need less prompting and, in fact, become increasingly impatient with the delay it entails. The solution to this problem is to let operators set the prompting level that they want.

One technique for setting the prompting level is to have the computer analyze the content of operator interactions — errors, requests for help, delays — and set the prompting level accordingly. For most microcomputer programs, this technique is impractical. However, it is feasible to let operators set the prompting level themselves — for example, by using a menu, or by entering a prompting code (Figure 7-1).

• *Let operators change their minds.* Operators should always be able to escape from where they are in the data-input sequence, without being required to carry on mechanically to the end. They may realize that an error has been made or decide to do something different. These are the operator's prerogatives. The machine is lower in the social hierarchy. It has the status of a slave. Obedient slaves do not compel their masters to stay on the path simply because they have started that way. No, masters can turn around or walk on the grass or even in the flowers if they want to.

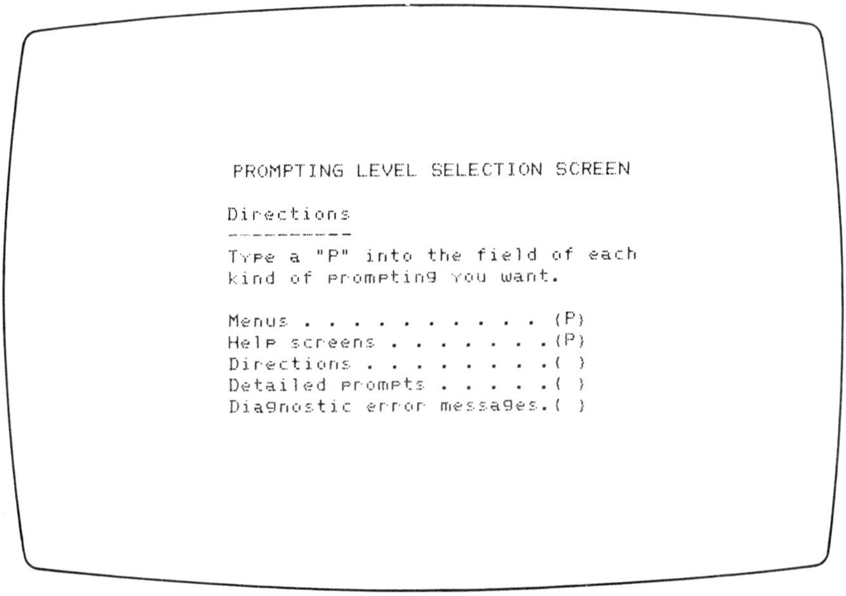

```
PROMPTING LEVEL SELECTION SCREEN

Directions
-----------
Type a "P" into the field of each
kind of prompting you want.

Menus . . . . . . . . . . (P)
Help screens . . . . . . .(P)
Directions . . . . . . . .( )
Detailed prompts . . . . .( )
Diagnostic error messages.( )
```

Figure 7-1 A screen that permits the operator to set up the program to provide a desired level of prompting. Other ways of adjusting the prompting level are to use a menu, to use an operator-entered prompting code, and to analyze operator inputs to determine what prompting level is needed.

- *Provide error-correction features.* Operators will make errors. Often, they will recognize their errors and want to correct them. Make it easy for them. Operators need to be able to correct the error as they are filling in a field, after they have completed the field, or at any time (say, 5 years) later. Actually, there are three separate stages at which operators should be able to make these corrections. These are discussed in detail in the next section.

The bottom line on this is that the operator is in charge, sets the rules, and more or less has the right to be arbitrary. The computer, on the other hand, is the slave, follows the rules, and must be helpful and obedient.

2. Give Your Computer a Good Personality

Can a computer have a personality? If you read fiction or go to the movies, the answer is obvious. The computer personality is often depicted as *threatening*. Hal (the computer in *2001, A Space Odyssey*) is coolly threatening: programmed to mimic emotion, but never excitable

— nonetheless, he is a killer. Not very nice. At the opposite extreme are the "genuine people personality" (GPP) androids produced by the Sirius Cybernetics Corporation of Douglas Adams' *Hitchhiker's Guide to the Galaxy* (see the Bibliography). These androids are programmed to be cheerful and helpful, and to do everything you would expect from a good guide at Disneyland. However, they sing off-key and are so jarringly unresponsive that people hate them. And then we have R2D2 and C3PO . . .

Many people perceive computers as threatening. You, of course, do not. Nor do most people who know enough about them to make them carry out their will the way a good slave should. However, people who do not control them that way have a rather different perception of them. The computer is fast, can be demanding, and can threaten one's ego and livelihood. If, on top of this, the computer also seems to be patronizing or arrogant, working with it can be altogether unpleasant. Here are some undesirable personality traits a computer may exhibit, along with descriptions of how the computer might show those traits.

* *Demanding.* The computer times the rate at which you enter data and tells you with a flashing message and beeping signal that you should speed things up.

* *Insulting.* You make a data-entry error and the computer displays this message:

      DATA ENTRY ERROR — NEXT TIME USE THE PROPER FORMAT!!

* *Patronizing.* The program requests you to enter your first name. From that point on, whenever it wants something, it prints your name familiarly in the prompt, as if addressing an old friend. For example:

      PLEASE ENTER THE DATE, PHIL.

This is interesting the first time but gets old very quickly.

* *Anthropomorphic.* Then there is the game program that carries on a dialog with you in which it refers to itself as "I" or "me," and calls you by the first name it collected from you earlier. Who gave a computer the right to refer to itself with personal pronouns? They are supposed to be reserved for intelligent, conscious entities.

Much of the foregoing is, quite frankly, a statement of the author's opinion about the proper way for a computer to refer to itself and to its program user. The research into this matter is limited, but what is known suggests that you should limit your computer's mimicry of human traits. More specifically:

- The computer should never reprimand a program user for making an error.
- Prompts and error messages should avoid sarcasm.
- The computer should refer to itself as "the computer" or "the program," not "I" or "me." The other side of this is that the computer should not carry on a dialog with the operator in which it patronizingly displays the operator's name.
- The computer should refer to itself as what it is — a computer — and carry on its work efficiently, as an obedient and uncomplaining slave.
- The computer is *not* human and should not display the personality qualities of a human being — criticism of the operator, sarcasm, humor, use of pronouns in referring to itself, evocation of the operator's name.

There will be exceptions to these suggestions, of course — especially in game and entertainment programs. If you wish to make an exception, be sure that you know what you are doing. Better yet, test your computer's personality on your audience before you make it final.

3. Assure Consistency among Inputs, Displays, and Forms

The principle of consistency discussed in Chapter 3 applies very much during data input. Consistency helps the operator learn and remember things.

To illustrate this point, suppose you are designing a management information system. Data are collected on forms. These forms are then handed to an operator who sits down at a computer and enters the data through the keyboard. Later on, the operator may access the data base to check its accuracy against the forms or simply to see what is there. In this little scenario, the original data have three different manifestations:

1. The data-entry form
2. The data-input screen
3. The data-base review screen

These three manifestations of the data (Figure 7-2) should be as much alike, or consistent, as possible. That is, form should look like entry screen should look like data-base display. Though their functions differ, from the operators' viewpoint, all are more or less the same thing. Operators will make comparisons among these data manifestations. They will enter data from form to screen or from form to data-base review display. They will compare information in the data-base display against the entry form. The more these three things are alike, the easier it is for them.

The same principle applies in somewhat smaller matters — for example, in the formats used for expressing written language, dates, numeric quantities, and so forth. Operators should not be forced to make a translation as they enter data or review entered data against raw data. Such inconsistencies add confusion and invite errors.

4. Avoid Needless Entries

Never require operators to enter the same information twice. This goes equally for data and for giving the system "set-up" parameters such as the number of disk drives. Once data have been entered, the computer can keep them in temporary storage (RAM), or permanent storage (on disk). When the program needs the same information for some other purpose, data should be accessed directly. Requiring operators to reenter such data is forcing them to do what should be the program's job. This is needless extra work for operators.

Information may change slightly when used for different purposes within the program. When this happens, operators should be given the option of changing it or accepting a default value. For example, suppose your program needs a system date to keep track of different files of information. The operators enter a system date when they start the program up, and that becomes the default value. Later, the operators are given the option of accepting this default date or entering another. They are not forced to reenter the entire date each time.

While the system date and certain other parameters are likely to change often, the system set-up parameters — items such as number of disk drives, printer characteristics, control characters used — will change rarely. Many programs must be customized to fit a particular hardware configuration. Several parameters must be set, a process which can be time-consuming. Make it possible for operators to set these parameters once; do not require users to reset parameters with each use of the program. This is needless extra effort.

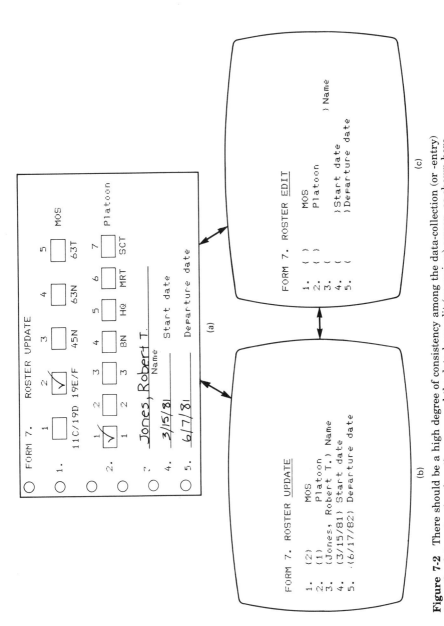

Figure 7-2 There should be a high degree of consistency among the data-collection (or -entry) form, the data-entry (or -input) screen, and the data-base-edit (or review) screen, as shown here. This makes it easier for the operator to relate the three to one another.

133

5. Pick an Area of the Screen for Data Entry

If you use a data-collection form, your data-entry screen should look as much like it as possible. This is the notion of *form-screen correspondence*. Each item of data on the form has a corresponding data-entry field on the screen. Operators transfer the data from the form to the screen, field by field. After they have filled in all the fields on the screen, they can make a direct comparison between the screen and the original form. The positions of each data item are the same and a comparison can be made very quickly.

Full-screen data entry, as described above, is the preferred method. Full-screen data entry is not always practical. If you are not using data-entry forms, the notion of form-screen correspondence is not valid. If the operator must enter many discrete, unrelated items of data, there is not much point in full-screen data entry either. And in some cases, even if you are using data-collection forms, it may not be practical to write software for full-screen data entry.

If you do not use full-screen data entry, be consistent in the way you permit data to be entered. Many programs use one of the bottom five lines of the screen; the advantage is that you can have a display on the top of the screen and collect data at the bottom. If you are writing a program which will often require the user to extract information from display screens and make data entries based on that information, then it is logical to collect information from one of the lower lines of the screen.

Inputs are sometimes collected from the center of the screen. When this is done, the input area is in the middle of the display area, which may cause conflicts. However, if the program does not require the operator to use displayed information in making his entries, screen center is the most logical place to collect inputs.

Avoid taking inputs from varying screen locations. Be consistent. The operator should know where the input line is without having to search the screen. The best way of assuring this is to keep the input line in one place.

THE INPUT-VALIDATION SEQUENCE

Errare humanum est.

Saying

The input-validation sequence is the process by which inputs are taken from the operator, tested, and eventually accepted (or rejected) by the computer. There are five steps in this process:

1. *Prompting.* The operator is prompted to make the input.
2. *Data entry.* The operator makes the input to the computer.
3. *Error test.* The computer tests the operator's input for errors. If an error is found, the process returns to step 1, prompting. If not, the process moves on to step 4, editing.
4. *Editing.* The operator is given a chance to modify the input.
5. *Data acceptance.* The computer accepts the data for use.

The logic of these five steps is shown in Figure 7-3.

The input-validation sequence is, literally, a *dialog*. It starts with a question, or prompt, from the computer. Operators answer the question by making an entry. The computer next performs an error test to decide whether the entry is acceptable. It lets operators reconsider their half of the dialog and change (edit) it, if necessary. Finally, the computer accepts the data as legitimate and stores them away in memory somewhere. We can imagine the human and computer carrying on a less formal dialog that accomplishes the same functions:

```
COMPUTER:   Who was that lady I saw you with last night?
            (Prompt)
OPERATOR:   That was no lady. That was my niece. (Data entry)
COMPUTER:   I'm sorry. That answer doesn't make sense. I have
            no record of your niece in my data banks. (Error
            test)
OPERATOR:   It was my wife. (Data entry)
COMPUTER:   All right. Do you want to change your entry?
            (Error test, editing)
OPERATOR:   Yes. It was my broker. We were discussing
            commodities futures. (Editing)
COMPUTER:   Do you want to change your entry? (Editing)
OPERATOR:   No.
COMPUTER:   Fine. It won't be easy, but I'll try to swallow
            your explanation. (Acceptance)
```

That, more or less, is what goes on during a data-entry dialog. Now, let us take a closer look at some of the steps in the process.

1. Prompting ("Who Was That Lady I Saw You with Last Night?)

The prompt is a question. It must meet all the information requirements of what we would consider a reasonable question in normal human dialog.

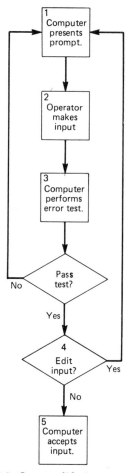

Figure 7-3 Input-validation sequence logic.

Bad Prompts. Some things which are often used as prompts, and which obviously do not meet this requirement, are the following:

* A flashing cursor
* A flashing question mark
* A prompt which says "Entry"

Good Prompts. So much for bad prompts. Here are some things a good prompt should do:

* State *what information* is required, briefly and specifically. For example:

```
ENTER THE PRICE OF CORN:
```

• If data must be entered in a particular format, *show the format* in the prompt. For example:

```
ENTER DATE (MONTH/DAY/YEAR):
```

• If there is a length limit to the entry, *show graphically in the prompt what the limit is.* The best way to do this is with an underline. For example:

```
ENTER YOUR LAST NAME: _____
```

The limit may also be shown with parentheses:

```
ENTER YOUR LAST NAME: (                        )
```

• If a default value will automatically be entered in case operators make no entry of their own, show the default on the prompt line. For example:

```
ENTER THE FILE NAME: SYS.DOCS
```

Operators should be able to verify the default value with a single keystroke and not have to reenter it from the keyboard.

Often a program will require the operator to enter the same data in different places. When it does, prompt consistently everywhere. One way to do this is to put your data-entry statements into subroutines that can be called from anywhere in the program.

The foregoing guidelines all say the same thing: *Make sure the operator knows what you want.* This is what we expect when a stranger comes up to us and asks a question. If the question is phrased properly, it tells us what we need to know to answer properly. If the question is vaguely worded or incomplete, or if it allows several interpretations, we cannot answer properly.

Contextual Prompting. Note that the context in which a data entry is requested often provides implicit prompting. For example, if your program requires the operator to enter the price of IBM stock at Friday's closing for the last 20 weeks, then you need only to prompt fully the first entry and make sure that the operator understands that nineteen more such entries are required (Figure 7-4). From that point on, the data-entry context provides the cues the operator requires. You are

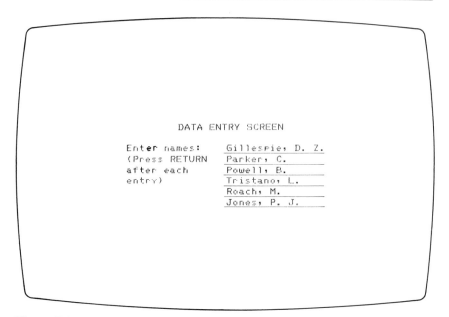

Figure 7-4 An example of contextual prompting. The prompt for the top field indicates the required entry, and additional full prompts are not required for the fields below.

in the best position to judge when context will provide the implicit prompting you need. If in doubt, provide full prompting. This will assure that there is no confusion.

Help Screens. If the stranger referred to above speaks a language or a dialect that we do not know, then our best attempts to communicate may fail. It would help the stranger to have a phrase book of our language. A help screen in a computer program is like a phrase book for a language. Both fill us in on what we need to know to carry on an effective dialog. As you plan data-entry and design prompts, consider providing optional help screens that will aid the operator to understand the program. If the data entries are complex in form, content, or in their relationships to one another, it may not be enough to provide only prompts on your data-entry screens. Additional information may be required. This information can be provided in a user's guide, in the program, or in both places.

Programmers have resisted providing help screens, but operators love them. Generally, operators can master a program more quickly when they can get quick answers to their questions. Help screens can provide quick answers; they must be *optional,* however. You should not require every operator to view them every time the program is used. As operators gain skill, they will want to refer to help screens less frequently. After they have mastered the program, they will not want to use them at all. If imposed on operators, help screens will be a patience-trying inconvenience.

A help screen explains things. It can contain text, graphics, examples, or anything else that will make the picture clearer to the operator. It might contain a set of directions; a filled-in data-entry screen; an explanation of content, format, and length limitations of a particular data entry; a definition of the semantic and syntactic rules that must be followed; or anything else that will be helpful. It explains what the operator must know to make the entry correctly. Help screens are a part of user documentation and are discussed in greater detail in Chapter 11.

2. Data Entry ("That Was No Lady. That Was My Niece.")

Display the Entry. Display (or "echo") the operator entry back on the screen. This provides operators with the feedback that they need to be sure that an entry has been taken by the computer. Without such feedback, they cannot be sure. Uncertain operators tend to make duplicate entries, often producing unintended results. If you have ever attempted to operate a computer without a functioning visual display, you understand the problem.

Permit Error Correction during Data Entry. A second reason for displaying the entry is to permit operators to identify their errors. Skilled keyboard operators will detect many of their errors through their hands; they know when they have made an error without looking at the output. However, many errors will go undetected unless they are observed. You must therefore make it possible for operators to observe and correct an entry before it becomes final. They must be able to back up the cursor, make changes, move the cursor forward without making changes, and so forth, and perform basic editing functions.

The entry should not be accepted by the computer until the operator verifies it by pressing the Return key or its equivalent. This principle also applies to single-key entries (e.g., menu selections). Some microcomputer BASICs permit the detection of a keystroke without requiring the operator to press the Return key (e.g., using the GET or INKEY$ statement). This permits fast input and is ideal for such applications as games. However, it gives the operator no chance to identify and correct errors. It is best to display the entry and require operator verification with the Return key.

Keep Entries Short. Keep operator entries as short as possible. Entries that are made repeatedly should be a maximum of 5 to 7 characters long — the shorter, the better. One way to reduce length is to use abbreviations, although these take longer to learn than the original words. A better technique is to permit the operator to enter either the original word or its first few characters. For example, if the operator is accessing a file named "vegetable," permit the entry of either the entire word or just its first few characters (e.g., "veg").

Permit Entries in Their Natural Form. Permit operators to make entries in the form that is most natural for them. This applies to dates, units of measure, quantities, names, or anything else that might be represented differently within the computer than in normal, written communication. For example, do not require an operator to enter leading zeros unless the zeros are truly significant — do not require operators to enter a date such as 02/04/85. Let operators enter the date as they would write it, and have the computer put the leading zeros in, if it needs them.

Keep the Operator Posted on Delays. If an operator entry will cause an extended delay — 5 seconds or more — then display a message (or other sign) such as the following to show that the program has not stopped:

```
PROCESSING DATA. PLEASE STAND BY.
```

As operators gain experience, they will worry less about delays. Even experienced operators worry when a program takes too long to do something, thinking that the delay means a problem with processing, memory, or something else.

Break up Long Strings. Chapter 6 recommended that in displaying long strings, you break them up into groups of no more than 5 characters. This makes them easier for the operator to process. The same principle applies during data entry. The operator should be able to enter the string as several separate fields. This is what you would do, naturally, in entering such a string as a telephone number; that is, you would type in 1-800-000-1010 (rather than 18000001010). Apply this principle also to strings that do not have natural divisions. For example, permit entry of the first twenty letters of the alphabet as follows:

```
ABCDE FGHIJ KLMNO PQRST
```

3. Error Test ("I Have No Record of Your Niece. . . .")

Assume that operators will make every possible error; among other things, they might do the following:

- Enter numbers where letters are requested, and vice versa.
- Exceed length limits.
- Enter nothing.
- Enter inappropriate punctuation.
- Enter control characters.
- Press the Reset key (or its equivalent).
- Make semantic errors.
- Make syntactic errors.
- Do exactly what you tell them not to do.

Error-Testing Philosophy. You must assume that any error, however improbable, will in fact occur. This is admittedly a pessimistic philosophy, based on the premise that one ought to expect the worst in order to guard against it. A more optimistic philosophy assumes operators will act responsibly — and is folly. This is not meant as an insult to the fine, intelligent people who use microcomputer programs. Rather, it is based on the desire to spare you the anguish of the telephone call in which an operator describes to you the bizarre sequence of keystrokes that permitted all the valuable files to be purged, that made the disk unreadable, and that sent the disk drives into self-destructive frenzy.

Anticipate Errors. The first step is to anticipate what errors can occur. These will vary with the program. Next, you must devise error tests to trap these errors when they occur. It is easy to check for such errors as illegal length (using too many characters), range (extending beyond alphanumeric limits between which an entry must lie), and semantic inequality (typing an entry which is not within the program's vocabulary). Many errors are more difficult to detect; these may require a software interpreter to do the job properly.

Error Messages. Write error messages that apply to each error you test for, and display the appropriate messages when an error occurs. Guidelines for writing and displaying error messages are given below.

- *Display the message as close to the offending entry as possible.* During data entry, the logical place for the operator to look for feedback information is where the entry has just been typed in. It is not always feasible to display error messages this way. It is difficult, for example, with full-screen data entry on a crowded display. In that case, it might be necessary to overwrite part of the display to present the error message. If you do not put the error message beside the offending entry, select a part of the screen for displaying error messages and *use the same location for all of them.* (Remember the principle of consistency.)

- *Use an audio signal to alert the operator that an error has occurred.* Even if not viewing the display, the operator will be alerted. Audio signals become irritating, especially if they occur frequently. They also have a social dimension. If the operator uses the program in a social setting, repeated beeps produced by entry errors announce those errors to the world. This can be embarrassing, raise the anxiety level, and interfere with learning and performance. Consider permitting operators to turn the audio off in such cases — providing that they will still be able to identify and correct their errors.

- *The error message should do three things: (1) alert the operator that an error has occurred, (2) identify the error, and (3) tell the operator how to recover.*

- *Alerting signals must differ from the customary background.* A flashing message can serve this purpose, but it will not be alerting if the screen is filled with other flashing messages. The same is true of other alerting techniques, such as arrows, color, or boxing. To alert the operator, the signal must be unique. Ideally, an audio signal should alert the operator that an error has occurred, and a video alerting technique (such as flashing) should be used to attract attention to the error message on the screen.

- *The error message must identify what is wrong.* If identification of the error will permit the operator to figure out what to do next, then that is all the message needs to contain. However, if the nature of the error is still ambiguous, then more information must be provided. For example, it is not enough to tell the operator that an entry is "too large." This does not convey how much too large, or what the acceptable range of values is. Perhaps the operator should know this information, but in general it is not reasonable to make this a requirement. It is best to make the error message specific. For example, the identification part of the error message could read as follows:

```
ENTERED VALUE IS TOO LARGE. ACCEPTABLE RANGE IS FROM 0 TO
255.
```

The final part of the message is the *recovery action*. This tells the operator what to do to get out of a fix. The recovery action may be to reenter data, to select a legal program option, to restart a program, or to take some other action. Whatever it is, do not assume that the operator will automatically know. Define the action, even if it is obvious. For example, the recovery action for the earlier error message would be the following:

REENTER DATA

Figure 7-5 shows several acceptable error messages to illustrate the points discussed above.

* *Make error messages brief and explicit.*   Do not attempt to punish the operator for mistakes. Avoid humor. Jokes inside a computer get stale very quickly, and there is always the possibility that some operators will get the idea that the computer is making fun of them. Be factual, and leave personalities to people.

* *Provide an escape route.*   Suppose that in the midst of data entry the operator decides to quit. There should be an easy way to exit from the data-entry sequence without carrying on mechanically to the end. This is an operator convenience. It is also a way out for inexperienced users who cannot figure out what to do. Without it, such users may find themselves trapped so that the only escape is to exit from the program by brute force — by interrupting the program and restarting. Interrupting and restarting can have disastrous consequences and the temptation should be minimized.

   Provide a standard escape procedure — such as entering a blank or the escape (ESC) key — that will return the operator to a safe harbor (e.g., the last control menu).

4. Editing ("Do You Want to Change Your Entry?")

Permit the operator to edit entries before they become permanent. Operators often change their minds or recognize data-entry errors after the fact. Therefore, it is important for them to be able to change earlier entries. In any program that builds a data base through keyboard entries, editing should be possible at three different stages:

1. *Screen editing during initial entry.*   As operators type data in, they should be able to back up, make changes, or rewrite the entire field if they want to. This form of editing was discussed under "2.

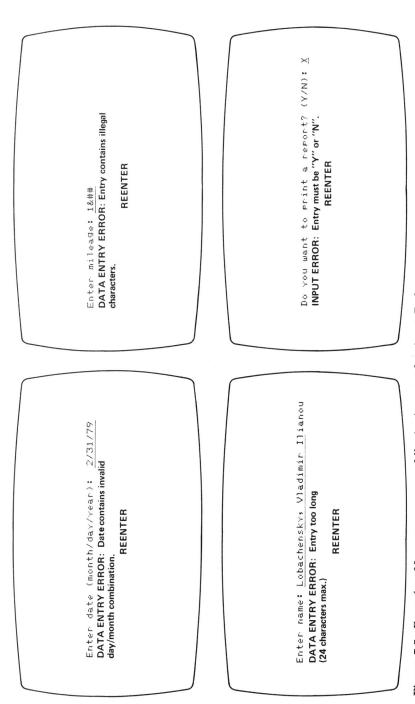

Figure 7-5 Examples of four error messages, following incorrect data input. Each error message contains three parts: (a) alert, (b) error identification, and (c) recovery action.

144

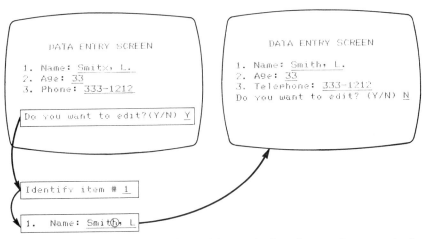

Figure 7-6 An example of page editing. After entries have been made, a prompt asks whether the operator wants to edit (bottom line of screen). After entering Y for yes, the operator is prompted to identify the item number to change. The program then permits reentry of data, producing the corrected screen on the right.

Data Entry," above. It is easy to provide this editing capability, as it is built into most programming languages. However, with ingenuity, a misguided programmer can obliterate it.

2. *Block or page editing.* This type of editing occurs after a series (i.e., a block or page) of entries have been made (Figure 7-6). After making the entries, operators are prompted to indicate whether they want to change any of the information entered. If they respond "yes," then the computer prompts them to indicate which item, by line number, location, or other reference. The computer then permits operators to reenter the data for the selected item, just as during data entry. That is, the data-entry prompt is presented as before — on the screen or in the designated input location — and all the same error tests are made. After operators complete the entry, they are again prompted to indicate whether they have any changes. If so, the process just described recurs. If not, the program moves on to the next phase.

3. *Data-base editing.* Data-base editing is the process whereby the operator accesses an existing data base and edits it. This occurs after data entry has ended. Data input and data-base editing are not directly related. However, it is often advisable to integrate them together. The data-base editing process is described in greater detail in the next chapter. Guidelines are given there for the design of data-base editing utility programs.

If your program requires a data base to function properly, then these three editing capabilities are essential. Screen editing during initial data entry is easy. Block or page editing is more difficult. Data-base editing, if done properly, is the most difficult of all. Without these three capabilities, the operator will be handicapped in maintaining the data base.

PREVENTING DISASTERS (SOME HINTS ON AVERTING WORLD WAR III)

Certain keyboard entries can have far-reaching consequences. For example, the keystrokes that activate a file purging program can, if made mistakenly, destroy part or all of an important data base. If the file is not backed up, this may be a major disaster. In a menu-driven program, pressing the wrong key will select the wrong subprogram. The consequence is not serious — only a delay.

Now imagine yourself in a missile control center. You are the officer who, distracted by a spilled coffee cup, strikes the key that corresponds to the menu selection for "fire all missiles." Improbable, perhaps, but this would be a disaster of the first degree.

These examples illustrate how important it is for you to be aware of such traps in your program and to take measures to protect the operator against them. If you do not, using your program may be like walking through a mine field.

First, identify the points in your program where a wrong turn or entry error may cause a problem. The following are examples of such points in a data-base management program.

- *Using menus.* Selecting the wrong option will cause a delay.
- *Loading files.* Loading a new file may destroy the file currently in memory and also cause a time delay.
- *Purging files.* Doing this by mistake will destroy the files.
- *Printing reports.* This will cause a delay and tie up the printer.
- *Creating a new file.* If done improperly, the new file may wipe out existing files.

This list is not meant to be comprehensive, but to illustrate the kinds of things to look out for in a typical program. The list will vary with the type of program you are designing.

After you have identified the danger points, write software that will enable the operator to *verify* the entry before the program proceeds.

```
                    *WARNING*
        You have selected the PURGE option.
        It will DESTROY your files.
        If you want to continue, type
        in the word "PURGE" and
        press the Return key: _____
```

Figure 7-7   A screen designed to protect the operator from the serious error of purging files by mistake. Before purging actually occurs, the operator must verify the decision by typing in the word "purge" and then pressing the Return key. Purging or other actions that will significantly affect the data base or a phase of program operation should never proceed on the basis of a single keystroke; these actions should require operator verification first.

You must prevent the program from proceeding based on one or two keystrokes. Rather, the operator action must require *two* steps: initial selection, and a verification.

When error consequences are not severe, the initial selection may be one keystroke, and the verification pressing the Return key. This is how menu options should be selected, as discussed earlier in this chapter.

When error consequences are severe, display a warning screen to operators after they have made their initial selection. Require operators to read the warning and verify their choice before proceeding. If they have second thoughts, they can back out. For example, if operators initially select a purge files routine, display a message such as that shown in Figure 7-7. When the operators see this screen, they can continue with purging or change their minds and back out. Whatever happens, they have been given ample warning.

.

Eight

Utilities

This chapter contains a catalog and brief descriptions of several support programs. For want of a better name, these programs are called *utilities*. Utilities are more than just the useful aids you might infer from their label. They are important and sometimes essential tools. The utilities covered in this chapter are the following:

- *System-setup utility.* Used to set up a program to match a particular hardware combination. It is used for such things as defining the number and location of disk drives and printers.
- *Create-new-files utility.* Used to plan and create a new set of data files.
- *Edit-data-base utility.* Used to access and edit the data base.
- *Print-data-base utility.* Used to access and print out part or all of the data base.
- *Copy-data-base utility.* Used to transfer data files from one data disk to another.
- *File-compression utility.* Used to remove old, inactive records from a data file in order to make file space available.

The first utility concerns *system setup*. All the remaining utilities concern *data-base maintenance*. If you design programs that will be used with only one hardware configuration, you can forget the first utility. If none of your programs employs a data base, you can forget the rest.

The following are general guidelines for designing utility programs:

- Assume an unsophisticated operator.
- Permit the operator to perform all utility functions within the main program (i.e., without exiting it to use some other program).
- Do not require the operator to use operating system commands or outside programs to perform utility functions.
- Do not require the operator to modify program code.

These guidelines and the utilities themselves are illustrated and discussed in greater detail in the sections that follow.

SYSTEM-SETUP UTILITY

If your program will be used with a number of different hardware configurations, provide a utility that permits operators to define the setup parameters for the configuration and then save them to disk. In the future, when the program is used, read these parameters from disk. Do not require operators to enter them manually each time the program is used.

Write a utility program that permits operators to enter the parameters through the keyboard. Do not require operators to modify the code of the program. Generally, you should not assume that they will know how to do this or be able to do it successfully, even if you provide detailed directions. It is unwise to have operators modify the program code. Strange, surprising, and often unintended things happen when they do. Leave programming to programmers, and operating to operators.

On the setup display, make the entries as straightforward as possible. Do not expect the operator who does the setup to be able to extract information from a reference manual, to speak hexadecimal, or to know complex technical jargon. Permit the operator to make entries in as direct and straightforward a way as possible.

What parameters should be included in these programs? It is impossible to compile a complete list, but the following are some typical examples:

• Disk drive parameters, e.g., number of drives, slot numbers of controller cards

• Printer parameters, e.g., slot numbers of controller cards, line feed requirement, control codes

• Modem parameters, e.g., slot number of interface card, control codes

Not all programmers see the point of such utilities. For example, there is a fairly popular word-processing program which has no utilities for defining disk or printer parameters. Each time users want to save a file to disk, or read one, they must use commands from the operating system (specifying disk drive). Invariably, when two disk drives are used, the operator will attempt to read from or save to the wrong disk drive. Using a printer is even more awkward. To print out a file, the operator must exit the program; enter keyboard commands to activate the printer card; and then reenter the program, load up the file, and work through three levels of subprograms before the file can be printed. This program does work reliably, but this does not excuse its poor design. How much nicer it would be if it could learn and remember about its disk drives and printers, and did not require the operator to run around the flagpole five times in order to perform the simplest task.

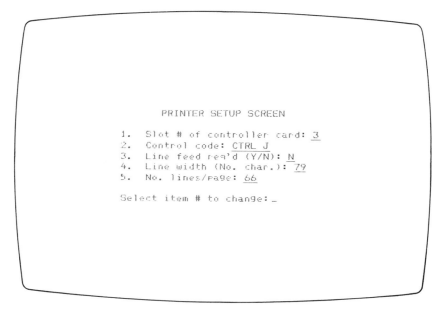

Figure 8-1 A screen for defining printer parameters. It should be possible for the operator to set these and similar program set-up parameters once, and not have to reenter them each time the program is used.

Of course, not every parameter needs to be saved to disk. The ones that do are those that are fixed, or that will change very rarely. If a parameter will change every time the operator uses the program, that parameter should not be saved in a file. If it will change only once in every ten uses, or even once in five uses, save it.

Here are some guidelines for designing the setup utility program:

- Classify the types of parameters into different functional areas, such as disk drives, printer, modem.
- Design a separate input screen for each parameter in a particular functional area. For example, have a screen for disk-drive setup, one for printer setup, etc.
- On the screen, list the parameter on the left and its current value on the right.
- Permit the operator to access any display parameter and reset its value, within legal limits.

Figure 8-1 shows an example of a screen for setting up printer parameters.

When you deliver your program, set all parameters at their "minimum" values. Do not assume that the user has any hardware which might be considered optional. For example, set number of disk drives to one, no modem, no printer, and so forth.

DATA-BASE-MAINTENANCE UTILITIES

This section discusses several utilities that are important in programs that use a data base. Typically, the data base is entered through a keyboard, maintained in files, and processed to generate on-screen or hard-copy reports. A wide range of different types of programs use a data base in this manner, including management information systems, word processors, and portfolio management programs, to name a few.

The program's data base, whatever its form, has a life cycle: It is created, information is added to it, it is edited, and eventually, part or all of it is purged. The program operator interacts with it throughout its life cycle. Data-base utilities can considerably simplify this interaction.

It is arguable that each utility discussed below is superfluous, since a competent programmer, or perhaps a clever operator, could find a way to accomplish the function the utility serves without using a separate program. Depending upon the computer, and the sophistication of its operating system, this may or may not be true. For example, it is probably true that any microcomputer that readers of this book might use for maintaining a data base would have a copy program which would permit files to be transferred from one disk to another. This would entail going outside the main program, however, would require use of operating system commands, and might require deletion of unwanted files from the target disk afterward. Creating or purging files is possible with some microcomputers, but is more difficult than copying files. Still more difficult is editing or printing a data base, or doing a file compression. These latter three functions require considerable sophistication on the part of the operator.

As noted earlier, your program should not require a sophisticated operator, should permit the operator to perform utility functions within the main program, and should not require the operator to use outside programs to accomplish a function that your program depends on. Abiding by these principles assures that you remain in control of things and that errors will be minimized.

Each data-base-maintenance utility is discussed below.

Create-New-Files Utility

Permit the operator to create new files within the main program. Make file creation as simple as possible. How simple file creation can be depends upon the program itself. For example, in a typical word-processing program, the operator will create a file by assigning a file name and saving the named file to a disk. That is all there is to it. Usually, the operator must be careful not to use a name that has been used previously — to avoid overwriting an old file. (The program should really check for this sort of thing and warn the operator if it is about to occur.) In assigning the name, the program should not require the operator to use operating system commands, such as disk-drive indicators. These should be taken care of automatically through the setup program, as described earlier in this chapter. It should not be necessary for the operator to define file characteristics — such as file size — that can be tracked or computed automatically by the computer. All that should really be required in a program such as this is a *name*. That name should be anything that the operator wants to use, up to, say, 24 characters or so. Programs that require their operators to use syntactically constraining labels — such as "SYS.DOC9," "PL4-WORD2," or "LBL.FL4.SPEEDI" — are distinctly unfriendly since their use of language is unnatural.

Creating files in some programs should and will require a good deal more than just a file name. For example, a program for managing a large, complex data base will have several files and will require operators to define the fields, record formats, and number of records in each file. Where disk space is limited, they may have to trade off some file sizes against others. Creating such files requires a major planning effort during which the operator decides what files to use, what information to store in each one, and how much disk space to allot to each file in order to make them all fit on the storage medium used.

When you recognize the complexities of a program such as this, you have two choices as a designer. The first is to adopt the "one size fits all" philosophy and design the files so that the operator has no control over them. This philosophy is defensible when one size really will fit all, or the vast majority, and when your operators will be too unsophisticated to plan their own files. The second choice is to give operators the flexibility of planning their own files and trading them off against each other. This gives operators much greater freedom and on this basis is more friendly. On the other hand, if the operators are naive, the programmer can only be considered naive for permitting those operators to dabble in arcane matters. (Remember the sorcerer's apprentice in the movie *Fantasia*.)

If you do decide to permit operators to plan their files, design a data-entry screen that lets operators lay out their file size specification and immediately see the results displayed before them. For example, if the file sizes must be traded off against each other to meet a storage limitation, display the sizes of all files on the same screen, along with the

```
              DATA FILE DEFINITION SCREEN

                              User-defined
         File name            size (K bytes)
         _____           _____

         1.  Master file           56
         2.  Historical file      288
         3.  Buffer                12
         4.  Working file         400
                                 _____

                         Total   756

         Maximum file space available: 512 K.
         Your specification is 244 K too large.

         Select item # to change:_
```

Figure 8-2   A data-entry screen that permits the operator to trade off the sizes of files against each other. This screen uses the familiar spreadsheet technique and will save the operator a lot of work in doing the file setup.

bottom-line total of all file sizes (Figure 8-2). This is the familiar "spreadsheet" technique, and it permits operators to fine-tune the numbers until they come out exactly as desired.

After the specification has been laid out and the operator is satisfied with it, it is time for you to create the files. Creating files can produce the sort of profound and irreversible changes discussed at the end of Chapter 7. For example, if you create files on a data disk that already has them, you may overwrite the existing files. To prevent this from occurring, warn the operator before actually writing the new files on the disk. If there is a danger of destroying existing files, give the operator the chance to switch disks or exit before continuing.

Test the disk before writing to it. Verify that there are no files on it that will be destroyed.

It is always a good idea to put an identification file on any data disk. This file should include the disk label and the date the file was last updated. The existence of this file on a particular disk means that the file has been used in the past and should not be overwritten.

Edit-Data-Base Utility

If human error did not exist, then edit utilities would be unnecessary. Since this is obviously not the case, they are. As discussed in Chapter

7, the operator should be able to edit entries at three stages: (1) when initially typing them in, (2) after completion of a block or page of entries, and (3) any time later. The first two types of editing were discussed in Chapter 7. This section covers the third, which could be called "historical editing," that is, the editing of information that was entered in the past.

This edit utility serves at least two purposes: as a "window" into the data files, and as a tool for correcting errors in the data base. The first purpose is at least as important as the second, for often an edit utility will be used simply to view information in the files and no changes will be made.

Provide a utility program that will permit operators to access any data previously entered, in order to modify or delete it. Permit them to access old records by means of a logical reference system such as date, alphabetic order, or numeric sequence. Record numbers can be useful, but to know which record to look for, operators must keep a separate, written record.

Operators should be able to move backward and forward through the file, one record at a time, as if they were paging through a book, without having to go back to a menu. For example, permit operators to page forward through the file by pressing the F key, or backward by pressing the B key.

Display the record in the same form in which it was originally entered (see Figure 7-2). This will make it easier for operators to interpret the record and find what they are looking for. By all means, avoid presenting records in their raw form, i.e., as a series of run-on characters without labels or separators. This format is satisfactory during program development, but it is difficult and trying for operators to use on a regular basis.

In designing your edit program, consider why and how often it will be used. A common reason for using edit programs is to correct errors that have been discovered downstream. For example, a printed report or a display may contain questionable results. A probable cause for this is erroneous data or a data-entry error. Operators will use the edit program to locate the raw data that led to the report. They will check these data, perhaps against a data-entry form, and see if the data contain any errors. If they do find errors, then they will want to correct the record on the spot; they will reenter part or all of the record, just as during initial data entry. This scenario illustrates two points. First, it is important for operators to gain ready access to the records. Second, since editing is much like initial data entry, the programs should be similar in form and function. The more frequently the edit utility will be used, the more important it is to adhere to these two principles.

The edit utility should permit the operator to change any selected field within the record or to delete the record entirely. An edited record still exists and can be changed back to its original form if an error is made. A deleted record must be re-created from scratch. Therefore, do not make deletion a one-step process. Have the operator verify the command before executing it. (See "Preventing Disasters" in Chapter 7.)

Make the edit utility readily accessible from the data-input program. During data input, operators will often discover errors or inconsistencies that need correction; they should be able to correct these immediately by calling up the edit utility. In fact, some designers integrate the data-input and edit functions into a single program. With this arrangement, the program has two modes — data input or edit — and switching between them is only a matter of a few keystrokes. This arrangement assumes that edits will be made frequently. If edits will be made infrequently, it makes more sense to have separate programs for data input and editing. However, in no case should these programs be more than a few keystrokes apart.

Print-Data-Base Utility

A print-data-base utility permits the operator to generate a hard copy of all the records in a file that meet certain criteria. This is similar to what a data-base management system (DBMS) does. A DBMS will usually permit the operator to specify certain search parameters (e.g., time window, content of one or more fields) and produce a printed report that shows the results in a fully labeled, stand-alone format. These reports are what a DBMS is designed to create.

Generally, a print-data-base utility will not be this sophisticated. The operator will be able to specify fewer selection parameters, and the printed report will not be designed for permanent use. For example, the operator might be able to specify a range of record numbers to print out, and the resultant report would contain one set of field headings with raw data printed beneath (Figure 8-3).

The print-data-base utility permits the operator to print out summaries of records in a particular file based on a simple specification, such as a range of dates or record numbers. The resultant summary serves much the same purpose for operators as a program listing does for a programmer: In one place, it provides a complete summary of all information. Users (operators or programmers) can refer to the summary, identify individual items, and cross-reference items that are far apart. Further, they do not experience the delays entailed in searching through the data base, or program listing, on the CRT.

```
○    DATA BASE PRINTOUT
     Form #: 4
○    Dates: 1135 to 1139

     Julian            Data fields
○    Date    Ref #     F1    F2    F3
     1135    42102     01    08    08
     1135    41102     01    08    08
○    1135    43002     01    08    08
     1135    38602     01    08    08
     1135    38702     01    08    08
○    1138    32002     01    06    06
     1138    33002     01    08    08
     1138    40802     01    08    08
○    1138    37702     01    08    08
     1138    43502     01    08    08
     1138    38402     01    08    00
○    1139    36002     01    08    08
     1139    40202     01    08    08
     1139    40402     01    08    08
○    1139    42602     01    08    08
     1139    42902     01    08    08
```

Figure 8-3   A sample data-base printout. Data-base printouts are extremely handy for keeping track of what is in the files. They do not have to be fancy. All they need is some identification information at the top and column headings to label the information that is printed out.

The data-base printout is probably most useful for error detection. The operator can lay the printout on a table, examine it at leisure, annotate it with pencil, make the necessary cross-references, and collaborate with others, if need be, to find what is wrong. When a large data base must be searched for errors, a printed report is a definite asset. When the files are small and the edit utility provides ready access to the files, the ability to generate a hard copy is less important.

Here are some guidelines for designing a simple data-base-print utility.

• Put a title at the top.
• Print the record selection parameters (e.g., range of dates or record numbers displayed).
• Print the report in columnar form, with a heading at the top of each column.
• Separate columns by two or more blank spaces.
• Print the search or selection fields by the left margin so that the operator can refer to them while reviewing the report.

Copy-Data-Base Utility

Have any of the following things ever happened to you?

- Your golden retriever mistook one of your floppy disks for a flying saucer toy and lovingly placed it on your left knee, complete with teeth marks and drool.
- A delivery person proved that it was possible to fit an 8-inch floppy disk through your 6-inch mail slot.
- You received a floppy disk in the mail with a cover letter stapled to it.
- Your favorite disk drive died, taking several data files with it.
- Using the copy utility that came with your computer, you managed to copy a blank disk onto a source disk.

These and similar experiences convince us in a very basic way about the importance of having a good, foolproof copy utility. Programmers have these problems and so does everyone else.

It is essential to provide operators with a utility that they can use to back up their data files. Disks will wear out or be damaged and become unreadable. When this happens, if no backup is available, operators are in serious trouble.

The importance of backing up data files is universally acknowledged. File-copy utilities are probably available for any microcomputer that a reader of this book might use. If they are available, and if they are simple to operate, then they can probably fulfill this requirement. However, even if such utilities do exist, it is wise to write one of your own in case either of these two conditions exists:

1. The operators are naive, inexperienced, or careless.
2. The utility, if used incorrectly, can destroy the source disk.

Ideally, the copy utility should be turn-key and foolproof. Copy utilities provided by a computer's manufacturer are usually faster than one you can design yourself. Usually they are more prone to disaster as well, since they are designed simply to copy and have only limited safety tests, if any, built in. If the users of your program will be naive, or inexperienced, think twice about trusting a data base to a standard copy program. You would probably be better off designing a turn-key copy program of your own.

Here are some design guidelines:

- *The prompts should be directive.* They should prompt the operator concerning disk insertions, keys to press, and so forth. This is preferable to requiring the operator to decide how copying will take place and then executing the plan. The plan may be incorrect, the decisions may be wrong, and errors can result in disaster.

• *The utility must be error-proof.* It should not be possible to destroy the original of the disk, to copy data to a program disk, or to over-write a data disk that is more current than the one being copied from.

The following is a suggested sequence for a two-drive, turn-key copy utility to follow. Figure 8-4 shows the copy logic. This sequence commences when the operator selects the copy utility with a control command.

• Prompt the operator to insert the source disk into the appropriate drive (say, drive 1).

• Prompt the operator to insert the target disk into the appropriate drive (say, drive 2).

• Verify the files on the source disk. If one or more is missing, exit the program and present error message to operator. Otherwise, continue.

• Extract the date of the latest update from the source disk.

• Attempt to read the target disk identification (ID) file. If the file is for the program disk, or another disk that should not be copied to, exit the program and present an error message to the operator. Otherwise, continue.

• If the ID file is present on the target disk, test whether its date is earlier than that of the source disk. If it is not, exit and present an error message to the operator. Otherwise, continue.

• Execute the copy from the source disk to the target disk.

• When the copy is complete, display a "copy-complete" message.

File-Compression Utility

A file-compression utility is a program that permits you to clear the deadwood out of your file. It is like a purge program, but more discriminating. Whereas a purge program will eliminate every record, a file-compression program will eliminate only those that meet certain criteria. Generally, it will then move all the remaining records up to the front of the file, leaving the empty space at the end. A file-compression utility is important for three reasons:

1. It rids the file of records that are no longer valuable.
2. It makes empty space available.
3. It keeps the file from choking on itself.

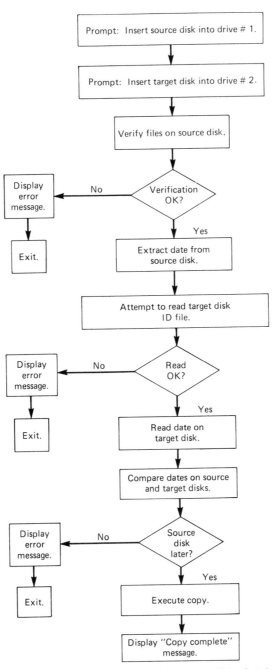

Figure 8-4 Logic for a two-disk copy utility that is relatively foolproof. The program disk must have an ID file and the data disk must have a file with the system date. Before copying occurs, three conditions must be met: (a) files must exist on a source disk, (b) there must be no ID file on the target disk, and (c) the date on the target disk must be earlier than that on the source disk.

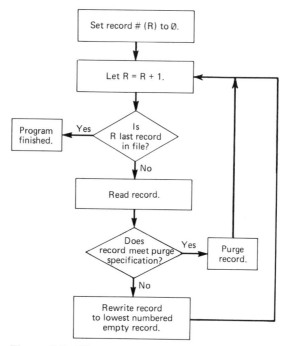

Figure 8-5 File compression logic. The program starts at the lowest-numbered record and works its way up. It reads each record and tests its contents against the operator's purging specification. If the record meets the specification, it is purged. If not, it is rewritten to the lowest-numbered empty record available.

Not all programs need a file-compression utility. This utility becomes important when your data base is large and it is impractical to rid the file of old records in some other way. For example, a compression utility makes good sense in a program that is used to keep track of the transactions of an active stock trader. In a single year, the trader might make several thousand stock trades, and keeping records of all these forever would be impractical. For tax purposes, they can be printed out in hard-copy form. But from time to time, the stock trader will want to get rid of the older transaction records, move the newest ones up to the front of the file, and make room for new records. Alternatively, file compression has little relevance in a word-processing program since the operator can keep the files up to date without the computer's help.

File compression may be thought of as selective purging. Typically, the operator will enter a specification which defines the basis on which records are to be purged. For example, the operator enters a cutoff date such that all records older than that date are purged. The specification may require that several conditions be met before a record is purged. After the specification is entered, the program starts at the lowest-numbered record in the file and reads each record, testing it against the specification. If it meets the conditions, the record is purged. If not, the record is moved as close to the front of the file as possible, based on the file space available. File-compression logic is illustrated in Figure 8-5.

Purging, of course, is much simpler. The computer simply goes through the file, record by record, eliminating each record as it goes. File purging is, to borrow a term from medicine, a traumatic event that greatly insults the file. If the file were a living entity, its life would be over. File compression is less traumatic. The patient would still be breathing, at least. Obviously, if either file compression or purging is done improperly, the result is disaster. Neither procedure should be performed until the source disk has first been copied and the backup disk is stored safely away.

Since either purging or file compression will make irreversible changes to a file, the operator must be forewarned and required to verify the action before the program proceeds. (See "Preventing Disasters" in Chapter 7.)

Either of these programs has important human factors implications for the operator. In programs with large data files, utilities which can compress or purge files may save the operator countless hours of labor. At the same time, the use of these programs is hazardous, at best, and the programmer must build in warnings and safety devices to prevent the operator from destroying valuable data. Unfortunately, the programmer has no control over the most important requirement of all — that of backing up data files before purging or compressing.

Nine

Program Control

This chapter addresses program control. Program control is the manner in which the operator interacts with the computer to get it to do something. To exercise control, the operator engages in a two-way conversation, or dialog, with the computer. The essence of dialog is two-way communication. The computer side of this dialog is carried on through its displays and through the prompts or questions that it asks. The human side is carried on through the keyboard or other input devices.

The chapter is divided into four sections. The first section gives an overview of program control and introduces the two major classes of program control dialog — computer-initiated and operator-initiated. The second section discusses two common computer-initiated control techniques — question and answer and menu selection. The third section discusses operator-initiated control techniques. The final section discusses some ways that computer-initiated and operator-initiated control dialogs can be combined to produce a hybrid control technique.

OVERVIEW OF PROGRAM CONTROL

Which Control Technique Is Best?

Program control can be exercised in many different ways; one of the most popular ways with microcomputers is to use menus. A menu is a list of program options. To use it, the operator selects the option, usually by typing in its number or letter, and the program then executes the command. Menus can work well when the tasks that operators perform are structured and predictable. The typical menu-driven program will have no more than a few dozen menu options, with each option corresponding to a separate subprogram. For example, menu control can be effective with data-base management systems since the functions these programs perform are fairly predictable. That is, files must be planned, data entered, reports generated, and the data base maintained. The task is structured enough so that one can list the different things that must be done on a sheet of paper and group them by category.

The tasks performed by many programs cannot be structured so neatly. The operating system and command language of your computer are examples. Using them, you can construct an infinite number of different programs. What the programmer does is new each time and cannot be fitted into boxes. Even if someone could devise a program that would permit you to generate code through menus, doing so would be slow and tedious.

These examples illustrate that no single control technique can be considered the best in every application. Which is best depends upon the type of user and upon the task that must be performed within the program.

Control versus Data-Entry Dialogs

First, let us divide dialogs into two types: data entry, and program control. A *data-entry* dialog involves operator entry of data into a computer and the related display of information to the operator. In a typical data-entry dialog, the operator is prompted (or should be) to enter data, enters it, it is echoed back on the screen, it is error-tested by the computer, and eventually it is accepted into the data base. A *control* dialog is similar to this but is performed for a different purpose. The objective of a control dialog is to exercise control over what the computer does, not to put data into the data base. In a control dialog, the computer says something such as, "Which of these things should I do?" and the operator says "Do number 5." In certain types of control dialogs, the operator does not wait to be asked by the computer, but just says, "Run the regression program" or something similar.

This chapter is concerned exclusively with control dialog. Data-entry dialogs were discussed in Chapter 7.

Computer-Initiated and Operator-Initiated Dialogs

Now we come to another important distinction — that between *computer-initiated* and *operator-initiated* dialogs. In any conversation, one participant must start things rolling and keep them on the right track. (Certain dialogs among people are exempt from this principle, particularly those of a political, religious, or artistic nature, but we will ignore them for purposes of this discussion.) The initiator is the person who talks first. For example, the salesperson who calls you up on the phone attempting to sell you life insurance is the initiator of a conversation which may be very short. However, you found out what was offered, and it was up to you to make a decision. In computer terms, programs which present you with a menu or ask you a question are carrying on a computer-initiated dialog.

You may, of course, prefer to initiate conversations about life insurance on your own terms. Your strategy might be to decide what you want, call several different salespeople, and try to find yourself the best deal. This puts you in the driver's seat. The analogy to a computer dialog is the blank screen with the flashing cursor into which you type a command directing the computer to provide you with some information or perform some function. This would be an operator-initiated dialog.

The next section of this chapter discusses computer-initiated dialogs. The section following discusses operator-initiated dialogs. Computer-initiated dialogs are much more common on microcomputers than are operator-initiated dialogs, although both are possible. In general, it takes a more sophisticated programmer to create an operator-initiated dialog, and a more sophisticated operator to engage in one. The reasons for this will be obvious when you read the sections that follow.

COMPUTER-INITIATED DIALOGS

This section discusses two common types of computer-initiated dialogs.

1. *Question and answer* (*Q&A*). The computer poses a question and the operator responds with an answer.
2. *Menu selection.* The operator selects one of a number of options displayed by the computer.

These are probably the most common types of computer-initiated dialogs used on microcomputers, and they are fairly representative of the genre as a whole.

Question-and-Answer Dialog

Description. Question-and-answer dialog is the simplest control technique. In it, the computer asks a question, which usually has a binary answer, such as "yes" or "no." The operator must respond to this question with one of the two legal alternatives. The following are three examples of this technique.

1. Computer wants to know whether to use old file or new.

```
COMPUTER:  Do you want to load old file? (Y/N)
OPERATOR:  (Types in) N
```

2. Computer wants to know whether to present output on video display or printer.

```
COMPUTER:  Should output go to CRT (C) or Printer (P)?
OPERATOR:  P
```

3. Computer wants operator to verify displayed information.

```
COMPUTER:  Is this information correct? (Y/N)
OPERATOR:  N
```

Number of Alternatives. Question-and-answer dialog is invaluable for answering those simple little questions that come up during programs, provided there are only two possible answers. You can stretch this technique to work for questions with more than two answers, but this is awkward and not usually done. For example, suppose the program could send output to either CRT or printer, or to both. A three-way Q&A prompt could be constructed as follows:

```
COMPUTER:  Should output be sent to CRT (C), Printer (P), or
           Both (B)?
OPERATOR:  B
```

A three-way question such as this could be asked as a combination of two binary questions. One way of doing it is as follows:

```
COMPUTER:  Should output be sent to CRT? (Y/N)
OPERATOR:  Y
COMPUTER:  Should output be sent to printer? (Y/N)
OPERATOR:  Y
```

Three-way or more questions can be answered more efficiently with other control techniques. The most logical candidate is the menu.

Use for General Control. How good is Q&A dialog for general control of a program? This question can perhaps best be answered with a "real-world" example. Suppose that an operator is a passenger in a taxicab and the driver is a computer. The operator has just left Joe's Bar and entered the taxi. He wants to go down the street to the first corner, turn right, and stop midway in that block to visit the Ritz Hotel, where Count Basie's band is playing. The taxi driver does not know the Ritz, and so the operator must give her directions. The driver can do three things: start, turn (left or right), or stop. To get the operator to the Ritz, a dialog must occur. In the dialog that follows, Q&A dialog is restricted to questions with two alternatives, since this is most typical.

```
COMPUTER:  Do you want to start? (Y/N)
OPERATOR:  Y
(Taxi starts moving.)
COMPUTER:  Do you want to stop? (Y/N)
OPERATOR:  N
COMPUTER:  Do you want to turn? (Y/N)
OPERATOR:  Y
COMPUTER:  Which way — Left (L) or Right (R)?
OPERATOR:  R
(Taxi swerves around corner. Count Basie's band is heard
in the distance.)
COMPUTER:  Do you want to stop? (Y/N)
OPERATOR:  Y
(Music is blaring out of the Ritz onto the street. The
operator's heart races as he reaches for his wallet.)
```

The inefficiency of this technique for general control of a program is obvious. The program has a limited repertoire of control commands. To find out what the operator wants, the program must present each of these to the operator, in turn. If the operator rejects one, it goes on mechanically to the next. Obviously, it would be much more efficient for all concerned if the operator could give the taxi driver the address of the Ritz and be done with it. Unfortunately, Q&A dialog does not work that way.

It is also clear that this type of dialog offers no shortcuts and requires every user to answer several questions every time he or she uses the program.

Logical Decision Making — Where Q&A Works Best. Q&A dialog is ideally suited for certain types of logical decision-making processes that can be reduced to sequences of binary choices. An example of such a process is electronic equipment troubleshooting. The electronics technician sits before the computer with a list of symptoms The computer poses questions and the technician answers. Based on responses, the problem can be narrowed down to a particular defective module. Using this technique, the computer becomes, in essence, an automated troubleshooting chart. Few real-world processes lend themselves to this sort of systematic mapping from symptoms to cause, but if the mapping can be made, the Q&A approach is highly effective.

Open-Ended Q&A Dialog. In the type of Q&A dialog just described, the legal answers are always displayed in the prompt and only those answers are acceptable. What is to prevent Q&A dialog from being more flexible? For example, why not permit operators to type in any answer they like?

The only limit to what can be accomplished with Q&A dialog is the programmer's ingenuity. As the constraints on how it is legal for operators to respond expand, so does the complexity of interpreting their responses. In the limited type of Q&A dialog discussed earlier, legal responses were one of two displayed letters. In principle, the vocabulary could be expanded beyond this to mnemonics, words, short sentences, or full, natural language. As this progression is made, computer interpretation becomes successively more difficult. The same is true of the computer's ability to handle the required processing. There is an enormous difference in the difficulty of writing a program that can simulate a well-defined decision tree and one that must interpret responses and show true artificial intelligence. The latter is generally beyond the capability of microcomputers.

There are several programs which seem to mimic natural language. Perhaps the most famous of these is ELIZA, a program originally developed at M.I.T. on a mainframe computer and which, playing the role of a psychiatrist, seems to carry on an open-ended dialog with its "patient." Subsets of this and similar programs have been made available for microcomputers, and these show that it is possible to have a microcomputer program give the appearance of carrying on a simple conversation.

Note that, as the number of possible responses to a question expands beyond what can be displayed in the prompt, the nature of the dialog changes from being computer-initiated to being operator-initiated. When operators no longer feel constrained to respond to a prompt in a very narrow fashion, they take control of the dialog.

Conclusions. Here are some conclusions about Q&A dialog.

- It is best used for soliciting the answers to a few binary questions.
- It should be considered as a general control technique only in highly structured programs.
- It should be limited to very simple programs or to programs involving logical decision making.
- If you want to drive a programmer crazy, assign her or him to write a DBMS or word processor program using this control technique.

Menu Selection

Description. In menu-driven programs, the computer displays a list of program options and the operator selects one option. This is usually done by typing in the number or letter of the desired option, but it is also commonly done by pointing at the option with a light pen or finger (on a touch-sensitive screen), pressing a function key, or in other ways. Following operator selection, the program calls the subprogram or executes the function that the operator has selected. Menu-selection dialog is computer-initiated since the operator must respond to computer menus and cannot create any. The following are two examples of program control menus:

1. This menu is used for program selection. When the operator picks an option, the menu disappears and the display for the selected program appears.

```
                        MAIN MENU

        1.  Update files.
        2.  Analyze data base.
        3.  Print reports.
        4.  Edit data base.
        5.  Exit program.

                SELECT OPTION #:  ___
```

2. This menu is used to select a function to be performed on data being displayed graphically. This menu is displayed continuously on the top of the screen.

```
                   GRAPHIC CONTROL MENU

        (X)   Change X axis.
        (Y)   Change Y axis.
        (N)   Select new variable.
        (H)   Print hard copy.
      (ESC)   Exit display.

             ENTER LETTER OF CHOICE:  ___
```

Human Memory Demands.   The menu-driven program makes little demand on human recall memory, although it does require the user to recognize and interpret the displayed menu options. There are no special control codes, command languages, or key sequences to memorize. All the operator must do is type in (or otherwise enter) a choice, and the command is executed.

Use for General Control.   Menu-driven programs are popular since they are easy to use, even for a naive operator. In order for it to be practical to use menus, the task the operator performs with the computer must be highly structured. Examples of programs which work well with menus are management information systems and data-base management systems. Examples of programs which do not lend themselves readily to the menu-driven approach are word processors, spreadsheet programs, and other programs in which the task is structured by the operator.

The menu control technique is often criticized by computer sophisticates for the limitations it puts on what the operator can do and for its lack of speed. These criticisms are valid, but they must be placed in perspective.

First, as noted, the menu technique requires tasks which are highly structured. With such tasks, the menu has undeniable advantages in terms of ease of learning and use. These advantages apply equally to computer novices and experts. The main advantage of menus is that they do not require the operator to memorize a great deal of information to use them effectively. This advantage is particularly important for the user — novice or expert — who does not use the program frequently. On the other hand, the frequent user will master the program functions and vocabulary and menus will be no particular asset.

Second, the speed of one particular control technique versus another (e.g., menus versus a command language) depends on several variables, the most important of which is the operator's experience. The advantages of operator-initiated control techniques such as command languages become evident only with highly sophisticated and experienced operators. These are operators who use a program frequently enough to learn it inside out. For them, the most effective way to call a program or perform a function is to tell the computer what they want directly, rather than to work their way through menus. Less sophisticated or experienced operators need more prompting and hand-holding, and will be able to perform better and sooner with menus.

To illustrate how menus work for program control, let us return to the adventures of our peripatetic operator, who has just, through a hole in the space-time continuum, found himself back at the front door of Joe's Bar. Spying the taxicab, and feeling a sense of déjà vu, he approaches, opens the back door, and seats himself. On the glass separating him from the driver is a dirty sheet of paper which reads as follows:

```
Your driver has just immigrated to New York from the planet
Tralfamadore. She does not understand spoken English, but she
does understand numbers. To control taxi movement, tell her the
number of what you want to do:


                        MENU

                1.  Start.
                2.  Stop.
                3.  Turn right.
                4.  Turn left.
```

The operator is not crazy about this arrangement, particularly since the driver's compartment is filled with a cloud of opaque gas, but taxicabs are hard to get, and he wants to get to the Ritz very badly.

```
OPERATOR:  1
(Taxi starts moving.)
OPERATOR:  3
(Taxi turns right.)
OPERATOR:  2
(The taxi stops. The operator gets out, steps onto the
sidewalk, and observes a gaping hole in the earth where
the Ritz used to be. He hears the sound of Count Basie's
band overhead and getting weaker as the Ritz rises into
the night sky. Another tear in the space-time fabric, he
thinks.)
```

Here are some conclusions about dialog:

• The program in which it is used must be highly structured, but it may be fairly complex.
• It places little demand on recall memory.
• Operators can learn to use such programs quickly.
• It is good for users — novice through expert — who do not use a program frequently.
• It is ideal for unsophisticated operators.

How to Design a Menu. The following are some general guidelines for designing menus:

• Title the menu. The more menus there are, the more important it is to do this. The title should be descriptive and should have the word "menu" in it — e.g., "Main Menu" or "Edit Menu."
• Limit the number of menu options. The ideal number is somewhere between four and six. In some programs, shorter or longer menus will be unavoidable. When a menu exceeds about ten items, it becomes, for all practical purposes, a directory. Rather than listing all programs on one long menu, organize your menus in levels or tiers. List functionally related subprograms on separate menus. For example, list all the subprograms for data-base editing — such as inserting, modifying, or deleting — on the same menu. The only time it makes

sense to have one long list of programs is if each one is totally unrelated to the others.

- On short menus, list the options according to their frequency of use — most frequent at top, least frequent at bottom. On long menus or directories, list the items in an order that operators will recognize, such as alphabetic, numeric, or chronologic order.

- It is desirable to be able to select the menu option with the first letter of the option label (e.g., select the "Edit" option by typing in E) since the operator can learn this more quickly than an option number. If only a few menus are used, and their options are semantically distinct, use *alphabetic* option selection throughout. As the number of menu options on each menu increases, the availability of unique semantic labels decreases. With such menus, permit option selection with *numbers* rather than letters. Permit the option to be selected with a minimum number of keystrokes — preferably a single letter or number — followed by a verification with the Return key or its equivalent.

- With long menus or directories, it may not be possible to display all options on a single screen. In these cases, permit operators to page or scroll through the menu to find the part they want. They should then be able to select the option with a number. However, on directories that contain information that is familiar to the operator — such as clients' names, merchandise, or titles — permit operators to select the option by typing in a portion of the label (e.g., typing in Chel to call Cheltenham). This way they can select the option without actually seeing it.

- Display a prompt line at the bottom of the menu for operator input. Make the prompt brief and explicit. For example, "Select option #."

Note that if you use numbers for menu selection, then any list of numbered items appearing on one of your display screens may be mistaken for a menu. Avoid numbered items on nonmenu displays, if possible. For example, in a list of instructions, precede each instruction by a bullet instead of a number.

Menu Control Structure. Most menu-driven programs have several menus that are organized together into an overall control structure, or *network*. In this network, the menus may be thought of as nodes (or crossroads), with each menu option linking the menu either to another menu or to a subprogram (Figure 9-1). Such networks can be designed in many different ways. It is not immediately obvious which is best. To determine this, we must define the criteria by which

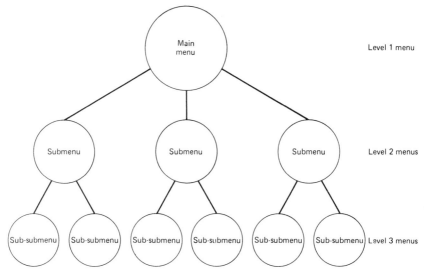

Figure 9-1　The control structure of a menu-driven program may be represented as a network in which the menus are nodes and each menu option links the menu either to another menu or to a subprogram.

to evaluate different control structures. When the primary goal is to make the program user-friendly, two such criteria are obvious:

1. *Speed.*　How quickly does the structure permit us to move around the program?

2. *Ease of learning and use.*

A simple way to assess speed is to count the number of keystrokes to get from any given menu to any other. The fewer the keystrokes, the easier transportation is, and the more efficient the program. Ease of learning and use of the program will be influenced by how logically the menus are organized. A key factor here is whether or not the menus are organized in a hierarchical fashion. This structure is usually both easy to learn and easy to use.

Perhaps the most common control structure in menu-driven programs is the familiar tree (Figure 9-2). This is a multilevel, hierarchical structure. The main menu is the highest node. Selecting a program from it leads to a level 2 node or menu, selecting an option from a level 2 menu leads to a level 3 menu, and so on. There are no links or crossovers between different menus at the same level. If an operator selects a level 3 menu, for example, in order to call another level 3 menu, it is necessary first to return to the previous level 2 menu

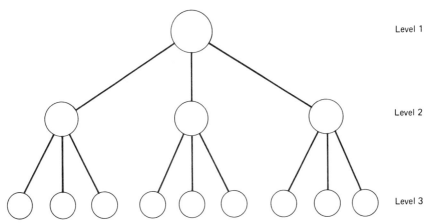

Figure 9-2 A strictly hierarchical menu control structure. Each node is linked only to the node above it. Moving from one branch to the next requires a return to the highest node, or main menu.

and then the main menu, and then work back down through another level 2 menu to the desired level 3 menu.

This structure has the advantage that it is symmetrical and therefore easy to learn. However, if it is several levels deep, moving between branches is very time-consuming. The obvious solution to this problem is to provide some shortcuts or links between different parts of the structure. One way of simplifying things is to provide an option on every menu that links it directly back to the main menu (Figure 9-3). This provides a shortcut that does not disrupt the functional integrity of the different branches of the structure.

Another, more radical, solution is to provide links between branches (Figure 9-4). However, this must be done consistently or the structure will begin to lose its symmetry. The more crossovers are permitted, the less predictable the structure and the more difficult it is for the operator to model it mentally and learn it.

What should be avoided is a structure with crossovers between branches that follow no particular pattern or rule. This is like having a road system in which some streets come to dead ends and others have cross streets. The more symmetric you make your structure, the easier it will be for the operator to learn it. If your control structure resembles a complex network, the operator will need a road map to find the way around it.

Try to keep things simple and hierarchical. Add a quick exit to the main menu when there are three or more levels. If this does not provide quick enough access to programs, then either use crossovers or switch to operator-initiated dialog.

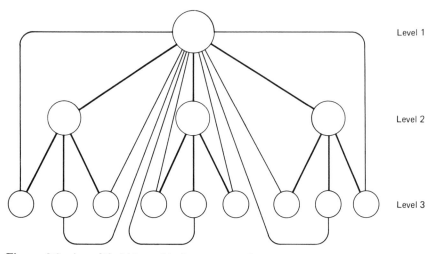

Level 1

Level 2

Level 3

Figure 9-3 A modified hierarchical menu control structure. Each node is linked not only to the node above, but also to the highest node. This permits faster movement around the program.

In designing a menu control network, sometimes you must make a depth-breadth trade-off, that is, decide whether to use longer menus with fewer options or shorter menus with more options. Make the trade-off in favor of longer menus. For example, if your program has a total of sixty-four different options, it is better to use two levels of menus with eight options each than three levels with four options each or six levels with two options each. No single menu should contain more than ten options, however.

OPERATOR-INITIATED DIALOGS

Description

In operator-initiated dialog, the operator types in a word, mnemonic, code, or other command, and the computer immediately carries out the command. This command may be to call a program, present a display, or perform some other computer function. The prompt line does not usually provide any operator cueing; the command typed in must come straight from the operator's recall memory.

The two types of computer-initiated dialogs discussed so far — question and answer, and menu selection — both display the legal control commands and permit the operator to move about the program one step at a time. The operator is kept on track by the computer, so to

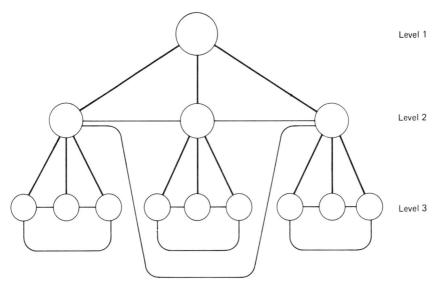

Figure 9-4 Another alternative menu control structure. In this one, each node is linked not only to the node above, but also to the node at the same level in other branches.

speak. In operator-initiated dialog, there are fewer constraints on what the operator can do. Simply by typing in the appropriate control code, the operator becomes free to move to any point in the program at any time.

Operator-initiated dialog can take many different forms. The major difference is in the type of information that is entered by the operator and interpreted by the computer. The most common types of entries are the following:

- *Words.* Names of programs, displays, or computer functions to be performed.

- *Letters, mnemonics, or abbreviations.* These represent the names of programs, displays, or computer functions.

- *Logical or mathematical expressions.*

- *Programlike languages.* For example, simple, English language — like commands to execute functions such as those performed within computer programs.

- *Action codes.* Short combinations of characters that tell the computer to perform certain functions.

- *Command language.* A formal control language like that used for programming.

Obviously, different types of entries imply different levels of complexity. The simplest form of operator-initiated dialog would consist of the operator typing in the name of a display and having it appear on the CRT. The most complex dialog would be one employing a formal command language such as Statistical Analysis System (SAS), which permits operators to make keyboard entries that have all the complexity of a formal programming language.

Use for General Control

Operator-initiated dialog gives operators greater control of the computer than does computer-initiated dialog. It should therefore be faster and more efficient. Right? While this is true in principle, such dialog has some serious drawbacks, particularly for unsophisticated users.

• Operators must carry the program's vocabulary (program names, abbreviations, etc.) around mentally. They receive little, if any, prompting from the program.

• Operators must have an internal mental map of how the program is structured, what it can do, and what strategy to employ in accomplishing their objectives. Unsophisticated operators will have few of these things.

• Frequent practice is required to maintain operator proficiency.

Operator-initiated dialog is essential in programs which require flexibility and operator control. A good example is word processors. Most of these require the operator to learn a special vocabulary consisting of command words, control codes, and mnemonics in order to control text composition, formatting, editing, and printing. With practice, operators gain proficiency using these programs, but many operators become frustrated and quit before they reach the required level. Simple, menu-driven word-processing programs have appeared for this reason. They take less time to master, but they have limited capabilities. Still, many operators prefer them because they are easy to learn and use.

Sophisticated users usually prefer operator-initiated dialog for the control and flexibility it gives them, just as the auto enthusiast might love a $125,000 Lamborghini for its exhilarating power and exquisite handling. However, this is not the sort of car you would lend to an inexperienced driver, since its complexity would probably get him or her in trouble. Instead, lend out the old station wagon, with its automatic transmission, mushy steering and ride, and simplicity.

Let us continue the saga of our operator, who at last report was observing the consequences of a rift in space and time. Through an intervention by a mysterious and unseen force, the rift has sealed, and our operator has been transported magically back once again to the front of Joe's Bar. His response is, "Oh, no, not again!" However, he is willing to try one more time. He opens the door of the taxi and steps in. This time things seem more normal. The taxi driver turns and stares at him expectantly, waiting for a command.

```
OPERATOR:  Start.
(Taxi moves forward.)
OPERATOR:  Turn right.
(Taxi turns.)
OPERATOR:  Stop.
(The taxi stops and the operator pays the driver, steps
out, and walks into the Ritz at last.)
```

Here, the driving commands were given in natural language. They could just as well have been abbreviations, mnemonics, or codes. If a command language were used, all three driving commands could have been combined into a single statement.

Conclusions

Here are some conclusions about operator-initiated dialogs.

• It is the fastest and most efficient technique for operators who are sophisticated and use a program regularly.

• It should not be used by unsophisticated operators or by operators who will use a program occasionally.

HYBRID CONTROL TECHNIQUES, OR HOW TO GET THE BEST OF BOTH WORLDS

An actual computer program will seldom rely entirely on one type of control technique. The programmer will employ a combination of dialog types — both computer- and operator-initiated — without giving it a second thought. For example, a word processor will often have a few menus, although the majority of its commands will be entered without prompting. On the other hand, one will encounter data-base management systems which are mainly menu-driven, but which permit the operator to select an item from a directory by typing in its name, or to compose a record on a single line by typing in the different fields and separating them by slashes. There is no rule that one control technique must be used throughout.

At the same time, there is a virtue in simplicity and consistency that cannot be denied. If the programmer does use different control techniques, there must be some underlying principle or rule that is followed so that the operator does not get confused. The operator should not, for example, have to select some programs with a menu and others by typing in program names.

Along with using different control techniques in different parts of the program, it is possible to have a completely — or partially — *redundant* control structure. One might, for example, design a program that is menu-driven but that can also function in a different mode using operator-initiated dialog. Why would one want to do this? The main reason is to accommodate operators who are working at different levels of skill. The inexperienced operator will prefer the menus. The experienced operator will prefer operator-initiated dialog.

Is it difficult to do this? Obviously, it is more difficult and time-consuming to write a program with two control structures than with one. Not many designers have done it, probably because of the time and effort involved. In addition, it is possible that many programmers have never thought of this idea before. It is worth considering. With all the interest these days in human factors, help screens, and good documentation, we ought also to build into our programs the ability to meet the needs of different types of operators.

Ten

Program Documentation

This chapter covers two types of program documentation. The first is documentation intended for the programmers who will maintain, troubleshoot, and update an existing program. This documentation is usually prepared by the program's author and is referred to as *system documentation*. Coverage of this topic is limited here to programs written in BASIC or similar languages, although many of the concepts will apply more broadly.

The second type of documentation is *user documentation*. This may be in written form, appear within the program, or be a combination of both. Such documentation must explain your program, initiate the new user, and provide the reference information the experienced user needs.

How important is system documentation? The answer depends upon several factors: program complexity; the availability of the program's author to troubleshoot, maintain, and update the program; and the program's probable life span. For simple programs that will be maintained by the original author for a limited period of time, it probably does not matter very much. For more complex programs that will not be maintained by the original author (or that have a team of authors) and that have a longer life span, system documentation is very important. It may make the difference between whether or not a program error can be isolated and corrected. System documentation may decide whether it is feasible to upgrade a program based on its original design or cheaper to write a new one from scratch.

What about user documentation? Here, the answer is more clearcut. It is accurate to say that user documentation will make the difference between whether your program can be used effectively or not. In fact, it is reasonable to go a step further and say that, if the program is not documented properly, it may not be usable at all. It follows from this that it is only sound practice to give as much attention to user documentation as to the program itself. If you do otherwise, you are cutting your own throat.

The user documentation provided with most microcomputer programs has not been distinguished for its completeness, quality, or ease of use. In fact, much of it to date has been awful. The situation does appear to be changing, however. In the 1970s, when the microcomputer revolution began, publishers could and did get away with anything. The documentation for your game might be a fourth-generation photocopy of an original that was incomplete and full of grammatical and spelling errors. If you attempted to follow the directions, procedures would not work and you could only set things right by using your ingenuity to fill in the missing steps or by making a long-distance call to the author, who might or might not be available. These days, documentation is often handsomer — offset printed, with illustrations, and contained in a nice binder — but still not up to the standard most of us would like.

The industry's awareness of the importance of documentation is increasing. This was inevitable, mainly because of market pressure. Publishers have discovered that programs people can use sell more copies. Good user documentation makes programs usable — ergo, there is more interest in making it good, or at least look good.

User documentation is increasingly becoming a selling point for software products. Programmers cannot afford to ignore it. If you do not want to write it yourself, then hire a good writer. If your publisher has a documentation department, so much the better. Of course, an outsider will never understand your program as well as you do, and it is unlikely that the resulting documentation will exercise all your program's capabilities. For this reason, it is always a good idea for a program's author to write the first draft of the user's guide. This will assure that nothing is overlooked. Even if you have not done this sort of thing before, you can do it. It is not that difficult. This chapter will tell you how.

SYSTEM DOCUMENTATION

Purpose

The purpose of system documentation is to support the maintenance, troubleshooting, and upgrading of a program. In a sense, maintenance encompasses all these, but this discussion will treat it as a separate topic. *Maintenance* is the routine, day-to-day work done on a program to customize it to fit the differing needs of program users, to make minor improvements, and to correct errors not discovered during program development. *Troubleshooting* is the diagnostic work a programmer goes through to localize, isolate, and correct program errors. *Upgrading* is the major modification of the program to enhance its capabilities; the resulting program may be a slight improvement over the original or a totally new program.

Although these functions differ, the documentation needs for all are basically the same. You must *provide enough information to enable the programmer to understand what is going on inside the program.* Since programs are written in code, not natural language, a program listing itself is not usually sufficient to provide this understanding. Several items of additional information must be provided to fill out the picture.

Audience Considerations

The first step in planning system documentation is to consider the audience, in order to decide how much detail to put in it. If you, the program's author, are the only one who will use the documentation, then it does not have to be as complete as if a stranger would use it. Documentation requirements are greatest when the program will leave your hands and be maintained by others. In this case, you must provide all the information that others will need to understand the program as well as you do. This is the impossible goal to strive for. For example, your documentation must make it possible for another programmer to do such things as the following:

• Modify the program's control structure to add a new subprogram.
• Modify the file structure.
• Determine the purpose of each function and subroutine and be able to modify it.
• Determine the assignment of any variable.

This list is not complete, but it provides examples of the kinds of things system documentation must communicate. This information, as well as a good deal more, can be communicated by providing the documentation items described under the headings that follow.

Overall System Description

The system description is intended to provide the programmer with an understanding of the program's purpose and structure. It is a high-level description of the program in both written and graphic form. It describes the purpose of the program, the content of each program module, and the relationships among modules. It also provides incidental information on the program, such as hardware requirements, operating system and programming languages used, machine language routines and utilities, and any special requirements.

Statement of Purpose. The first thing that should appear in the description is a statement of the program's purpose. Here is an example of such a statement for a management information system:

> The purpose of this program is to store data and generate reports which are provided to managers. The managers review these reports and evaluate sales productivity of individuals and determine the relative success of different product lines. Decisions are then made concerning salespeople incentives and rewards, and what product lines should be expanded or contracted to maximize profits.

It is no easy matter to state the purpose of a complex program in a few sentences. Doing it is very helpful to the programmer, however, because it answers the basic question of why the program was conceived and developed.

Program Structure. Name and define each program module and tell its purpose. For example, the hypothetical management information system might contain four program modules:

1. *Data entry.* Used by operators to enter data into the files.
2. *Report generation.* Used for printing reports.
3. *Data-base editing.* Used to access and maintain the data base.
4. *Utilities.* Used to create files, copy files, and produce hard copies of the data base.

Describe the subprograms in each program module in terms of their purpose and the function they perform. Incidentally, if your program is menu-driven, writing the overall description is usually simplified. Often, the program modules are the programs listed on the highest level or main menu. If so, list these and tell the purpose of each one. Then describe the individual modules in terms of the subprograms listed on the lower-level menus.

Provide a diagram which shows the relationships among the program modules (Figure 10-1). Note that this is not a flow chart; it is simply a diagram which shows relationships. The description and accompanying diagram do not have to be highly detailed, but they must provide enough information so that a programmer can use them as a map in determining where different functions are performed within the program. This is particularly important during program troubleshooting. For example, if a customer calls and says that a problem is occurring in a particular data-entry routine, the programmer should be able to identify the program module responsible for the problem.

Hardware and Software Requirements. Document the hardware and software environment in which the program is to operate. Specifically, provide a written description of any of the following that apply in your program:

• Operating system and programming languages used, and any modifications or patches that have been made to them.
• Any special routines that are called from within the program. For example, if you are accessing machine-language routines, identify them, tell their purpose, and indicate how they are called.

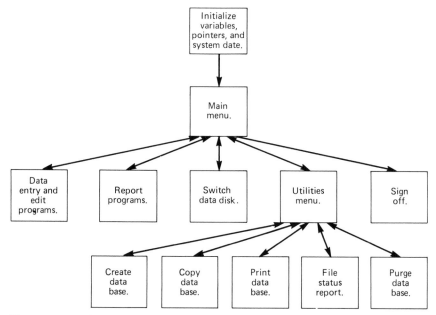

Figure 10-1   The relationships among different program modules. This shows the basic structure of the program, and is extremely helpful to the programmer. It should be accompanied by a written description.

- The hardware suite your program requires: computer, memory requirements, disk drives, printer, any special interfaces, and so forth.

Program Listing

The system overall description is a sort of index to your program. The program listing is the content of the program and what a programmer must work with. For this reason, it is important to provide this listing in a form that is informative, understandable, and easy to use. Here are some general guidelines for preparing a listing:

- *Use remarks liberally.*   Use remarks to indicate the purpose of each block of code, e.g., functions, subroutines, program modules, and submodules. Remarks are helpful even if the author is the only programmer who will ever use the listing. Without them, the stranger to your program may find it incomprehensible.
  If you are concerned about the impact of remarks on memory or program speed, use an optimization (remark remover and compression) routine before delivering the program. But always keep a fully remarked source code version of the program.

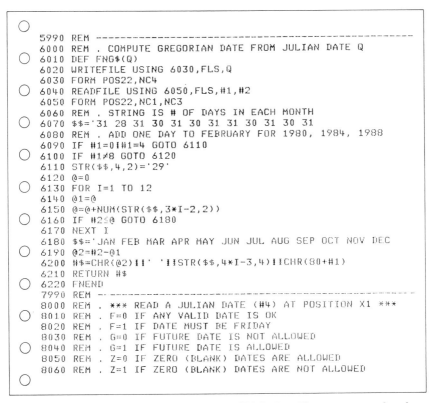

```
5990 REM --------------------------------------------------
6000 REM . COMPUTE GREGORIAN DATE FROM JULIAN DATE Q
6010 DEF FNG$(Q)
6020 WRITEFILE USING 6030,FLS,Q
6030 FORM POS22,NC4
6040 READFILE USING 6050,FLS,#1,#2
6050 FORM POS22,NC1,NC3
6060 REM . STRING IS # OF DAYS IN EACH MONTH
6070 $$='31 28 31 30 31 30 31 31 30 31 30 31
6080 REM . ADD ONE DAY TO FEBRUARY FOR 1980, 1984, 1988
6090 IF #1=0I#1=4 GOTO 6110
6100 IF #1≠8 GOTO 6120
6110 STR($$,4,2)='29'
6120 @=0
6130 FOR I=1 TO 12
6140 @1=@
6150 @=@+NUM(STR($$,3*I-2,2))
6160 IF #2≤@ GOTO 6180
6170 NEXT I
6180 $$='JAN FEB MAR APR MAY JUN JUL AUG SEP OCT NOV DEC
6190 @2=#2-@1
6200 #$=CHR(@2)II' 'IISTR($$,4*I-3,4)IICHR(80+#1)
6210 RETURN #$
6220 FNEND
7990 REM --------------------------------------------------
8000 REM . *** READ A JULIAN DATE (#4) AT POSITION X1 ***
8010 REM . F=0 IF ANY VALID DATE IS OK
8020 REM . F=1 IF DATE MUST BE FRIDAY
8030 REM . G=0 IF FUTURE DATE IS NOT ALLOWED
8040 REM . G=1 IF FUTURE DATE IS ALLOWED
8050 REM . Z=0 IF ZERO (BLANK) DATES ARE ALLOWED
8060 REM . Z=1 IF ZERO (BLANK) DATES ARE NOT ALLOWED
```

Figure 10-2 Section of a well-documented BASIC listing. The programmer has done several things to make this listing readable: One statement is printed per line. Remarks are used liberally; dashed lines separate the main code module at the top. The module is defined in line 6000. Line 6060 defines the string on line 6070. Line 6080 tells how leap years are handled in subsequent lines. Lines 8000 to 8060 define key variables.

• *Separate the listings of different subprograms.* It should not be necessary for a programmer to work through a 3-inch stack of paper. Finding a subprogram should be as easy as opening a notebook to an index tab or pulling a manila folder out of a file.

• *Print your listing so that it is readable.* A listing is most readable when there is one statement per line. If you tend to write long lines, then use a formatting utility to print each statement on a separate line and make the listing more readable.

Figure 10-2 shows a portion of a BASIC listing with sufficient remarks to make it readable.

The time to enter remarks is when you code the program, not afterward. Once you get in the habit, it becomes easy. This is an important habit to get into.

```
                              TABLE  1
O             FILE  NAME:  FORM  1                    REC=33
                                   NO.  OF  RECS.  =  1000
                      # of
O    Variable   Pos.   bytes   Format    Description  &  range

     S1          1      4       S         Reference  #  (1  to  99999)
O    D8          5      2       B2        Julian date
     B           7      2       B2        Bumper  #  (1  to  150)
     MO          9      2       B2        MOS  #  (1  to  2)
O    C(5)        11     10      5*B2      Crew  roster  code  numbers
     V           21     1       NC1       Vehicle  type  (1,  2)
     P(8)        22     8       8*NC1     PMCS  types  (each  0  or  1)
O    H           30     4       S         Total  hours
```

Figure 10-3 File documentation. This documentation identifies the file name, record length, number of records, and the content and length of each record field. Such documentation is essential when using data files.

File Structure

Prepare a written and graphic description of each text file used in your program. This description should list and illustrate all the following:

- File name
- Number of records
- Record length
- Type of file (record-oriented or sequential)
- Content, type, and length of each field
- Relevant variables
- (If applicable) subroutines used for reading and writing files

Figure 10-3 shows documentation for a text file.

Variable, Array, and Function Reference Tables

Prepare tables that define each variable, array, and function used in your program. These tables are intended for use by a programmer who is referring to a listing and wants to determine the purpose of a particular variable, array, or function. It should be possible for this programmer to go to a table, look up the item of interest, and answer the question immediately. If you are using the same variables throughout the program, then make one table. If variable assignments change with subprogram, make a separate table for each subprogram.

In addition to defining the variable, array, or function, provide any

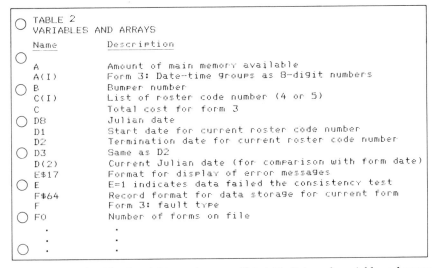

```
○  TABLE 2
     VARIABLES AND ARRAYS

     Name           Description
○
     A              Amount of main memory available
     A(I)           Form 3: Date-time groups as 8-digit numbers
○    B              Bumper number
     C(I)           List of roster code number (4 or 5)
     C              Total cost for form 3
○    D8             Julian date
     D1             Start date for current roster code number
     D2             Termination date for current roster code number
○    D3             Same as D2
     D(2)           Current Julian date (for comparison with form date)
     E$17           Format for display of error messages
○    E              E=1 indicates data failed the consistency test
     F$64           Record format for data storage for current form
     F              Form 3: fault type
○    FO             Number of forms on file
                    .
                    .
○    .              .
```

Figure 10-4 A table of variables and arrays. This table lists each variable and array in the program and describes what it is used for. Functions should be documented in this way also, either together with variables and arrays, or in a separate table.

additional information the programmer will need to use or interpret the variable in the program. For example, if you are using the real variable D to represent the date, and if you are storing the date in the form YYMMDD, then indicate the format in your notes for that variable. Figure 10-4 shows a table of variables and arrays.

Additional Documentation Items

Use your judgment in providing additional documentation. Keep in mind the goal of providing a programmer with the information needed to maintain, troubleshoot, and update the program. Always provide the programmer with a copy of the *user's guide*. This will help the programmer understand how the program operates, its input requirements, and the nature of its outputs. The following are suggestions for additional items to include in system documentation:

• *Detailed explanation of input requirements.* Explain the types of inputs and the range and length limits, and describe error tests.
• *Flow charts or other descriptions of the logic involved in key parts of the program.* The popularity of flow charts is waning and that of *formal design languages* is on the rise. However you feel about this matter, provide a formal, rigorous description of any programming procedures which are esoteric, subtle, or not obvious. Examples of

procedures which warrant such documentation are shifting pointers, compressing files, or performing sorts.

• *Formulas used in computations.* Give the formulas used and provide a written description of them, indicating what each variable stands for.

• *Program narrative.* A program narrative describes what is going on inside the program and is an adjunct to the program listing. The more remarks contained in the listing, the less the narrative is needed.

USER DOCUMENTATION

Setting the Level

The following conversation took place between a software publisher and a programmer whose new program had been accepted:

PROGRAMMER: I'm glad you like the program. How about my user's guide?

PUBLISHER: (After pausing) We'll have to rewrite it.

PROGRAMMER: I thought I'd saved you people work by writing it.

PUBLISHER: It will be helpful.

PROGRAMMER: What's wrong with it?

PUBLISHER: Nothing, more or less.

PROGRAMMER: I don't understand.

PUBLISHER: Well, it has more of some kinds of information than it needs, and less of others. It talks about complicated things like file structure, but not about simple things like how to get the program up and running.

PROGRAMMER: I wasn't sure what level to write it at. What do you assume about program users? I mean, what do you assume they know about computers?

PUBLISHER: We assume they know where the on–off switch is.

PROGRAMMER: That's all?

PUBLISHER: Not quite. We assume they can turn it on.

This publisher may underestimate program users; nevertheless the first principle of writing a user's guide is: Know thine audience.

Operators are usually less technically sophisticated than programmers, and so the user's guide must usually be written at a lower level than system documentation. The audience will, of course, vary depending upon the type of program. Some programs, such as programming utilities and linking loaders, are designed for use by programmers. If you are writing a user's guide for such a program, then you can assume that your audience is technically sophisticated. More commonly, however, users of microcomputer programs vary in sophistication from complete novices to technical experts. You must therefore write documentation that serves the needs of everyone.

Moreover, as people use a program, they gain skill and their needs change. New operators need a step-by-step tutorial that they can use to work through the program and that will help them to develop skill and confidence. Experienced operators no longer need this, but they do need quick access to important reference information for using the program.

In sum, the user's guide should serve the needs of all members of its audience and should accommodate itself to growth in skill. (This principle also applies to software design.) Writing a user's guide that does all this is not easy, but there are ways of doing it.

Internal versus External Documentation

User documentation comes in two forms: internal and external. Internal documentation consists of help screens, directions, and other explanatory information that the operator can access within the program. To use this documentation, the program must be up. External documentation is — well, external, i.e., outside the program itself. Its most typical form is the *user's guide*, although adventurous publishers are finding other ways to document their programs these days, including audio cassettes, videotapes, and video disks, as well as the familiar print medium.

All user documentation has the same purpose: to explain the features of your program and help the operator gain proficiency in using it. While the purpose of internal and external documentation is the same, each has unique strengths and limitations and is more suited to certain things than the other. The two documentation approaches should be considered complementary rather than competing alternatives. Internal documentation is best used to aid the operator's memory concerning procedures (e.g., how to start a new file) and program vocabulary (e.g., the commands required for text formatting with a word processor). The small text window and memory overhead of internal documentation combine to make it a poor candidate for presenting a lot of detail. However, there is no question but that it is useful for the

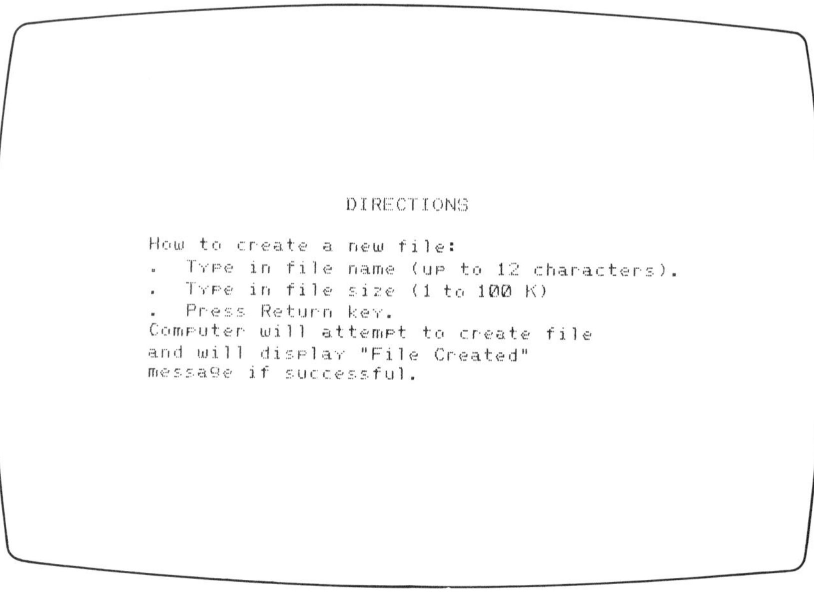

```
                    DIRECTIONS

   How to create a new file:
   .  Type in file name (up to 12 characters).
   .  Type in file size (1 to 100 K)
   .  Press Return key.
   Computer will attempt to create file
   and will display "File Created"
   message if successful.
```

Figure 10-5 An example of internal documentation — a help screen. This screen, accessed when the operator asks for help, gives the procedure for creating a new file.

operator to be able to access detailed information concerning procedures and program vocabulary while using the program — without having to leaf through a user's guide.

Figures 10-5, 10-6, and 10-7 illustrate three screens containing typical internal documentation. Each is accessed, at operator request, within the program. Figure 10-5 is a set of directions for the procedure of creating a new file. Figure 10-6 contains a summary of text-formatting commands for use in a word-processing program. Figure 10-7 contains guidelines for interpreting the results produced by a stock analysis program. These examples illustrate the type of information that internal documentation is best suited to present. More has been and can be done with internal documentation, but the cost effectiveness of such efforts must be examined critically. As noted in Chapter 7, the use of internal documentation is fairly new, and you should feel free to experiment. Creative people — and programmers are certainly included among them — must make their own rules to a certain extent.

What should be the relationship between internal and external documentation? In general, whatever is covered in internal documentation should also be covered in external documentation. This follows from the philosophy that internal documentation should be used

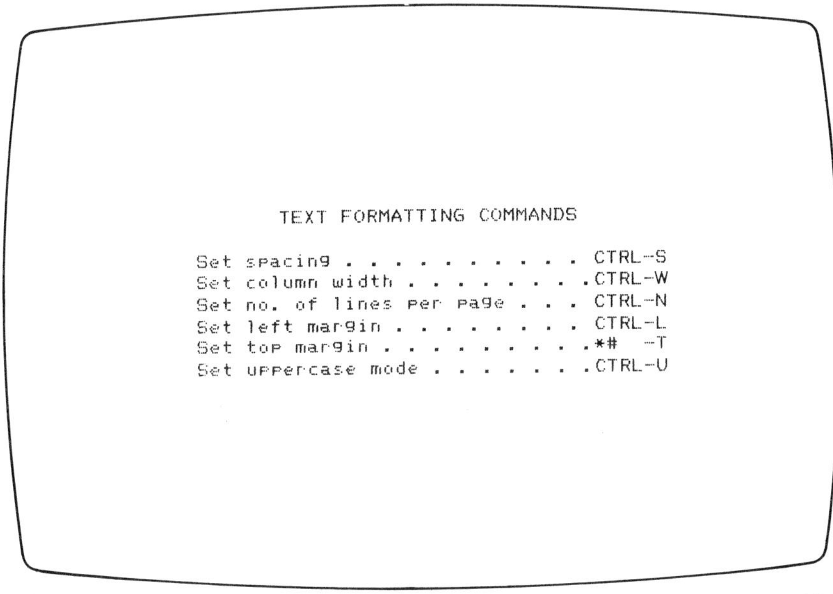

```
              TEXT FORMATTING COMMANDS

        Set spacing . . . . . . . . . . CTRL-S
        Set column width . . . . . . . .CTRL-W
        Set no. of lines per page . . . CTRL-N
        Set left margin . . . . . . . . CTRL-L
        Set top margin . . . . . . . . .*#  -T
        Set uppercase mode . . . . . . .CTRL-U
```

Figure 10-6 Another help screen. This one provides reference information needed for formatting text in a word-processing program.

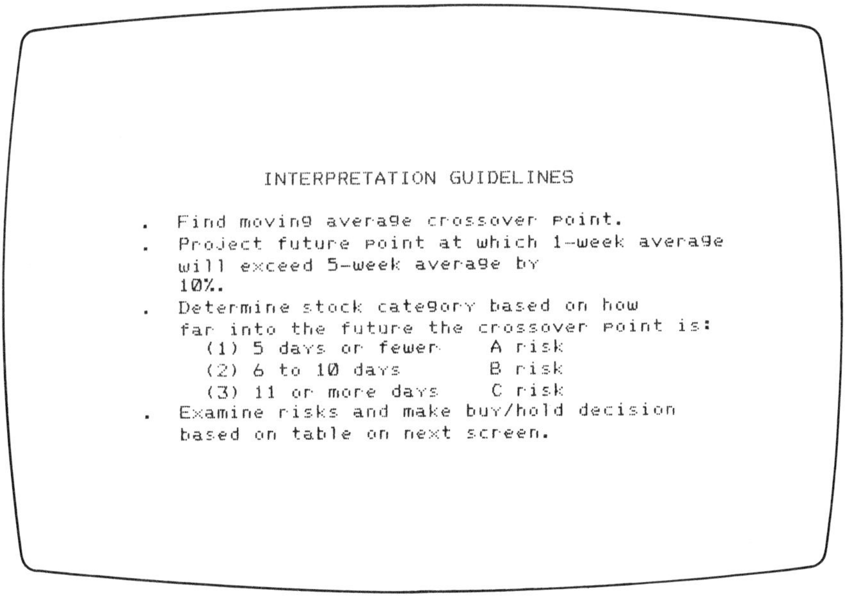

```
              INTERPRETATION GUIDELINES

        .  Find moving average crossover point.
        .  Project future point at which 1-week average
           will exceed 5-week average by
           10%.
        .  Determine stock category based on how
           far into the future the crossover point is:
             (1) 5 days or fewer    A risk
             (2) 6 to 10 days       B risk
             (3) 11 or more days    C risk
        .  Examine risks and make buy/hold decision
           based on table on next screen.
```

Figure 10-7 A third example of internal documentation. This screen, accessed when requested, gives guidelines for interpreting the graphs of price moving averages in a stock market analysis program.

mainly to jog the operator's memory. Full coverage of a program's features should be contained in the external documentation. Internal documentation, then, may be thought of as a subset of external documentation. The various help screens, directions, and so forth that make up the internal documentation may, in fact, also appear in the external documentation.

Naturally, there will be exceptions to this rule. In extremely simple programs, documentation requirements are minimal. You may be able to get along with only one type of documentation. Users of entertainment programs such as games seldom read anything before getting started, and it may make sense to provide only internal documentation for some such programs. On the other hand, if the procedures for using the program are complex, and the program is short (e.g., a program for computing the internal rate of return on an investment), then maybe the program should have exclusively external documentation.

The User's Guide

This section describes the content of a sort of ideal program user's guide. This is the type of user's guide that should be prepared for a program that will be used in serious, everyday applications. Examples of such programs are data-base management systems, word processors, and budget management and analysis programs. This user's guide contains much more than would be needed for simple programs such as games. In following the recipe below, use only what you need, but be sure that you do not leave out any of the essentials.

A Tutorial and Reference. As noted above, the user's guide must work at two levels:

1. As a step-by-step *tutorial* which guides new users until they gain the basic skills and confidence needed to operate the program effectively

2. As a *reference* which provides experienced users with the information needed to use the program effectively and increase their proficiency

There are two basic ways of meeting these needs. The first is to provide separate tutorial and reference sections in the guide. The second is to integrate tutorial and reference information and use page format to highlight information so that the document can be read at two different levels. Both techniques are valid, but the first is somewhat simpler to prepare. For this reason, this section will focus on the first option, although some examples of the second technique will be given.

Figure 10-8 The program user's guide will be used while sitting at a small computer or terminal. It should be structured for ease of use, preferably in a binder in which the pages will lie flat.

Physical Structure and Format. The following are suggestions for the physical structure and format of the guide:

• Prepare the guide with a spiral *binder* or in the form of a loose-leaf notebook so that, when opened, its pages lie flat. The guide will be used by operators sitting before a small computer, with hands occupied by the keyboard (Figure 10-8). Spiral or loose-leaf binding makes a document easy to handle with one hand, and using the document does not interfere with the computer task the operator is performing. If a document is stapled or bound so that its pages will not lie flat, the operator must hold it open with one hand, and turning pages is awkward.

• Break up the text into short *paragraphs*. This makes it easier to read and helps operators keep track of their place when looking back and forth between the computer and the guide.

• Provide *tabs* to help operators locate different major sections of the guide. They should not have to refer to the table of contents or index

QUICK REFERENCE CARD
Summary of Text Writer commands

[B] Start file.

[C] Quit Text Writer.

[D] Load new file.

[E] Save file to disk.

[F] Call help screen.

[G] Split display.

[L] Print file.

[N] Merge documents.

[O] Access DOS.

Figure 10-9 An example of a quick-reference card. This card contains key reference information important for use during the program. It is analogous to a help screen (see Figure 10-6) but is in the form of external documentation.

to locate major sections. Consider color-coding different sections if tabs cannot be used.

- Use *graphics* liberally. Graphics combined with text are more effective for conveying concepts than text alone. Use graphics to convey high-level concepts, such as a program's organization, as well as the literal details of a program, such as its display screens. One rule is that you should never talk about a display screen without showing it. In general, the pages of your user's guide should contain a minimum of about 25 percent graphics, and the rest text. Use foldouts, if necessary, so that the reader can view an illustration that is referred to in the text without turning the page.

- Provide *quick-reference information,* in convenient form, that the operator can use apart from the guide. For example, provide a reference card (Figure 10-9) that lists the key commands in your word-processing program. If procedures are complex, consider providing a job performance aid (JPA), which provides a step-by-step procedural summary of the task (Figure 10-10).

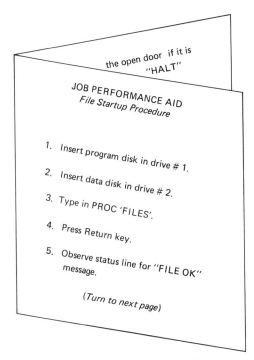

the open door if it is
"HALT"

JOB PERFORMANCE AID
File Startup Procedure

1. Insert program disk in drive # 1.
2. Insert data disk in drive # 2.
3. Type in PROC 'FILES'.
4. Press Return key.
5. Observe status line for "FILE OK" message.

(Turn to next page)

Figure 10-10   A job performance aid. The JPA is like the quick-reference card, but it describes the steps in a procedure. This is similar to the internal documentation in Figure 10-5.

• Write in the *active voice,* with *short sentences, concrete words,* and *numerous examples.* For good advice on how to write, buy Strunk and White's *The Elements of Style* (see the Bibliography), which is arguably the best book anyone has ever written on how to write expository prose that is simple and direct. This little book is a gem — informative, witty, and short.

Content of Guide.   The typical user's guide has three major sections:

1. Introduction
2. Tutorial
3. Reference material

The content of each of these sections is described in greater detail below.

Introduction.   The introduction should (1) introduce the reader to the program, and (2) explain the guide and how it is used. The required information may be organized in several different ways, and under different headings. The following are suggested headings and their content:

* **"Objectives of This Guide"** Explain what the guide is intended to do. For example, a guide such as the one described here is intended to (1) introduce the reader to the program, (2) help develop hands-on skill in using the program, and (3) provide necessary reference information for using the program after basic skills have been developed.
* **"How This Guide Is Organized"** List each major section of the guide, state its objectives, and describe its content. For example:

  Section 2 of this guide is a tutorial. Its objective is to help you develop basic hands-on skill in using the program. It is divided into nine parts. Each part contains hands-on exercises for you to follow while using your computer.

* **"How to Use This Guide"** This section contains the strategy for using the guide. The strategy reflects the structure of the guide — and vice versa. That is, the guide contains tutorial information to aid the new user as well as reference information to help the experienced user. Thus, the "How to Use This Guide" section offers advice such as the following:

  First, review the *equipment requirements* section to assure that your equipment is properly set up for using the program.
  If you are using the program for the first time, start with Chapter 1, which contains directions for using the *demonstration* program. The demonstration will familiarize you with the main features of the program.
  Next, go on to Chapters 2 through 9. Each of these chapters contains a tutorial dealing with a different aspect of the program. Read these chapters in order, and perform the exercises on your computer as you work your way through them.
  After completing the tutorial, review Chapter 10. Chapter 10 contains an alphabetic listing of the *key terms* used in the program. If you need to refresh your memory about a particular term, look it up in the alphabetic listing in Chapter 10.
  An *index* is provided to help you locate the terms and topics covered in this text. Use this to gain quick access to information.
  A *quick-reference card* is contained on the last page of this guide. Tear this out and keep it handy when you are using the program. It lists the special commands you will need to use the program.

* **"Definitions of Terms"** If you are using any special terms that need definition, list them and provide short definitions. Definitions

are usually in order if you have written a technical or scientific program that uses a vocabulary from a particular discipline, such as statistics, physics, or engineering.

- **"Equipment Requirements"** Identify the type of equipment required to use the program in terms of such things as type of computer, memory size, special processors, interfaces, disk drives, printer, modem, and so forth. If the equipment will operate in more than one configuration — for example, with or without a printer, or with either one or two disk drives — identify the preferred and alternate configurations. Here is an example of such an equipment requirement statement:

> This program is designed for use with a 64K Sirius computer with either two or three disk drives. A 132-column printer is recommended, but optional, as all printed reports have equivalent screen displays.

- **"Program Overview"** Briefly describe each of the major modules of your program in terms of its *purpose, content,* and *relationship* to other subprograms. The objective of this section is to familiarize the reader with the program modules and the relationships among them. It should prepare the reader for the program tutorial, which appears later in the user's guide.

The reader will use the overview to develop a framework for understanding your program. As the tutorial progresses, the reader will fill in the details. If you do not provide the framework in a preview, the reader will have to build one. If possible, provide a diagram which shows each program module and its relationships to every other module (e.g., Figure 10-1). This is fairly easy if you have a menu-driven program. In this case, prepare a diagram which shows each menu and its links to other menus. This will illustrate the program's structure nicely.

Tutorial. An important part of your user's guide is a program tutorial. Guidelines for preparing this tutorial are given below:

- Divide the tutorial into sections. Each section corresponds to one program module.
- Break up the sections into blocks that can be completed in about 1 hour by an inexperienced operator sitting before a computer. By breaking up your tutorial this way, you permit the user to complete it at an individual pace. If the tutorial is continuous, often the operator will have to break off in the middle and will lose the continuity of the exercise.

- Each section should start with a paragraph describing the module covered, its purpose, and its features. If the program is menu-driven, a convenient way of doing this is to present the menus accessed during the program and to describe each of the menu options.

- Give step-by-step instructions that will allow the reader to make entries, view displays, work through the program, and explore each of its features. The tutorial should be highly detailed and should not require the reader to make any assumptions or inferences in order to proceed. Rather, it should be in "cookbook" form.

- Describe each input that the operator must make, e.g., show each prompt line with completed entries.

- Illustrate the types of error messages that will occur with incorrect entries, and require the operator to experience some of these.

- Show the types of displays that will appear on the screen. Require the operator to make entries to call up these displays.

In short, *require operators to exercise every major facet of the program*. One of the major objectives of the tutorial is to help operators gain self-confidence in using the program. They will never develop confidence unless they actually work through the program, step by step, making inputs, generating reports, making errors, correcting them, and getting to the point where they have a feeling for the program "in their hands."

In writing the tutorial, bear in mind the publisher's advice to the programmer in the example earlier in this chapter. Assume that the reader knows where the on-off switch is and can turn the computer on. Unless you have strong evidence to the contrary, this is where you should set the level of your tutorial. This means that you must tell the reader even the most obvious things: which way to insert disks into drives, how to shut drive doors, the difference between moving the cursor with the space bar and with the cursor keys, and so forth.

The tutorial can be used for reference purposes — *if* you format it properly. The difference between a tutorial and reference information is that the tutorial is highly detailed and may take an entire page to make one point. Reference information, on the other hand, will make its point very concisely. You can make a tutorial useful for reference purposes by highlighting key points with graphic techniques such as boxes, a two-column format with the points listed in the left margin, colored type, or other imaginative techniques to make certain portions of the text stand out (Figure 10-11). The reader who wants to use the tutorial for reference purposes thus can readily spot a highlighted item, determine quickly whether or not it is of interest, and take the

Deleting and Retrieving Text

You will frequently want to delete text. For example, you will want to delete text if you make a mistake, if you change your mind about what you've written, or if you want to make changes to an old file.

There are several ways to delete text. We'll try the methods to see how they work.

Deleting Using the (DELETE) Key

The (DELETE) key removes text, which can never be retrieved.

When you use the (DELETE) key, you can never get your characters back.

Use the arrow keys to move the cursor just to the right of the last word, b u s i n e s s, in the second paragraph of PAPERSAVER.

What you do...

Press the (DELETE) key.

What you get...

One character is deleted from the word.

The longer you hold down the (DELETE) key, the more characters you will delete. Go ahead and use the (DELETE) key to remove characters and words in the second paragraph. Remember that when you delete with this key, your words are gone forever.

Deleting Using the ⓐ and ⊝ Keys

When you delete text by holding down the ⓐ key and pressing the ⊝ key, it can be retrieved by holding down the ⓐ key and pressing the ⊟ key.

In this method of deletion, characters can be retrieved.

Use the arrow keys to move the cursor to the right of the last word, m o n e y, in the third paragraph. **Apple Writer always deletes from the end of a specified text to its beginning.**

What you do...

Hold down the ⓐ key and press the ⊝ key.

What you get...

Characters are deleted as the cursor moves back over them, from right to left.

Keep holding down the ⓐ and press ⊝ several more times.

The entire word, m o n e y, is deleted.

Now suppose you didn't really mean to delete that word! Well, all is not lost. You can retrieve the word from memory.

Figure 10-11 An example of a tutorial which is formatted so that it can be used for reference purposes as well. This is a page from a tutorial in a word-processing program. It is highly procedure-oriented. The tutorial is contained in the right column. Key points and highlights are given in the left column. After working through the tutorial, the operator can refer to the key points in the left column for assistance in remembering the more detailed procedure on the right. (*Reprinted from the user's manual for the Applewriter II, copyright 1982, with permission from Apple Computer, Inc.*)

appropriate action. You can achieve a similar effect by sprinkling descriptive paragraph headings liberally throughout the text.

Reference Information. The final section of the user's guide contains reference information. The content of this reference information will vary with the program. Always provide an *index*. Also provide an *appendix* for each major class of reference information. For example, provide an appendix which summarizes the special commands required to use the program, the formulas used in generating reports, and a summary of any unique program input requirements.

A Good Example to Emulate

It is difficult to convey in this short chapter just what a user's guide should be like. It is even more difficult to write one. Nothing is more helpful than good examples of the genre, and there are probably none finer than those written for the Apple IIe computer. Apple released the Apple IIe with a set of user's manuals which are user-oriented, easy to read, and fully validated. These manuals constitute a milestone in the history of the microcomputer industry. Whether or not you use an Apple, your time would be well spent reviewing these manuals, particularly the *Applesoft Basic Programmer's Reference Manual*.

Eleven

Program Testing

Program testing is performed to assure the quality of the software product. The objectives of this testing are to identify any defects, or errors, in the program, and to assure that the program is usable by its intended audience. A program which has errors in it cannot be considered either usable or user-friendly. Being error-free is no guarantee that the program will be usable, although it is certainly a precondition.

Defects are inevitable in all but the most trivial programs. As a program grows larger, the probability of errors, and the effort required to find them, increase proportionately. If the programmer does not make sufficient effort to test the program, errors will remain and the program will be full of unpleasant surprises.

Errors vary in significance. Some, such as a misspelled prompt, do not significantly affect program performance and are not serious. Others, such as a file-writing routine which sometimes destroys records, are very serious. The former may be tolerable, but not the latter. However you test your program, you must identify and correct the serious errors that will prevent it from functioning properly.

There are many different program testing techniques. This chapter will avoid the theory and offer you a program testing strategy. It is possible, though unlikely, that you will want to adopt and apply verbatim the strategy described here. Your testing strategy should be tailored to the type of program, its user audience, and the consequences of the most serious error that can occur. You should take these factors into account and adapt this strategy to your needs.

Though there is more than one way to test a program, some testing principles are universal. The first of these is the familiar divide-and-conquer principle that was introduced in Chapter 4. In testing, we always start with the smallest program module, test it, then move upward in the scale of complexity to the level at which modules are combined, and so forth (Figure 11-1). There are many, many levels in a program and we must test them all systematically. Only at the end do we test the entire program as a unit.

The second principle is human myopia. This principle holds that every individual involved in a programming enterprise has blind spots that make it impossible for her or him to discover certain types of errors. This is because each individual develops habitual, stereotyped ways of doing things and will not explore every error path. Other people, with different biases, will use the program differently and explore different error paths. This is why it is so important for program testing to involve a team of individuals with different backgrounds and computer skills.

The program testing process is often described as having three phases, and the following discussion is based on this convention.

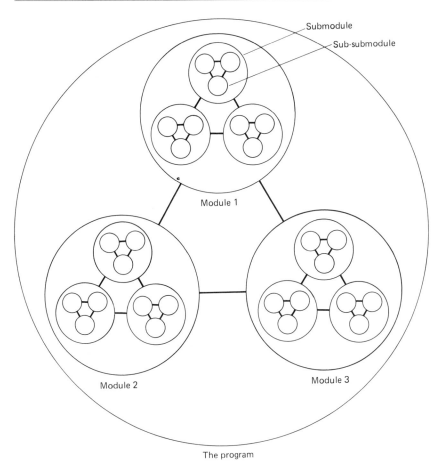

Figure 11-1 Program modules, and the relationships among them, can be represented as circles within circles, with each circle linked to others. Program testing begins with the smallest modules and moves gradually to larger and larger modules, until the entire program is tested in the end. A defect in any module, at whatever level, affects program performance.

- *Phase 1: module testing.* During this phase, individual program modules are tested.

- *Phase 2: integration testing.* During this phase, modules are combined and tested together. Phases 1 and 2 are usually carried out by programmers and uncover routine programming errors, design errors, and shortcomings in the program specification. By the end of phase 2, all the technical problems in the program should be uncovered and corrected.

- *Phase 3: acceptance testing.* During this phase, the program is put through its paces by representatives of its target audience. The objective of phase 3 is to determine the program's shortcomings from the user's viewpoint and to correct these shortcomings. The concern is not so much with technical errors as with program usability. A program may be technically sound, but unusable. (This has been known to occur.) Sometimes program developers overlook phase 3 and never validate their program with its intended audience. When this blunder is made, the result may be a program that works fine when operated by its developers but not when operated by its intended users. The developer who makes this blunder will tend to blame the program's failure on operators, which really misses the point. The program must be fitted to the operators, not the other way around. Making it usable is the programmer's responsibility.

The testing strategy described in this chapter consists of these three phases. Each phase is discussed in greater detail in the sections below.

PHASE 1: MODULE TESTING

Informal Testing

Programming is rather like building a house with bricks. A difference is that programmers must make their own bricks, or lines of program code. A module may be a single line of code, such as a short subroutine, or several hundred lines designed to perform a particular function.

Programmers test their modules informally as they create them. This procedure will uncover the errors that programmers anticipate and test for, but it will miss those they overlook. The primary goal of programmers is to get the program up and running, not to test it. Though they may be very conscientious, they will seldom test systematically or thoroughly.

Formal Testing

Program modules must be tested by someone other than the programmer. It does not make sense to send very small program modules out for testing, but does make sense when a module consists of, say, all or most of a complete subprogram. When the program's author has completed the module and is satisfied, it should be submitted to someone else for testing.

The Expert Operator. An effective technique for testing a module is to use a second programmer, or a team of programmers, as expert operators. Programmers have the sophistication to know how and what to test for, and they are ideally suited to do this job. Further, they are effective at diagnosing problems and communicating with the program's author.

Expert operators should test each module to determine whether or not it is performing according to the design specification. It is *not* their job to troubleshoot the program code. Rather, their job is to identify defects and bring them to the author's attention. The author then makes the fixes. The tester is essentially a foil for the program's author. More a helper to the author than a critic, the tester relieves the author of worrying about and carrying out all the routine testing that is required during program development.

If the program is complex, it is best to use a team of expert operators rather than one individual. Each tester will have a slightly different point of view and different blind spots. The more perspectives brought to bear on the program, the greater the likelihood of uncovering its defects.

A tester does not have to work at the job full-time. In fact, if a team of programmers is working together on different projects, they can perform the testing function for each other while carrying on their own program development efforts.

A Testing Strategy. What program testers do is sometimes described as running little controlled experiments. In practice, their behavior is similar to scientific research. They develop hypotheses about the types of errors that will occur, create artificial data sets to test their hypotheses, enter their data, and obtain results. If the results are not what they should be according to the specification, then their hypotheses are satisfied and the error they anticipated has occurred.

Of course, the trick in program testing, as in scientific research, is to develop the right hypotheses and carry out the appropriate tests. Knowing what questions to ask takes ingenuity and experience. For the experienced tester, as for the scientific researcher, planning the experiment is a more routine matter. The most difficult part is to frame the questions, i.e., to anticipate what might go wrong in the program.

Teams are almost always better at this than individuals. Three people sitting around a table can usually stimulate each other's thoughts and develop a more complete list of possible problems than one person working alone. However, the potential success of a meeting in stirring up original ideas is very much a function of the personalities involved and their particular working styles. Some programmers work well in teams, and others work better alone.

Iterative Testing. During program development, testers will usually test a program module several times. They will test it initially when the author first delivers it and will report defects to the author.

The author will then attempt to correct the defects and resubmit it to the testers. This cycle may be repeated several times.

Record Keeping. It is important for testers to maintain records so that they can repeat tests which earlier caused the program to misbehave. One simple and effective technique for record keeping is to maintain a manila folder for each program module, containing a log of defects observed and dates. Each time the module is tested or retested, the tester can refer to the log to determine what things to test for. The folder is also handy for storing hard copies of printed reports, printouts of display screens, and whatever else the tester needs to keep track of. Some testers prefer notebooks, or other types of records. The form of the records is not really important. What *is* important is that they are kept.

Test Management. A program module will generally move through the following stages of development:

* Not started
* In process (being programmed)
* Undergoing module (phase 1) testing
* Undergoing integration (phase 2) testing
* Undergoing acceptance (phase 3) testing

If your program has more than a few modules, keep a written record of the progress of each module. You can do this by preparing a chart which lists the modules down the side and the testing phases across the top (Figure 11-2).

If a module is progressing satisfactorily, it should move gradually through the various steps. Some reverses are inevitable, but the general movement should be forward, or left to right, on the chart. Record keeping consists of writing a date in the appropriate cell of the matrix. A chart such as this is helpful because it tells you at a glance how program development is going. It will also keep you from overlooking tests that need to be performed.

PHASE 2: INTEGRATION TESTING

Description

During integration testing, individual program modules are combined and tested as a unit. In the usual description of testing procedures,

TEST STATUS CHART

Module name	Not started	In process	Phase 1	Phase 2	Phase 3,
Main driver	—	$11/1$	$11/22$	$12/6$	
File create	—	$11/15$	$11/27$	$12/18$	
Data input • Form 1	—	$12/21$	$1/6$		
• Form 2	—	$1/6$	$1/13$		
• Form 3	—	$1/4$	$1/11$		
• Form 4	—	$1/5$	$1/21$		
Reports • Table 1	✓				
• Table 2	✓				
• Table 3	✓				

Figure 11-2   A test status chart, such as this, is helpful in managing the development of complex programs. The status of each module is shown on the chart by writing the date the module entered the testing phase identified at the top of the column.

integration testing is broken out conveniently as a unique and logical phase of the testing process. The problem with this is that a program is not usually made up of logical modules that can be tested individually and then combined together. What a module consists of changes depending upon what level you slice things at. A program of any complexity at all is a hierarchical structure, with many levels of organization.

At the lower levels of organization — e.g., single lines of code, subroutines, short sections of code which perform functions — integration testing is performed by the program author. Typically, it is only at the higher levels of organization — e.g., complete subprograms — that outside testers become involved. The program author will, of course, perform such testing also, but not in the same way as the outside tester.

Relation to Module Testing

In practical terms, integration testing is indistinguishable from module testing. The tester will continue to work with the program and attempt to identify defects. These will be reported back to the author, who will revise the program and resubmit it to the tester, who will test it again, return it to the author, and so on, in a cycle that will end only when the tester is satisfied.

Getting Ready for Acceptance Testing

When the tester is finally satisfied, then the program is ready for acceptance testing by real (i.e., nonprogrammer) operators. Acceptance testing should not start until the program's author and all those involved in testing are satisfied that the program is clear of defects. Acceptance testing is not intended to reveal program defects and should not be used for that purpose. The version of the program that is used for acceptance testing should, in the program developer's opinion, be finished and publishable. However, keep in mind that the acceptance testers will probably soon reveal the fallacy of this opinion.

PHASE 3: ACCEPTANCE TESTING

Purpose

The purpose of acceptance testing is to determine how well typical operators can use the program. This will be a function of the program's basic design and the quality of the human-computer interface. Note that this purpose differs from that of phases 1 and 2, which focus on the detection of programming and design defects that have nothing to do with the program's use by an operator. It is true that acceptance testing often will lead to the discovery of technical flaws, as some will slip through earlier tests. However, it is important to bear in mind that phase 3 is not focused on or primarily intended to uncover such defects. Rather, its concern is with the human-computer interface itself. In short, phase 3 is where you test how well you have human-factored your program.

Degree of Completeness of Program

Acceptance tests should be conducted on a complete program. The realities of program development are such that this will often be impossible, and acceptance testing must occur concurrently with module and integration testing. If this is the case, whatever modules are subjected to acceptance testing should be in complete form, and with adequate user documentation. You cannot conduct a proper acceptance test with less.

Choosing the Operators

Select operators who are typical of the eventual users of the program. They should have the background, technical knowledge, and skills that you expect in the target audience. Unless this audience includes programmers, do not include programmers in acceptance testing. Programmers are not typical users — they can overcome many obstacles that nonprogrammers cannot. Using programmers would compromise the fairness of acceptance testing.

Number of Operators

The number of operators to use in acceptance testing depends upon the program and its complexity. The minimum number recommended for acceptance testing is about five. For a very simple program, you might be able to get away with fewer, but this is risky. For most programs, ten is about the right number.

Training the Operators

Give all operators appropriate training for using the program and provide them with user documentation. Assign them specific operator tasks to perform. The nature of these tasks depends upon the program. Make up a set of work assignments for all testers that requires them to exercise all the features of the program. If testing all the features is left to the operators, many things will be missed. It is your responsibility to assure that the program is fully tested.

The Operator's Log

Instruct all operators to keep a log of their experiences in using the program. In this log, they should record the following information:

* Identification information (name, program module, date)
* Any errors that occur (line number, error code, description of error)
* Problems experienced in using the program (e.g., data input, display interpretation, control)
* Suggestions for improvements

The operator's log is a sort of diary, to be completed as each task assignment is performed. It is a record of both objective information concerning program defects (e.g., error code numbers) and the operator's subjective experiences in using the program (e.g., difficulties in entering data, interpreting displays, controlling what goes on).

The objective information can be acted on directly — the programmer can correct the defect. The subjective information must be interpreted by programmers and designers. This interpretation can be aided greatly by interviewing the users on an individual basis to question them about their experiences. The log will not be as complete as the verbal description users give when you interview them.

Program Modifications

At intervals during testing, interview all operators and check their logs. After interviewing several users, get together with the design team and decide what program changes, if any, to make to the program. The primary concern is the human-computer interface. Routine program errors can be taken care of easily enough, but it is much more difficult to revise a design to improve its human-computer interface.

A program may be functionally sound, but operators may have difficulty using it. They may, for example, find the program control method awkward to use — that it takes too may keystrokes to get from one part of the program to another. They may feel that error messages are unclear, or that the program is too unforgiving of operator errors. In short, they may point out any of the interface problems that this book was written to prevent.

In reviewing operators' remarks and logs, be particularly alert to comments that reflect any of the following major classes of problems:

- *Level at which the program is written.*   How difficult is the program to use? Do typical operators feel that it is beyond their capabilities? This may be the case if you have used a sophisticated control technique or have departed from conventions. Other possible causes include poor prompting, obscure displays, and poor documentation.

- *Task performance.*   Has the program been designed to aid operators in performing specific tasks? Each of these tasks usually involves several steps. If the program is poorly designed, performing a task may require too many steps, may involve detours, or may have traps which permit the task to be aborted unintentionally. How difficult it is to perform a task is not so much a function of individual input routines, displays, or the control technique, but the combination of all these things.

- *Input routines.*   How successfully can operators enter data? Recover from errors? Correct errors they have made?

- *Output.*   Are the displays well designed? Should any displays be redesigned for greater clarity or ease of use? Should some displays be

combined, and others divided? Should additional displays be provided? Are any displays unnecessary?

- *Program control.* Is the control technique logical, straightforward,
  and easy to use once learned? If the program is designed for occa-
  sional users, can the control technique be learned quickly? Is the
  control structure logical and easy to understand?

- *User documentation.* Does program documentation — both internal
  and external — successfully help the operator use the program? The
  acid test of this is whether operators can employ the program using
  documentation alone, and without getting outside help from members of the design team. Documentation is fully as important as the
  program, and program testing should address its shortcomings as
  well as those of the program. The solution to many problems may lie
  in documentation, not a revision to the program.

Beta Testing

The acceptance tests described above involve operators who work
closely with the design group. A small group of operators participates,
and each uses the program according to a plan. These operators are
essentially an extension of the design group.

At some point, everyone on the program development team — programmer, expert operators, operators participating in acceptance tests
— will be (more or less) satisfied with the program and its documentation. At that point, the program is ready for further acceptance tests,
by a larger group of operators in a much less controlled environment.

There are two basic approaches to what to do once a program has
reached this stage. The first is to distribute it to beta testing sites, i.e.,
locations where the program will be put through its paces by operators
who are totally independent of the design group. There are organiza-
tions and people who are expert at wringing out a program this way,
and who invariably uncover shortcomings that are not observed during
the testing conducted by the program developer.

The second approach is to publish the program and let users do the
beta testing for you. This approach is often criticized as cynical; if the
program is distributed full of defects, then certainly the approach is
cynical. On the other hand, if the program is simple and acceptance
testing has been thorough, there is a good chance that all serious
defects have been identified and corrected. If the publisher maintains a
responsive customer service organization (preferably a hot line) which
promptly responds to user problems; if every defect, however small, is
corrected; and if users are provided with upgraded versions of the
program at little or no cost — then this approach is defensible.

You can never expect to ship a perfect program, unless that program is of a trivial nature or you have an infinite amount of time and money to spend on its testing. Still, you must ship the best program that you can and take care of your customers from that point on.

Ultimately, what and when you ship is a reflection of your own attitude about the quality of things. Whether you follow the testing strategy described in this chapter or some other strategy makes much less difference than the care you take in testing and the standards you set for yourself.

Bibliography

Adams, D.: *The Hitchhiker's Guide to the Galaxy*, Pocket Books, New York, 1979.

Albert, A. E.: "The Effect of Graphic Input Devices on Performance in a Cursor Positioning Task," *Proceedings of the Human Factors Society 26th Annual Meeting*, 1982, pp. 54–58.

Alden, D., R. Daniels, and A. Kanarick: "Keyboard Design and Operation: A Review of the Major Issues," *Human Factors*, vol. 14(4), 1972, pp. 275–293.

Anderson, J. R., and G. H. Bower: "Recognition and Retrieval Processes in Free Recall," *Psychological Review*, vol. 79(2), 1972, pp. 97–123.

Bailey, R. W.: *Human Error in Computer Systems*, Prentice-Hall, Englewood Cliffs, N.J., 1983.

———: *Human Performance Engineering: A Guide for System Designers*, Prentice-Hall, Englewood Cliffs, N.J., 1982.

Ballantine, M.: "Conversing with Computers — The Dream and the Controversy," *Ergonomics*, vol. 23(9), 1980, pp. 935–945.

Barnard, P., N. Hamond, A. MacLean, and J. Morton: "Learning and Remembering Interactive Commands," *Proceedings, Human Factors in Computer Systems*, March 1982, pp. 2–7.

Bartlett, J., and J. Walter (eds.): *Conference Proceedings: International Conference on Systems Documentation, January 22–23, 1982*, Association for Computing Machinery, New York, 1982.

Bell, T.: "Talk to Me," *Personal Computing*, September 1983.

Benbasat, I., A. S. Dexter, and P. S. Masulis: "An Experimental Study of the Human/Computer Interface," *Communications of the ACM*, vol. 24(11), 1981, pp. 739–751.

Billingsley, P. A.: "Navigation through Hierarchical Menu Structures: Does It Help to Have a Map?" *Proceedings of the Human Factors Society 26th Annual Meeting*, 1982, pp. 103–107.

Black, J. B., and T. P. Moran: "Learning and Remembering Command Names," *Proceedings, Human Factors in Computer Systems*, March 1982, pp. 8–11.

Booher, H. R.: "Relative Comprehensibility of Pictorial Information and Printed Words in Proceduralized Instructions," *Human Factors*, vol. 17, 1975, pp. 266–277.

Borman, L., and R. Karr: "Efficient for Computers or Easy for People? Evaluating the 'Friendliness' of a Timesharing System," *Proceedings, Human Interaction and the Computer Interface*, January 1982, pp. 31–34.

Bury, K. F., J. M. Boyle, R. J. Evey, and A. S. Neal: "Windowing Versus Scrolling on a Visual Display Terminal," *Human Factors*, vol. 24(4), 1982, pp. 385–394.

Butterbaugh, L. C.: "Evaluation of Alternative Alphanumeric Keying Logics," *Human Factors*, vol. 24(5), 1982, pp. 521–533.

Cakir, A., D. J. Hart, and T. F. M. Stewart: *Visual Display Terminals. A Manual Covering Ergonomics, Workplace Design, Health and Safety, and Task Organization*, Wiley, New York, 1980.

Card, S. K.: "User Perceptual Mechanisms in the Search of Computer Command Menus," *Proceedings, Human Factors in Computer Systems*, March 1982, pp. 190–196.

———, W. K. English, and B. J. Burr: "Evaluation of Mouse, Rate-Controlled Isometric Joystick, Step Keys, and Text Keys for Text Selection on a CRT," *Ergonomics*, vol. 21(8), 1978, pp. 601–613.

———, T. P. Moran, and A. Newell: "The Keystroke-Level Model for User Performance Time with Interactive Systems," *Communications of the ACM*, vol. 23(7), 1980, pp. 396–410.

———, ———, and ———: *The Psychology of Human-Computer Interaction*, Lawrence Erlbaum, Hillsdale, N.J., 1983.

Chapanis, A.: *Man-Machine Engineering*, Brooks/Cole, Monterey, Calif., 1965.

———: *Research Techniques in Human Engineering*, Johns Hopkins, Baltimore, Md., 1959.

Christ, R. E.: "Review and Analysis of Color Coding Research for Visual Displays," *Human Factors*, vol. 17, 1975, pp. 542–570.

Clarke, A. C.: *2001: A Space Odyssey*, The New American Library, New York, 1968.

Cohill, A. M., and R. C. Williges: "Computer-Augmented Retrieval of Help Information for Novice Users," *Proceedings of the Human Factors Society 26th Annual Meeting*, 1982, pp. 79–82.

Craik, F. I. M., and E. Tulving: "Depth of Processing and the Retention of Words in Episodic Memory," *Journal of Experimental Psychology: General*, vol. 104(3), 1975, pp. 268–294.

Crowder, R. G.: *Principles of Learning and Memory*, Lawrence Erlbaum, Hillsdale, N.J., 1976.

Curtis, B.: "A Review of Human Factors Research on Programming Languages and Specifications," *Proceedings, Human Factors in Computer Systems*, March 1982, pp. 212–218.

—— (ed.): *Tutorial: Human Factors in Software Development*, IEEE Computer Society, New York, 1981.

Dainoff, M. J., and A. Happ: "Visual Fatigue and Occupational Stress in VDT Operators," *Human Factors*, vol. 23(4), 1981, pp. 421–438.

deKleer, J., and J. S. Brown: "Mental Models of Physical Mechanisms and Their Acquisition," in J. R. Anderson (ed.), *Cognitive Skills and Their Acquisition*, Lawrence Erlbaum, Hillsdale, N.J., 1981.

Diffrient, N., A. R. Tilley, D. Harman, and J. C. Bardagjy: *Humanscale 1/2/3, 4/5/6, 7/8/9*, M.I.T., Cambridge, Mass., 1981.

Durding, B. M., C. A. Becker, and J. D. Gould: "Data Organization," *Human Factors*, vol. 19(1), 1977, pp. 1–14.

Durrett, J., and J. Trezona: "How to Use Color Displays Effectively," *BYTE*, April 1982.

Eastman Kodak Company: *Ergonomic Design for People at Work: Volume I*, Lifetime Learning Publications, Belmont, Calif., 1983.

Egly, D. H.: "Cognitive Style, Categorization and Vocational Effects on Performance of REL Database Users," *Proceedings, Human Interaction and the User Interface*, January 1982, pp. 91–97.

Ehrenreich, S. L.: "Query Languages: Design Recommendations Derived from the Human Factors Literature," *Human Factors*, vol. 23(6), 1981, pp. 709–725.

Elkerton, J., R. C. Williges, J. A. Pittman, and J. Roach: "Strategies of Interactive File Search," *Proceedings of the Human Factors Society 26th Annual Meeting*, 1982, pp. 83–86.

Engel, S. E., and R. E. Granda: *Guidelines for Man/Display Interfaces*, Technical Report TR 00.2720, IBM, Poughkeepsie, N.Y., December 1975.

Freeman, P., and A. I. Wasserman (eds.): *Tutorial on Software Design Techniques*, IEEE Computer Society, New York, 1980.

Fuller, R. G.: *Maintenance Performance Systems (Organizational). I&ES Operating Manual*. Technical Report 465-12, Anacapa Sciences, Inc., Santa Barbara, Calif., December 1981.

Funk, K., and E. McDowell: "Voice Input/Output in Perspective," *Proceedings of the Human Factors Society 26th Annual Meeting*, January 1982, pp. 218–222.

Gade, P. A., A. F. Fields, R. E. Maisano, C. F. Marshall, and I. N. Alderman: "Data Entry Performance as a Function of Method and Instructional Strategy," *Human Factors*, vol. 23(2), 1981, pp. 199–210.

Glass, R. L.: "Real-Time: The 'Lost World' of Software Debugging and Testing," *Communications of the ACM*, vol. 23(5), 1980, pp. 264–271.

Gold, B.: *Maintenance Performance Systems (Organizational). IBM 5120 Programmers Reference Manual. Volume 1: General Program Description. Volume 2: Program Listing*, Technical Report 465-16, Anacapa Sciences, Inc., Santa Barbara, Calif., January 1982.

Goldman, S. R., and J. W. Pellegrino: "Processing Domain, Encoding Elaboration, and Memory Trace Strength," *Journal of Verbal Learning and Verbal Behavior*, vol. 16, 1977, pp. 29–43.

Goodwin, N. C.: "Cursor Positioning on an Electronic Display Using Lightpen, Lightgun, or Keyboard for Three Basic Tasks," *Human Factors*, vol. 17(3), 1975, pp. 289–295.

Granda, R. E., R. C. Teitelbaum, and G. L. Dunlap: "The Effect of VDT Command Line Location on Data Entry Behavior," *Proceedings of the Human Factors Society 26th Annual Meeting*, 1982, pp. 621–624.

Grandjean, E.: *Fitting the Task to the Man*, Taylor and Francis, London, 1971.

———, W. Huntirg, and M. Piderman: "VDT Workstation Design: Preferred Settings and Their Effects," *Human Factors*, vol. 25(2), 1983, pp. 161–175.

———, ———, G. Wotzka, and R. Sharen: "An Ergonomic Investigation of Multipurpose Chairs," *Human Factors*, vol. 15(3), 1973, pp. 246–255.

——— and E. Vigliani (eds.): *Ergonomic Aspects of Visual Display Terminals*, Taylor and Francis, London, 1980.

Harris, D. H.: *Fundamentals of Human Factors for Engineering and Design*, Anacapa Sciences, Inc., Santa Barbara, Calif., 1983.

——— and F. B. Chaney: *Human Factors in Quality Assurance*, Wiley, New York, 1969.

Hemenway, K.: "Psychological Issues in the Use of Icons in Command Menus," *Proceedings, Human Factors in Computer Systems*, 1982, pp. 20–23.

Hendricks, D. E., P. W. Kilduff, P. Brooks, R. Marshak, and B. Doyle: *Human Engineering Guidelines for Management Information Systems*, U.S. Army Materiel Development and Readiness Command and U.S. Army Human Engineering Laboratory, Washington, D.C., 1983.

Hiltz, S. R., and M. Turoff: "Human Diversity and the Choice of Interface," *Proceedings, Human Interaction and the User Interface*, January 1982, pp. 125–130.

Hirshon, B.: "Putting Color Graphics on Paper," *Digital Design*, July 1983.

House, R.: "Comments on Program Specification and Testing," *Communications of the ACM*, vol. 23(6), 1980, pp. 324–331.

Isensee, S. H., and C. A. Bennett: "The Perception of Flicker and Glare on Computer CRT Displays," *Human Factors*, vol. 25(2), 1983, pp. 177–184.

Jayaraman, M. J., M. J. Lee, and M. Konopasek: "Human-Computer Interface Considerations in the Design of Personal Computer Software," *Proceedings, Human Factors in Computer Systems,* March 1982, pp. 58–62.

Jeffries, R., A. A. Turner, and P. G. Polson: "The Processes Involved in Designing Software," in J. R. Anderson (ed.), *Cognitive Skills and Their Acquisitions,* Lawrence Erlbaum, Hillsdale, N.J., 1981.

Kamins, S.: *Applesoft BASIC Programmer's Reference Manual,* Apple Computer, Inc., Cupertino, Calif., 1982.

—— and M. Waite: *Apple Backpack: Humanized Programming in BASIC,* McGraw-Hill, New York, 1982.

Kantowitz, B. H., and R. D. Sorkin: *Human Factors: Understanding People-System Relationships,* Wiley, New York, 1983.

Kennedy, P. J.: "Development and Testing of the Operator Training Package for a Small Computer System," *Proceedings of the Human Factors Society 26th Annual Meeting,* 1982, pp. 715–719.

Kernighan, B. W., and P. J. Plauger: *The Elements of Programming Style,* McGraw-Hill, New York, 1974.

Klensin, J. C.: "Short-Term Friendly and Long-Term Hostile?" *Proceedings, Human Interaction and the User Interface,* January 1982, pp. 105–110.

Kroemer, K.: "Human Engineering the Keyboard," *Human Factors,* vol. 14(1), 1972, pp. 51–63.

Lachman, R., J. L. Lachman, and E. C. Butterfield: *Cognitive Psychology and Information Processing,* Lawrence Erlbaum, Hillsdale, N.J., 1979.

Langley, P., and P. Simon: "The Central Role of Learning in Cognition," in J. R. Anderson (ed.), *Cognitive Skills and Their Acquisition,* Lawrence Erlbaum, Hillsdale, N.J., 1981.

Ledgard, H., J. A. Whiteside, A. Singer, and W. Seymour, "The Natural Language of Interactive Systems," *Communications of the ACM,* vol. 23(10), 1980, pp. 556–563.

Liebelt, L. S., J. E. McDonald, J. D. Stone, and J. Karat: "The Effect of Organization on Learning Menu Access," *Proceedings of the Human Factors Society 26th Annual Meeting,* 1982, pp. 546–550.

Lientz, B. P., and E. B. Swanson: "Problems in Application Software Maintenance," *Communications of the ACM,* vol. 24(11), 1981, pp. 763–769.

Ling, R. F.: "General Considerations in the Design of an Interactive System for Data Analysis," *Communications of the ACM,* vol. 23(3), 1980, pp. 247–254.

Martin, J.: *Design of Man-Computer Dialogues,* Prentice-Hall, Englewood Cliffs, N.J., 1973.

——: *Design of Real-Time Computer Systems,* Prentice-Hall, Englewood Cliffs, N.J., 1967.

Mayer, R. E.: "The Psychology of How Novices Learn Computer Programming," *Computing Surveys*, vol. 13(1), 1981, pp. 121–141.

————: "A Psychology of Learning BASIC," *Communications of the ACM*, vol. 22(11), 1979, pp. 589–593.

———— and P. Bayman: "Psychology of Calculator Languages: A Framework for Describing Differences in User Knowledge," *Communications of the ACM*, vol. 24(8), 1981, pp. 511–520.

McCormick, E. J.: *Human Factors in Engineering and Design*, McGraw-Hill, New York, 1976.

McTyre, J. H.: "Legibility Comparison of 7 by 7 and 7 by 9 CRT Dot Matrices," *Proceedings of the Human Factors Society 26th Annual Meeting*, 1982, pp. 710–714.

Meister, D.: *Human Factors: Theory and Practice*, Wiley, New York, 1971.

Metzger, P. W.: *Managing a Programming Project*, Prentice-Hall, Englewood Cliffs, N.J., 1981.

Military Specification: Human Engineering Requirements for Military Systems, Equipment and Facilities (MIL-H-48655B), Department of Defense, Washington, D.C., January 1979.

Military Standard 1280: Keyboard Arrangements (MIL-STD-1280), January 1969.

Military Standard 1472B: Human Engineering Design Criteria for Military Systems, Equipment, and Facilities (MIL-STD-1472B), Department of Defense, Washington, D.C., December 1974.

Military Standard 1472C: Human Engineering Design Criteria for Military Systems, Equipment and Facilities (MIL-STD-1472C), Department of Defense, Washington, D.C., May 1981.

Military Standardization Handbook: Human Factors Engineering Design for Army Materiel (MIL-HDBK-759), Department of Defense, Washington, D.C., 1981.

Miller, D. P.: "The Depth/Breadth Tradeoff in Hierarchical Computer Menus," *Proceedings of the Human Factors Society 25th Annual Meeting*, 1981, pp. 296–300.

Miller, G. A.: "The Magic Number Seven, Plus or Minus Two: Some Limits on Our Capacity to Process Information," *Psychological Review*, vol. 63, 1956, pp. 81–97.

Miller, R. B.: "Response Time in User-System Conversational Transactions," *Proceedings of the AFIPS Fall Joint Computer Conference*, vol. 33, 1968, pp. 267–277.

Moreland, D. V.: "Human Factors Guidelines for Terminal Interface Design," *Communications of the ACM*, vol. 26(7), 1983, pp. 484–494.

Morgan, C. T., J. S. Cook, A. Chapanis, and M. W. Lund (eds.): *Human Engineering Guide to Equipment Design*, McGraw-Hill, New York, 1963.

Mourant, R. R., R. Lakshmanan, and R. Chantadisai: "Visual Fatigue and Cathode Ray Tube Display Terminals," *Human Factors*, vol. 23(5), 1981, pp. 529–540.

Nagin, P., and H. F. Ledgard: *BASIC with Style: Programming Proverbs*, Hayden, Rochelle Park, N.J., 1978.

Neal, A. S., and W. H. Emmons: "Operator Corrections during Text Entry with Word Processing Systems," *Proceedings of the Human Factors Society 26th Annual Meeting*, 1982, pp. 625–628.

Newell, A., and P. S. Rosenbloom: "Mechanisms of Skill Acquisition and the Law of Practice," in J. R. Anderson (ed.), *Cognitive Skills and Their Acquisition*, Lawrence Erlbaum, Hillsdale, N.J., 1981.

Newman, W. M., and R. F. Sproull: *Principles of Interactive Computer Graphics*, McGraw-Hill, New York, 1979.

Norman, D. A.: "Design Rules Based on Analyses of Human Error," *Communications of the ACM*, vol. 26(4), 1984, pp. 254–258.

————: "Some Observations on Mental Models," *Five Papers on Human-Machine Interaction*, Technical Report ONR-8205, Center for Human Information Processing, La Jolla, Calif., May 1982, pp. 2–9.

————: "The Trouble with UNIX," *Datamation*, November 1981.

Paivio, A., and I. Begg: *Psychology of Language*, Prentice-Hall, Englewood Cliffs, N.J., 1981.

Pastoor, S., E. Schwartz, and I. Beldie: "The Relative Suitability of Four Dot-Matrix Sizes for Text Presentation on Color Television Screens," *Human Factors*, vol. 25(3), 1983, pp. 265–272.

Posner, M. I.: "Short Term Memory Systems in Human Information Processing," *Acta Psychologica*, vol. 27, 1967, pp. 267–283.

———— and S. J. Boies, "Components of Attention," *Psychological Review*, vol. 78, 1971, pp. 391–408.

Ramsey, H. R., and M. E. Atwood, *Human Factors in Computer Systems: A Review of the Literature*, Technical Report SAI-79-111-DEN, Science Applications, Inc., Englewood, Colo., September 1979.

————, ————, and J. R. Van Doren: "Flowcharts versus Program Design Languages: An Experimental Comparison," *Communications of the ACM*, vol. 26(6), 1983, pp. 445–449.

Rogers, S. P., and C. J. Jarosz: *Evaluation of Map Symbols for a Computer-Generated Topographic Display: Transfer of Training, Symbol Confusion, and Association Value Studies*, Anacapa Sciences, Inc., Santa Barbara, Calif., December 1982.

—— and M. C. McCallum: *Application of Coding Methods in Development of Symbology for a Computer-Generated Topographic Display for Army Aviators*, Anacapa Sciences, Inc., Santa Barbara, Calif., March 1982.

Rumelhart, D. E., and D. A. Norman: "Analogical Processes in Learning," in J. R. Anderson (ed.), *Cognitive Skills and Their Acquisition*, Lawrence Erlbaum, Hillsdale, N.J., 1981.

Savage, R. E., J. Habinek, and T. Barnhart: "The Design, Simulation, and Evaluation of a Menu Driven User Interface," *Proceedings, Human Factors in Computer Systems*, March 1982, pp. 36–40.

——, ——, and N. J. Blakstad: "An Experimental Evaluation of Input Field and Cursor Combinations," *Proceedings of the Human Factors Society 26th Annual Meeting*, January 1982, pp. 629–633.

Scapin, D.: "Computer Commands in Restricted Natural Language: Some Aspects of Memory and Experience," *Human Factors*, vol. 23(3), 1981, pp. 365–375.

Schwarz, E., I. Beldie, and S. Pastoor: "A Comparison of Paging and Scrolling for Changing Screen Contents by Inexperienced Users," *Human Factors*, vol. 25(3), 1983, pp. 279–282.

Shackel, B.: "Dialogues and Language — Can Computer Ergonomics Help?" *Ergonomics*, vol. 23(9), 1980, pp. 857–880.

Shneiderman, B.: *Software Psychology: Human Factors in Computer and Information Systems*, Winthrop Publishers, Inc., Cambridge, Mass., 1980.

Simpson, H.: "A Human-Factors Style Guide for Program Design," *BYTE*, April 1982, pp. 108–132.

——: *Maintenance Performance Systems (Organizational). Information and Evaluation System Design Specification, Volume I*. Technical Report 465-6, Anacapa Sciences, Inc., Santa Barbara, Calif., June 1981.

——: *Maintenance Performance Systems Program Development Specification*, Anacapa Sciences, Inc., Santa Barbara, Calif., August 1980.

——: "Printers '77," *Digital Design*, October, 1977.

——: "Terminals: CRT's, Printing and Graphic," *Digital Design*, January 1978.

—— and J. C. Gutmann: *Maintenance Performance Systems (Organizational). I&ES Evaluation Plan*, Technical Report 465-9, Anacapa Sciences, Inc., Santa Barbara, Calif., August 1981.

Smith, M. J., B. G. F. Cohen, and L. W. Stammerjohn: "An Investigation of Health Complaints and Job Stress in Video Display Operations," *Human Factors*, vol. 23(4), 1981, pp. 387–400.

Smith, S. L.: "Color Coding and Visual Search," *Journal of Experimental Psychology*, vol. 64(5), 1962, pp. 434–440.

————: *Man-Machine Interface (MMI) Requirements Definition and Design Guidelines: A Progress Report*, Technical Report ESD-TR-81-113, MTR-8134, The Mitre Corp., Bedford, Mass., February 1981.

———— and A. F. Aucella: *Design Guidelines for the User Interface to Computer-Based Information Systems*, ESD-TR-83-122, MTR 8857, The Mitre Corp., Bedford, Mass., March 1983.

Stammerjohn, L. W., M. J. Smith, and B. G. F. Cohen: "Evaluation of Work Station Design Factors in VDT Operations," *Human Factors*, vol. 23(4), 1981, pp. 401–412.

Steele, R. W.: "Evaluating Small Systems Applications Software," *Microcomputing*, June 1980.

Stewart, T.: "Communicating with Dialogues," *Ergonomics*, vol. 23(9), 1980, pp. 909–919.

Strunk, W., and E. B. White: *The Elements of Style*, Macmillan, New York, 1959.

Suther, T. W., and J. H. McTyre: "Effect on Operator Performance at Thin Profile Keyboard Slopes of 5°, 10°, 15°, and 25°," *Proceedings of the Human Factors Society 26th Annual Meeting*, January 1982, pp. 430–434.

Tullis, T. S.: "An Evaluation of Alphanumeric, Graphic, and Color Information Displays," *Human Factors*, vol. 23(5), 1981, pp. 541–550.

Turner, J.: "The Structure of Modular Programs," *Communications of the ACM*, vol. 23(5), 1980, pp. 272–277.

Tyler, S. W., S. Roth, and T. Post: "The Acquisition of Text Editing Skills," *Proceedings, Human Factors in Computer Systems*, 1982, pp. 324–325.

Van Cott, H. P., and R. G. Kinkade (eds.): *Human Engineering Guide to Equipment Design*, U.S. Government Printing Office, Washington, D.C., 1972.

Vonnegut, K.: *Slaughterhouse Five*, Dell, New York, 1969.

Wasserman, A. I.: "Information System Design Methodology," *Journal of the American Society for Information Science*, vol. 31(1), January 1980.

Weizenbaum, J.: "ELIZA — A Computer Program for the Study of Natural Language Communication between Man and Machine," *Communications of the ACM*, vol. 9(1), 1966, pp. 36–45.

Williges, B. H., and R. C. Williges: *User Considerations in Computer-Based Information Systems*, Technical Report CSIE-81-2, Virginia Polytechnic Institute and State University, Blackburg, Va., September 1981.

Woodson, W. E.: *Human Factors Design Handbook*, McGraw-Hill, New York, 1981.

"Xerox's Star: Word Processing, 'Typesetting,' Documentation, Business Graphics, Multi-Level Math, Electronic Communication, and More All Come Together in a Revolutionary New Video Terminal Workstation," *The Seybold Report*, vol. 10(16), 1981, pp. 16–1, 16–18.

Index

ABOUT THE AUTHOR

Henry Simpson is a senior scientist at Anacapa Sciences, Inc., a human factors research firm in Santa Barbara, California. Previously, he was West Coast editor of *Digital Design* magazine. For several years before that, he was a research engineer and project director at Human Factors Research, Inc. He has conducted research, acted as a consultant to industry, and developed a number of management information systems and other programs for microcomputers. His articles on microcomputers have appeared in several magazines.